In the
Company
of Jesus

In the Company of Jesus

Characters in Mark's Gospel

ELIZABETH STRUTHERS MALBON

Westminster John Knox Press
Louisville, Kentucky

Book design by Sharon Adams
Cover design by Lisa Buckley

First edition
Published by Westminster John Knox Press
Louisville, Kentucky

This book is printed on acid-free paper that meets the American National Standards Institute Z39.48 standard. ♾

PRINTED IN THE UNITED STATES OF AMERICA

00 01 02 03 04 05 06 07 08 09 — 10 9 8 7 6 5 4 3 2 1

Library of Congress Cataloging-in-Publication Data
Malbon, Elizabeth Struthers.
    In the company of Jesus : characters in Mark's gospel /
        Elizabeth Struthers Malbon.
        p. cm.
    Includes bibliographical references and index.
    ISBN 0-664-22255-2 (alk. paper)
        1. Women in the Bible. 2. Men in the Bible. 3. Bible.
        N.T. Mark—Criticism, Narrative
    I. Title.

BS2585.6.W65 M35 2000
226.3'066—dc21   00-040812

For two exceptional characters in my life:

my daughter,
Annemarie Struthers Malbon

and her namesake, my sister,
Helen Marie Struthers

Contents

Preface

This book is a collection of seven previously published essays on the topic of Markan characterization. Characterization is a special interest within narrative criticism, which is part of the broader field of literary approaches to the New Testament. The first chapter offers an overview of key elements of narrative as approached by narrative criticism—characters, settings, plot, and rhetoric—and thus serves to introduce the six chapters focused specifically on characters in the company of Jesus in Mark's Gospel. Three chapters explore aspects of the story of the followers of the Markan Jesus—the twelve disciples, women, at times the crowds, and even, implicitly, the hearers/readers. One chapter examines the Jewish leaders as characters in Mark. Another chapter investigates—within a number of Markan literary contexts—one minor character, the poor widow who gives two small coins, while the final chapter makes observations about the range of minor characters within the overall pattern of Markan characterization.

The central thesis of the closely connected chapters is that Mark is a story (whatever else it is—religious literature, for example!), and that central to the working of a story is the interaction and interrelation of its characters. No character derives meaning in isolation from other characters. In line with norms of ancient literature, the individual characters of Mark are mostly typical, one-dimensional characters rather than the psychologically complex characters of modern and postmodern novels, but the author of Mark's Gospel has included a broad range of characters in the company of Jesus. The richness of Markan characterization is in the interplay, comparisons, and contrasts *between* these characters and in their reaching out to the hearers/readers, both ancient and contemporary.

The essays included here were first published between 1983 and 1994 in two books and four different journals,[1] yet they are very closely connected. In fact, the project was originally imagined as a book, a second book, to follow my book on Markan narrative space.[2] My life, however, moved in other directions. I have taken courage to think again of these essays as a book from conversations with colleagues, known and unknown, at professional meetings, who have told me that people are still reading the essays and finding them helpful for themselves, their students, and—in some cases—their churches. As an author at home in literary—and especially narrative—criticism, I knew my work had an "implied audience," but I am most grateful to

---

1. The essays are presented here with minimal changes. Minor repetitions remain. Greek words have been transliterated and translated. Spelling, capitalization, punctuation, headings, and citations of references—adapted by an array of copy editors—have been made consistent throughout. References to previously "forthcoming" materials that have now come forth have been updated. Where appropriate, additional reference has also been made to later editions of materials cited here, but the discussion itself is still with the materials originally cited. A few minor errors that slipped past the fallible author and fallible editors the first time have also been corrected.

2. Elizabeth Struthers Malbon, *Narrative Space and Mythic Meaning in Mark*, New Voices in Biblical Studies (San Francisco: Harper & Row, 1986; reprint, The Biblical Seminar 13; Sheffield: Sheffield Academic Press, 1991).

those members of my real audience who have identified them-selves to me.

When I first began to bring these essays (back) together, I started writing material on the central character, Jesus, which I imagined might become the final essay in the collection. Not too surprisingly, the character Jesus turned out to be rather more complex than the others, and the material likewise grew longer and longer and more and more disproportionate to the other essays. Thus, not too surprisingly, I have come to imag-ine my work differently again, and *this* book concerns itself with characters in the company of Mark's Jesus, both follow-ers and foes, both exemplars and enemies. Even when he is not the central focus, however, the Markan Jesus is still the central character: all other characters are portrayed in relation to him-and in relation to one another. The interrelations of the char-acters around Mark's Jesus are the focus of this book.

Chapter 1, "Narrative Criticism: How Does the Story Mean?" sets the context for my approach by presenting a sketch of narrative criticism. After briefly tracing the roots of narrative criticism in the New Criticism and structuralism and introducing several key narrative elements (implied author and implied reader, characters, settings, plot, and rhetoric), I exemplify these elements in a commentary on Mark 4:1–8:26. Further reading on narrative criticism, both general and bib-lical, is suggested in the Appendix to Chapter 1. This method-ological overview sets the stage for the Markan characters in the company of Jesus.

Literary analysis of the Gospel of Mark reveals that the Markan portrait of the followers of Jesus is both complex and composite: complex in portraying both the success and the fal-libility of followers; composite in including not only the twelve disciples but also the crowd, certain exceptional individuals like Bartimaeus and Jairus, and women. Chapter 2, "Fallible Fol-lowers: Women and Men in the Gospel of Mark," focuses on two questions concerning the women: (1) How do the women

characters shed light on what it means to follow Jesus? and (2)
Why are women characters especially appropriate for the role
of illuminating followership? By providing a complex and composite image of followers—fallible followers, women and
men—the author of the Markan Gospel is able to communicate clearly and powerfully to the hearer/reader a twofold message: Anyone can be a follower; no one finds it easy.

The threefold thesis of chapter 3, "Disciples/Crowds/
Whoever: Markan Characters and Readers," is closely related
to chapter 2. First, the disciples of the Markan Jesus are portrayed with both strong points and weak points in order to
serve as realistic and encouraging models for hearers/readers
who experience both strength and weakness in their Christian
discipleship. Second, the crowd is also portrayed in the Gospel
of Mark in both positive and negative ways in relation to Jesus
and serves to complement the disciples in a composite portrait
of followers of Jesus. Third, both separately and together, the
disciples and the crowd serve to open the story of Jesus and the
narrative of Mark outward to a larger group—whoever hears
or reads the Gospel of Mark. The focus of chapter 3 is the second assertion, for which detailed evidence from the Greek text
of Mark is presented, including a listing of specific references
to the disciples and the crowd in the Appendix to Chapter 3.

Chapter 4, "Text and Contexts: Interpreting the Disciples
in Mark," is more self-conscious about method. It approaches
the topic of differing interpretations of a text by considering
the differing contexts in which interpreters read it. A four-part
typology of contextual foci of interpreters is presented, based
on the intersection of two familiar distinctions: internal/
external and literary/historical. The typology is applied to
Werner Kelber's reading of the story of the disciples in Mark
as presented primarily in *The Oral and the Written Gospel*. Following the suggestions of intellectual historian Dominick
LaCapra, questions are raised about the possible "contextual
saturation of the meaning of the text." An alternative reading

of the story of the disciples in Mark is offered from the point of view of an alternative context. The conclusion suggests two images (advocacy and "complication") that give direction to the question of how to interrelate multiple readings of a single text resulting from multiple interpreters focusing on multiple contexts.

Chapter 5, "The Jewish Leaders in the Gospel of Mark: A Literary Study of Markan Characterization," has two starting points: the observations concerning characterization by Theodore Weeden (but not his interpretation of the disciples) and the work of Michael Cook concerning the Markan presentation of the Jewish leaders. From these starting points, the essay moves to literary observations about the Jewish leaders as they are characterized in Mark's narrative, focusing on scribes and Pharisees in Mark 1–10 and on chief priests, scribes, elders, and others in the passion narrative (Mark 11–16). From these literary observations, three inferences concerning Mark's portrayal of the Jewish leaders are drawn: (1) The Jewish leaders are unified as a group opposed to the Markan Jesus; (2) the distinctions among the Jewish leaders reflect a Markan literary pattern of narrative escalation; and (3) the exceptional members of the Jewish leadership groups are a key to a basic aspect of Markan characterization—that being a foe of the Markan Jesus is a matter of how one chooses to relate to him, not a matter of one's social or religious status and role, and the same is true of being a follower of Jesus.

Chapter 6, "The Poor Widow in Mark and Her Poor Rich Readers," reviews and adds to the varying interpretations of one small story of a Markan minor character, the poor widow who gives two coins to the temple treasury, as a way of raising an important methodological issue in the larger story of the New Testament or, more broadly, biblical interpretation. Examination of the interpretations presented in three representative commentaries—historical critical (Henry Barclay Swete, 1898), form critical (Vincent Taylor, 1952), redaction critical (D. E. Nineham, 1963)—and one intriguing article (by Addison Wright) preludes the reading of the story of the poor widow in six Markan narrative contexts. These multiple interpretations provide a basis for reflection on the methodological issue also brought out in chapter 4 (thus the overlap in their concluding paragraphs): how to deal with differences in interpretation. There are a wealth of readings of the poor widow's story, yet one must sometimes wonder whether our embarrassment of riches as readers is not akin to poverty: both can be paralyzing.

For the purposes of chapter 7, "The Major Importance of the Minor Characters in Mark," a "minor" character is one who lacks a continuing or recurrent presence in the story as narrated. The goal of the chapter is to suggest—illustratively, not exhaustively—that the minor characters of Mark do have major importance. (1) They, alongside the major characters, extend the continuum of potential responses to Jesus in an open-ended way, providing implicit narrative comparisons and contrasts with the responses of the continuing or recurrent characters and providing a bridge from the (internal) characters to the (borderline) implied audience. (2) They mark where the implied audience is to pause, reflect, connect; that is, they provide overall narrative punctuation—parentheses, exclamation points, and colons especially. These two functions are entirely intertwined.

The final chapter, which was both written and published last, also serves as an overall conclusion. Its many references to the previous chapters is simply the most obvious manifestation of their interconnectedness. Although each chapter focuses on a particular group of characters around Mark's Jesus (disciples, the crowd, women, religious leaders, minor characters)—or even on one particular character (the poor widow)—all the chapters interconnect because all the characters interrelate. The essays have been drawn together here for readers and scholars, students and teachers, laity and clergy, who seek to gain a deeper understanding of *how* Mark's story of the characters in the company of Jesus is so powerful and engaging that it has continued to draw its audience into the story to join them for nearly two thousand years.

Elizabeth Struthers Malbon
April, 2000

Acknowledgments

I thank the original publishers for permission to reprint the following essays of mine as chapters in this book:

1. "Narrative Criticism: How Does the Story Mean?" from *Mark and Method: New Approaches in Biblical Studies*, ed. Janice Capel Anderson and Stephen D. Moore (Minneapolis: Fortress, 1992), 23–49. Reprinted by permission of Augsburg Fortress Publishers.

2. "Fallible Followers: Women and Men in the Gospel of Mark," *Semeia* 28 (1983): 29–48. Reprinted by permission of Scholars Press.

3. "Disciples/Crowds/Whoever: Markan Characters and Readers," *Novum Testamentum* 28 (1986): 104–30. Reprinted by permission of Brill Academic Publishing.

4. "Text and Contexts: Interpreting the Disciples in Mark," *Semeia* 62 (1993): 81–102. Reprinted by permission of Scholars Press.

5. "The Jewish Leaders in the Gospel of Mark: A Literary Study of Marcan Characterization," *Journal of Biblical Literature* 108 (1989): 259–81. Reprinted by permission of Scholars Press.

6. "The Poor Widow in Mark and Her Poor Rich Readers,"
Catholic Biblical Quarterly 53 (1991): 589–604. Reprinted by
permission of the Catholic Biblical Association.
7. "The Major Importance of the Minor Characters in Mark,"
in *The New Literary Criticism and the New Testament*, edited by
Elizabeth Struthers Malbon and Edgar V. McKnight (Sheffield University Press/Trinity Press International, 1994), 58–
86. Reprinted by permission of Sheffield Academic Press.

I gratefully acknowledge the assistance of Scott Thomson,
graduate student in Science and Technology Studies in the
Center for Interdisciplinary Studies at Virginia Polytechnic
Institute and State University, in bringing the electronic files
of these articles into a common word-processing format.

In moving from electronic files to book, I have been delighted
to work with Vicki Hochstedler, freelance project manager,
and especially with Carey C. Newman, Editor Academic
Books, Westminster John Knox Press.

Abbreviations

AAR	American Academy of Religion
AnBib	Analecta biblica
BTB	*Biblical Theology Bulletin*
CBQ	*Catholic Biblical Quarterly*
ETR	*Etudes théologiques et religieuses*
FBBS	Facet Books, Biblical Series
GBS	Guides to Biblical Scholarship
HTR	*Harvard Theological Review*
Int	*Interpretation*
JAAR	*Journal of the American Academy of Religion*
JBL	*Journal of Biblical Literature*
JES	*Journal of Ecumenical Studies*
JR	*Journal of Religion*
JSNTSup	Journal for the Study of the New Testament: Supplement Series
JTSA	*Journal of Theology for Southern Africa*
LCL	Loeb Classical Library
LXX	Septuagint
NovT	*Novum Testamentum*
NRSV	NEW REVISED STANDARD VERSION
NTS	*New Testament Studies*

PNTC	Pelican New Testament Commentaries
RevExp	*Review and Expositor*
RSV	REVISED STANDARD VERSION
SBL	Society of Biblical Literature
SBLDS	Society of Biblical Literature Dissertation Series
SBLSP	*Society of Biblical Literature Seminar Papers*
TBT	*The Bible Today*
TDNT	*Theological Dictionary of the New Testament*, 10 vols., ed. G. Kittel and G. Friedrick, trans. G. W. Bromiley, (Grand Rapids: Eerdmans, 1964–1976)
ThTo	*Theology Today*
TZ	*Theologische Zeitschrift*
WMANT	Wissenschaftliche Monographien zum Alten und Neuen Testament
ZNW	*Zeitschrift für die neutestamentliche Wissenschaft und die Kunde der älteren Kirche*
ZTK	*Zeitschrift für Theologie und Kirche*

1

Narrative Criticism

How Does the Story Mean?

The questions we ask of the texts we read are as important as the answers we are led to. Most readers of the New Testament for almost two thousand years have asked religious questions: What does the text mean? What does it mean to me? to us? to our faith and our lives? The answers have reflected not only the different individual readers but also broader cultural shifts. The time and place of the readers or communities of readers have influenced their answers. What other types of questions have been asked by New Testament readers—especially scholarly readers?

Since the nineteenth century, most New Testament scholars have asked, What *did* the text mean? What did it mean in its original context? for its author? to its first hearers or readers? One could discuss three chief ways the question, What did the text mean? has been asked: source criticism, form criticism, and redaction criticism. Source, form, and redaction criticism might seem to be asking literary questions. Source criticism was first called literary criticism because it approached Matthew, Mark, and Luke as literary documents. Source criticism is, however, a search for literary sources and relationships in history. Which Gospel was written first? Which Gospel was the historical source for the others? These questions are primarily historical. Form criticism is concerned with the literary form of the small stories. However, form criticism a search for the sources behind the sources in history. What do the individual stories tell us about the history of the earliest churches? What may we attribute to the historical Jesus? Redaction criticism certainly has literary aspects. As the study of the theological motivation of the editing of earlier traditions, it is concerned with the Gospels as literary wholes. However, redaction criticism is a search for the theology of the churches of the Gospel writers in history. What *did* the text mean? To ask *what* did the text mean is to seek referential meaning. The text's meaning is found in what it refers to— what it refers to other than and outside itself.

In the past two decades an increasing number of biblical scholars (especially in the United States) have been asking a different question: *How* does the text mean? This question is literary; it represents a search for internal meaning rather than external (or referential) meaning. How do various literary patterns enable the text to communicate meaning to its hearers and readers? How do the interrelated characters, settings, and actions of the plot contribute to a narrative's meaning for a reader? The move from historical to literary questions represents a paradigm shift in biblical studies. A paradigm gives us our basic way of understanding things. When there is a paradigm shift, we are challenged to think of the old and familiar in a new way. The writer of Mark is no longer a cut-and-paste editor but an author with control over the story he narrates. The Jesus of Mark is no longer a shadowy historical personage but a lively character. Galilee and Jerusalem are no longer simply geographical references but settings for dramatic action. The account of Jesus' passion (suffering and death) is no longer the source of theological doctrine but the culmination of a dramatic and engaging plot.

The New Criticism and Structuralism

The shift to a literary paradigm by some biblical interpreters echoed a similar and earlier shift among interpreters of secular literature. In the 1940s the New Criticism argued that the key to reading a poem or a play, novel, or short story is to be found in the work itself. Historical information about the culture and biographical information about the author were pushed aside as external to the work. The New Criticism must be understood as a reaction to previous literary studies that gave such information primary importance. A similar reaction in biblical studies led many to move from redaction criticism to literary criticism. The final lines of a poem by Archibald MacLeish may be understood almost as a slogan for the New Critics: "A poem should not mean/But be."[1] A critic or reader must not be concerned with a poem's referential meaning, that is, its reference to some external world. She or he must attend to its being, its presence, its metaphoric power. The poem's power to speak to us depends neither on the author's intention nor on the reader's knowledge of the author's circumstances. It depends on the poem itself—its words, its rhythms, its images.

The New Criticism made its initial impact in New Testament studies on interpretations of the sayings and parables of Jesus. The "significance of forceful and imaginative language" in the synoptic sayings of Jesus was explored by Robert Tannehill.[2] Robert Funk considered "language as event and theology" in parable and letter.[3] Dan Via reflected on the "literary

1. Archibald MacLeish, "Ars Poetica," in *Collected Poems 1917–1954* (Boston: Houghton Mifflin, 1962), 50–51.

2. Robert C. Tannehill, *The Sword of His Mouth*, Semeia Supplements 1 (Philadelphia: Fortress; Missoula, Mont.: Scholars Press, 1975).

3. Robert W. Funk, *Language, Hermeneutic, and the Word of God: The Problem of Language in the New Testament and Contemporary Theology* (New York: Harper & Row, 1966).

and existential dimension" of the parables.[4] The surprising, challenging, world-shattering potential of the parables was the theme of John Dominic Crossan's work.[5] "A poem should not mean/But be"—and a parable should not refer but impel.

Structuralism is another critical approach that has influenced biblical literary criticism. Structuralism was born in linguistics and grew up in anthropology, literature, and other areas. Central to structuralism are three affirmations about language. First, language is communication. Language as communication involves a sender giving a message to a receiver; literature as communication means an author giving a text to a reader. Redaction critics focus on the sender or author, and reader-response critics focus on the receiver or reader. Structuralist critics in particular, like literary critics in general, focus on the text. By analogy, structuralist critics note that within a narrative text a "sender" gives an "object" to a "receiver." For example, in a traditional fairy tale the king gives his daughter in marriage to the most worthy suitor. (Much of the tale works out which suitor is most worthy.) In a synoptic parable a king gives a feast to—surprisingly—the poor and the outcast. This model of language as communication and narrative as language has been worked out by French structuralist A. J. Greimas.[6]

Second, structuralism stresses that language is a system of signs. No sign has meaning on its own. Signs have meaning

---

4. Dan Otto Via, Jr., *The Parables: Their Literary and Existential Dimension* (Philadelphia: Fortress, 1967).

5. John Dominic Crossan, *In Parables: The Challenge of the Historical Jesus* (New York: Harper & Row, 1973); Crossan, *The Dark Interval: Towards a Theology of Story* (Niles, Ill.: Argus Communications, 1975; reprint, Sonoma, Calif.: Polebridge Press, 1988).

6. A. J. Greimas, "Elements of a Narrative Grammar," trans. Catherine Porter, *Diacritics* 7 (1977): 23–40. For an explanation, see Daniel Patte, *What Is Structural Exegesis?* GBS (Philadelphia: Fortress, 1976), 41–43. For an adaptation and application to the parables, see Crossan, *Dark Interval.*

in relation to other signs. Analogously, no element of a literary work has meaning in isolation. Everything has meaning as part of a system of relationships. A narrative, that is, a literary work that tells a story, must be read in two ways to disclose its system of relations. It must be read diachronically, that is, "through time," from beginning to end. It must also be read (understood) synchronically, that is, as if everything happened at the "same time." For a synchronic reading, logical categories (good versus evil, order versus chaos, etc.) are more important than chronological categories. The interrelation of parts within a whole is the key. This approach has been worked out by French structural anthropologist Claude Lévi-Strauss and applied in detail to the spatial settings of Mark's Gospel.[7]

Third, structuralism focuses on language as a cultural code. This understanding of language builds on the other two. Through careful analysis of the oppositions expressed in a text, the even more basic oppositions implicitly supporting it are revealed. Daniel Patte, the foremost biblical structuralist, has illustrated this and other aspects of structuralism in relation to Paul's letters and Matthew's Gospel. Patte seeks to uncover the "system of convictions" of Paul and of Matthew.[8]

7. Claude Lévi-Strauss, "The Structural Study of Myth," *Journal of American Folklore* 68 (1955): 428–44; Lévi-Strauss, "The Story of Asdiwal," trans. Nicholas Mann, in *The Structural Study of Myth and Totemism*, ed. Edmund Leach, Association of Social Anthropologists Monographs 5 (London: Tavistock, 1967), 1–47. Elizabeth Struthers Malbon, *Narrative Space and Mythic Meaning in Mark*, New Voices in Biblical Studies (San Francisco: Harper & Row, 1986; reprint, The Biblical Seminar 13; Sheffield: Sheffield Academic Press, 1991).

8. Daniel Patte, *Paul's Faith and the Power of the Gospel: A Structural Introduction to the Pauline Letters* (Philadelphia: Fortress, 1983); Patte, *The Gospel according to Matthew: A Structural Commentary on Matthew's Faith* (Philadelphia: Fortress, 1987). See also Patte, *Structural Exegesis for New Testament Critics*, GBS (Minneapolis: Fortress, 1990).

Both the New Criticism and structuralism focus on the text itself—the language of the text and the text as language. Biblical literary criticism has been influenced by both approaches and shares this focus on the text. The first texts examined in detail by New Testament literary critics were the sayings and parables of Jesus. These short and powerful texts are in some ways comparable to the poems that intrigued the New Critics. The Gospels are the texts most explored by current New Testament literary critics. The Gospels are narratives, stories, in many ways not unlike the myths and folktales that structuralists often analyzed. New Testament literary criticism has become largely narrative criticism, a label employed by biblical critics but not by secular critics. To understand narrative criticism, we must consider the essential elements or aspects of narratives.

Narrative Elements

The distinction between story and discourse that was highlighted by literary critic Seymour Chatman has proved very useful to narrative critics. Story is the *what* of a narrative; discourse is the *how*. Story indicates the content of the narrative, including events, characters, and settings, and their interaction as the plot. Discourse indicates the rhetoric of the narrative, how the story is told. The four canonical Gospels, for example, share a similar (although not identical) story of Jesus, but the discourse of each Gospel is distinctive. The story is where the characters interact, the discourse is where the implied author and implied reader interact. Story and discourse are not really separable. What we have, in Chatman's words, is the story-as-discoursed. It is this about which narrative critics ask, How does the text mean?

The following elements or aspects of narrative (story-as-discoursed), although overlapping, are frequently distinguished by narrative critics: implied author and implied reader, characters, settings, plot, rhetoric. We will look at each in turn.

Implied Author and Implied Reader

The communication model of sender-message-receiver gives narrative critics a framework for approaching texts: author-text-reader. This simple model, however, soon proves inadequate for narrative analysis. Recent literary criticism has taught us to conceive of the author and the reader not as isolated entities but as poles of a continuum of communication. A real author writes a text for a real reader. An implied author, a creation of the real author that is implied in his or her text, presents a narrative to an implied reader, a parallel creation of the real author that is embedded in the text, and a narrator tells a story to a narratee. Of course, within a story a character may narrate another story to another character. This expanded model is often diagramed like this:[9]

real → | implied → narrator → narratee → implied | → real
author | author   reader | reader

Text or Narrative

Narrative criticism focuses on the narrative, but the implied author and the implied reader are understood as aspects of the narrative in this model. The implied author is a hypothetical construction based on the requirements of knowledge and belief presupposed in the narrative. The same is true of the implied reader. The implied author is the one who would be necessary for this narrative to be told or written. The implied reader is the one who would be necessary for this narrative to be heard or read.

The distinctions between the real and implied author and the real and implied reader are important for narrative critics, who

---

9. This diagram is based on that of Seymour Chatman, *Story and Discourse: Narrative Structure in Fiction and Film* (Ithaca, N.Y.: Cornell University Press, 1978), 151.

wish to interpret the narrative without reliance on biographical information about the real author and cultural information about the real reader. Of course, basic information about the cultural context is essential to any interpretation. The implied author and implied reader of Mark's Gospel, for example, were literate in *koine* (common) Greek and knew the Hebrew Bible (later to become the Old Testament for Christians) in the form of its Greek translation in the Septuagint. Narrative critics are eager to know as much as possible about the cultural contexts—especially of ancient works—in order to understand more completely the implied author and the implied reader of the narrative. However, narrative critics are wary of interpretations based on elements external to the narrative—including the intentions (known or supposed) of the real author.

The distinctions between the implied author and the narrator and between the narratee and the implied reader were developed in secular literary criticism for the close analysis of nineteenth- and twentieth-century novels. Ishmael is the narrator of *Moby Dick*, but he is the creation of the implied author. Most narrative critics of the first-century Gospels have not found these distinctions as useful. Most narrative critics have observed little or no difference between the implied author and narrator or between the narratee and implied reader of Matthew, Mark, Luke, and John. The implied author of *Moby Dick* knows more than Ishmael does, but a similar separation is not obvious in Mark. Thus some narrative critics use the terms *narrator* and *narratee*, while others employ *implied author* and *implied reader*.

The implied author/narrator may be characterized in various ways, according to the particular nature of the narrative. The implied authors/narrators of the Gospels are generally described as omniscient (all-knowing), or omnipresent (present everywhere), or unlimited. The implied author/narrator of Mark, for example, is able to narrate events involving any character or group of characters, including Jesus when alone. This implied author/narrator knows past, present, and future, as well as the inner thoughts and feelings of the characters. The Markan implied author/narrator is also reliable. The narratee/ implied reader may trust him (probably him) as a nondeceptive guide to the action and safely believe that what he foreshadows will be fulfilled. (Even a reliable implied author/narrator may be ironic, however.) In addition, the point of view of the implied author/narrator of Mark is aligned not only with the point of view of the main character, Jesus, but also with the point of view of God. From the point of view of the implied reader/narratee, you can't get any more reliable than that! The implied author/narrator begins: "The beginning of the good news of Jesus Christ [Messiah], the Son of God" (1:1). Ten verses later, God concurs, saying to Jesus, "You are my Son" (1:11). The interaction of the implied author and the implied reader is part of the discourse. The interaction of the characters is part of the story.

Characters

Characters are an obvious narrative element. A story is about someone—the characters. The actions are carried out by someone—the characters. Narrative analysis of characters is intertwined with narrative analysis of plot. The implied reader of the story-as-discoursed is frequently invited to admire, judge, or identify with the characters. Characters are brought to life for the implied reader by the implied author through narrating words and actions. These words and actions may be those of the character himself or herself, or those of another character, or those of the narrator. A character can be known by what she says and does; a character can be known by what other characters say to or about her and by what they do in relation to or because of her. A character can be known by what the narrator says about him—including names, epithets, and descriptions—or by what the narrator does in relation to him—including comparative or contrasting juxtapositions with other characters and the unfolding of the plot.

For example, the first mention of Judas Iscariot in Mark, at Jesus' appointing of the twelve, is followed immediately by the narrator's comment, "who betrayed him" (3:19). At the point when Judas's betrayal is being narrated, however, the narrator calls him "Judas Iscariot, who was one of the twelve" (14:10). This is characterization by the narrator's words and *actions*, that is, the ironic placement of these descriptions at moments of greatest contrast. The ironic contrast is extended by the immediate juxtaposition of the story of the unnamed woman who gives up money for Jesus (the anointing woman, 14:3–9) and the story of one of the twelve specially named men who gives up Jesus for money (Judas's betrayal, 14:10–11).

Some narrative critics distinguish characterization by "telling" and characterization by "showing." "Telling" involves the explicit words of a reliable narrator about a character. Anything else is "showing." "Showing" requires more from the narratee and implied reader and is thus more engaging. Most of the characterization in the Gospels is by "showing."

Some narrative critics find it helpful to identify the dominant traits of characters. A trait is a personal quality that persists over time. Sometimes such traits are explicitly named in a narrative. Frequently they are inferred from words and actions, as suggested previously. Some characters are portrayed with only one trait. Others are given a number of traits, or developing traits, or even conflicting traits.

E. M. Forster, novelist and literary critic, called these two types of characters "flat" and "round."[10] The distinction, which is sometimes elaborated, has proved to be extremely helpful for narrative critics. Flat characters are simple and consistent. Some flat characters appear but once, others again and again,

---

10. E. M. Forster, *Aspects of the Novel* (New York: Harcourt, Brace & Co., 1927; reprint, 1954), 103–18.

but their actions and words are predictable. Round characters are complex or dynamic. They may reveal new aspects of themselves or even change. The distinction between flat and round characters is not the same as the distinction between "minor" and "major" characters. The Jewish leaders are hardly minor characters in Mark, but they are flat. Nor is the flat/round distinction equivalent to negative versus positive. The Jewish leaders in Mark are flat and negative; the anointing woman is flat and positive. The disciples are round and both positive and negative; the Markan Jesus alone is a round, positive character. The flatness or roundness of characters, however, does affect the implied reader's response in praise, judgment, or identification. Round characters elicit identification in a way that flat characters do not.

Just as the point of view of the implied author/narrator is aligned and takes on a positive or negative value, so the point of view of each character or group of characters is given an evaluative point of view by the implied author. Norman Petersen has argued that the two evaluative points of view among Markan characters are "thinking the things of God" and "thinking the things of men."[11] The implied author, narrator, Jesus, and several minor exemplary characters represent the first (positive) point of view. The Jewish leaders and sometimes the disciples represent the second (negative) one.

New Testament narrative critics are generally aware of the differences in characterization between nineteenth- and twentieth-century psychological novels, for example, and the Gospels. The secular literary theory on which biblical narrative critics so often lean is not particularly supportive at this point. Ways of analyzing characterization in the Gospels are still being developed. Perhaps the current debate about the portrayal of the disciples of Jesus in Mark (Are they "fallible

---

11. Norman R. Petersen, "'Point of View' in Mark's Narrative," *Semeia* 12 (1978): 97–121.

followers" or final failures?[12]) will settle down somewhat as interpreters explore more thoroughly techniques of characterization in use in the ancient world. Vernon Robbins has instructively compared the portrayal of the Markan disciples of Jesus with the portrayal of the disciples of Apollonius of Tyana by Philostratus.[13] I have pointed out that characterization by "types" was conventional in ancient literature, including history writing as well as epic, drama, and other forms. Mark seems to continue this convention by presenting contrasting groups—exemplars to emulate and enemies to eschew. But perhaps Mark challenges this convention as well by presenting fallible followers with whom to identify.[14] More research remains to be done in this area.

Settings

Characters are the "who" of the narrative; settings are the "where" and "when." The shift from historical questions to literary questions has made a significant impact on the way interpreters think about the spatial and temporal settings of the Gospels.[15] The original questers for the historical Jesus

12. For the now classic exposition of the disciples as failed followers, see Theodore J. Weeden, Sr., *Mark—Traditions in Conflict* (Philadelphia: Fortress, 1971). See also Werner H. Kelber, *Mark's Story of Jesus* (Philadelphia: Fortress, 1979). For the view of the disciples as "fallible followers," see Robert C. Tannehill, "The Disciples in Mark: The Function of a Narrative Role," *JR* 57 (1977): 386–405, and Elizabeth Struthers Malbon, "Fallible Followers: Women and Men in the Gospel of Mark," *Semeia* 28 (1983): 29–48 [here chapter 2].

13. Vernon K. Robbins, *Jesus the Teacher: A Socio-Rhetorical Interpretation of Mark*, rev. ed. (Philadelphia: Fortress, 1992).

14. Elizabeth Struthers Malbon, "The Jewish Leaders in the Gospel of Mark: A Literary Study of Marcan Characterization," *JBL* 108 (1989): 259–81, esp. 275–81 [here chapter 5].

15. Elizabeth Struthers Malbon, "Galilee and Jerusalem: History and Literature in Marcan Interpretation," *CBQ* 44 (1982): 242–55;

combed the Gospels for information about the geography and chronology of Jesus' ministry. Early redaction critics of Mark argued that its confused geographical references indicate an author writing outside Galilee and Israel, probably in Rome. Later redaction critics speculated that the positive connotations of Galilee in Mark indicate Galilee as the locale of the community for which the Gospel was written.[16] The prediction of the destruction of the Jewish temple in chapter 13 of Mark—especially with its cryptic parenthetical phrase: "(let the reader understand)," 13:14—has been cited as evidence that Mark was written prior to 70 C.E. (the date of the temple's actual destruction by the Romans) *and* as evidence that it was written after 70 C.E.! The spatial and temporal settings of Mark give a clear picture of neither Jesus' time and place in history nor Mark's.

Literary critics, especially narrative critics, interpret these spatial and temporal references internally rather than externally. Together they form the background for the dramatic action of Mark's Gospel. And, in fact, settings often participate in the drama of the narrative. Places and times are rich in connotational, or associative, values, and these values contribute to the meaning of the narrative for the implied reader. For example, the Markan narrator says that Jesus "went up the mountain" (3:13) to appoint the twelve. Historical critics have searched in vain for a mountain in Galilee. But for the implied author and implied reader, who know their Bible, "the mountain" is where God comes to meet leaders of the people of God. Similarly, "the sea" is where God manifests divine power,

---

reprinted in *The Interpretation of Mark*, ed. William R. Telford (London: T. & T. Clark, 1995), 253–68.

16. Willi Marxsen, *Mark the Evangelist: Studies on the Redaction History of the Gospel*, trans. James Boyce et al. (Nashville: Abingdon, 1969). Werner H. Kelber, *The Kingdom in Mark: A New Place and a New Time* (Philadelphia: Fortress, 1974).

and "the wilderness" is where God manifests divine care in miraculously feeding the people of God. Thus the implied reader is shown (not told) that Jesus' power over the sea (4:35–41; 6:45–52) and miraculous feedings in the wilderness (6:31–44; 8:1–10) are divine manifestations.

Markan temporal settings also contribute significantly to the implied reader's appreciation of the narrative. Some temporal references are clearly allusive or symbolic. Jesus' testing in the wilderness for forty days (1:13) is an allusion to Israel's forty years of testing in the wilderness during the exodus. The twelve years of age of Jairus's daughter and the twelve years of suffering of the hemorrhaging woman intensify the Jewish flavor of the interwoven stories (5:21–43). Twelve is a number symbolic of Israel, with its twelve tribes.

In other cases the implied author uses temporal markers to pace the unfolding of the story. The first several chapters of Mark are peppered with the Greek adverb *euthus*, "immediately." (In English translation this is clearer in the Revised Standard Version than in the New Revised Standard Version.) The Markan Jesus rushes around—from baptism in the Jordan, to testing in the wilderness, to preaching and exorcising a demon in the Capernaum synagogue, to healing in Simon's house, to healing throughout Galilee. The Markan Jesus' first words tell of the urgency of the present time: "The time is fulfilled, and the kingdom of God has come near; repent, and believe in the good news" (1:15). The Markan narrator's first series of scenes *shows* this urgency. Immediately Jesus acts; immediately the implied reader is to respond.[17]

The pace of the Markan story-as-discoursed is dramatically different in the passion narrative, the story of Jesus' suffering and death. Everything slows down. Story time for the first ten chap-

---

17. On the larger issues of apocalyptic and temporality in relation to Mark's plot, see Dan O. Via, Jr., *The Ethics of Mark's Gospel: In the Middle of Time* (Philadelphia: Fortress, 1985), esp. 27–66.

ters is months and months, perhaps a year. Story time for the last six chapters is about a week. Moreover, everything becomes more specific. Instead of the "in those days" or "in the morning" of the first ten chapters, we now read "two days before the Passover and the festival of Unleavened Bread" (14:1) or "nine o'clock in the morning" (15:25; "the third hour [or watch]," RSV). The same specificity occurs spatially. Instead of "in the house," we find "at Bethany in the house of Simon the leper, . . . at the table" (14:3). A modern-day analogy would be a filmmaker's skillful use of slow-motion photography to suggest the profound significance of a climaxing series of scenes. The more detailed setting of scenes in time and space of the Markan passion narrative is the implied author's plea to the implied reader: slow down; take this in; to understand anything of the story, you must understand this. It is another form of urgency.

Spatial and temporal settings need to be mapped out in correlation with the plot of the narrative, just as characters need to be interpreted in terms of their roles in the plot. For the implied author and the implied reader, the elements of narrative—characters, settings, plot, rhetoric—are essentially integrated.

Plot

The plot is the "what" and the "why" of the narrative. What happens? Why? Then what happens? Why? These are questions of the plot. Biblical critic Norman Petersen presents a very fruitful distinction between Mark's "narrative world" and Mark's "plotted time." The "narrative world is comprised of all events described or referred to in the narrative, but in their causal and logical sequence." The "plotting of this world is to be seen in the ways its components have been selected and arranged in a sequence of narrated incidents."[18] Events are not

18. Norman R. Petersen, *Literary Criticism for New Testament Critics*, GBS (Philadelphia: Fortress, 1978), 49–50.

always plotted in the narrative in the order in which they would occur in the narrative world. The changes from narrative world to the plotted time of the narrative are part of the implied author's discourse with the implied reader.

Gérard Genette, a literary theorist, has worked out an intricate system for discussing the order, duration, and frequency of events in the plotted narrative.[19] An event may be narrated *after* its logical order in the narrative world (analepsis). An event may be narrated *before* its logical order in the narrative world (prolepsis). And, of course, events may occur in the same order in both. An event may be narrated with a longer, shorter, or equal duration in comparison with its duration in the narrative world. An event that occurs once in the narrative world may be narrated once or more than once. Changes in order, duration, and frequency are ways the implied author has of leading the implied reader through the story-as-discoursed to an interpretation.

Markan examples will clarify these distinctions. The three passion predictions that the Markan Jesus makes to his disciples (8:31; 9:31; 10:33) point proleptically to what will occur later—but still within the narrative. The Markan Jesus' prediction, echoed by the young man at the empty tomb (14:28; 16:7), that he will go before his disciples to Galilee, points proleptically to an event that is not narrated within the story-as-discoursed. The implied reader, however, has been cued to presume its occurrence in the narrative world (see, e.g., 13:9–13). This narrative technique contributes to the often-noted open ending of Mark's Gospel. A short but surprising and significant analepsis is narrated at 15:40–41. The Markan Jesus' twelve disciples have fled; he is crucified, bereft of their presence. But at the cross "there were also women looking on from a distance." Three are named, but "many other women"

---

19. Gérard Genette, *Narrative Discourse: An Essay in Method*, trans. Jane E. Lewin; (Ithaca, N.Y.: Cornell University Press, 1980).

are mentioned. At this crucial point the narrator tells the narratee that these women used to follow Jesus and minister to him in Galilee. *Follow* and *minister to* are discipleship words in Mark. So the implied reader learns at the last hour that Jesus had other followers, women followers, from the first. Moreover, these surprising followers stay to the last—although at a distance. Three of them are there at the empty tomb as well.

Conflict is the key to the Markan plot. As Markan characterization does not depend on psychological development within the characters, so the plot does not turn on high suspense and complicated intrigue among the characters. The plot moves by conflicts between groups of characters, or, rather, between God or Jesus and groups of characters. There are multiple conflicts, along several dimensions. The kingdom of God is in conflict with all other claims to power and authority. Jesus is in conflict with demons and unclean spirits. Jesus and the Jewish authorities are in continuing conflict over issues of authority and interpretation of the Law (Torah). Jesus and the disciples are in conflict over what it means to be the Messiah and thus what it means to follow him. All the conflicts have to do with power and authority. Where do ultimate power and authority lie? How should human power and authority be exercised? But all the conflicts are not the same. The disciples, for example, are not portrayed and evaluated by the implied author in the same way as the Jewish leaders are. And, of course, the Markan Jesus responds to the disciples very differently from the way he reacts to the other groups with whom he comes into conflict.

Thus the elements of narrative include the five Ws one might expect in the first paragraph of a news story: who (characters), where and when (settings), what and why (plot). To the extent that story and discourse can be separated analytically, these three are elements of story. A final narrative element is rhetoric, the how of the story-as-discoursed. Rhetoric refers to how the implied author persuades the implied reader to follow the story. Because narrative criticism (like literary criticism in general) asks, "*How* does the text mean?" narrative criticism takes a keen interest in rhetoric.

Rhetoric

Rhetoric is the art of persuasion. Persuasion, of course, works differently in varying contexts. Markan rhetoric is narrative rhetoric. By the way the story is told, the implied author persuades the implied reader first to understand, and then to share and extend, the story's levels of meaning. Mark's rhetoric is one of juxtaposition—placing scene over against scene in order to elicit comparison, contrast, insight. This juxtaposition includes repetition, not only of scenes but also of words and phrases; duality is widespread. Juxtaposition includes intercalation—splicing one story into another—and framing—placing similar stories as beginning and end of a series. In addition, juxtaposition includes foreshadowing and echoing of words, phrases, and whole events. Echoing and foreshadowing may be intratextual (within the text) or intertextual (between texts). The intertextual echoes heard in Mark's Gospel reverberate with the Septuagint. Symbolism involves the juxtaposition of a literal meaning and a metaphorical one. Irony involves the juxtaposition of an apparent or expected meaning and a deeper or surprising one. Repetition, intercalation, framing, foreshadowing and echoing, symbolism, and irony are favorite Markan rhetorical devices. They are part of the discourse of the narrative. Without the implied author's discourse, the implied reader could not receive the story. The story is never received directly but only as discoursed, only rhetorically.

The interwoven scenes of Jesus' trial before the high priest and Peter's denial (14:53–72) illustrate a number of these rhetorical techniques. The two stories are intercalated. The narrator first tells that Jesus was taken to the high priest (v. 53) and then that Peter followed "at a distance" into the courtyard of the high priest (v. 54). The scene between Jesus and the high priest and other chief priests is played out (vv. 55–65), and then the scene between Peter and the high priest's servant-girl and other bystanders is played out (vv. 66–72). The implied reader cannot forget the presence of Peter "warming himself at the fire" (v. 54) all the while Jesus endures the fiery rage of the high priest. Jesus' scene concludes with the guards taunting him to "Prophesy!" (v. 65). Peter's scene concludes with his remembrance of Jesus' prophecy of his denial (v. 72), an ominous echo of the earlier foreshadowing. It is sadly ironic that Peter's noisy denial of his discipleship in order to save his life is narrated almost simultaneously with Jesus' quiet affirmation of his Messiahship, although it will lead to his death. The rhetorical juxtaposition of these scenes—characters, words, actions, settings—in the unfolding plot pushes the implied reader not only to judge the two contrasting characters but also to judge himself or herself.

The order of stories or scenes in Mark 8:22–10:52 illustrates the rhetorical devices of repetition, framing, and symbolism. In this section of the narrative, the Markan Jesus three times predicts his passion and resurrection (8:31; 9:31; 10:33). After each prediction, the disciples manifest their limited understanding of serving and suffering as aspects of Messiahship and discipleship (8:32–33; 9:32–34, 38; 10:35–41). After each misunderstanding, Jesus renews his teaching on this topic (8:34–38; 9:35–37, 39–50; 10:42–45). Of course, each time Jesus teaches the disciples, the implied author teaches the implied reader. Repetition adds clarity and force.

Around these three three-part scenes (passion prediction units), other scenes (of teaching and healing) are set. Then all these scenes are framed by the only two Markan stories of the healing of blindness. At the beginning of the series, the two-stage healing of blindness at Bethsaida is narrated (8:22–26). At the close, the healing of blind Bartimaeus, who follows Jesus "on the way," is recounted (10:46–52). Blindness and sight are symbolic of misunderstanding and insight. As Jesus healed the blind man of Bethsaida in two stages, so he must teach the disciples in two stages about his Messiahship. At Caesarea Philippi, Peter tells that he "sees" Jesus' power and shows that he is "blind" to Jesus' suffering service (8:27–33). As the mighty deeds of chapters 1–8 were the first stage of Jesus' teaching, so the passion prediction units of chapters 8–10 are the second stage. The goal of the journey is for all— disciples and implied readers—to "see" as Bartimaeus does and to follow "on the way."

Understanding the narrative rhetoric is central to the work of the narrative critic because rhetoric is the how of the story's telling and "*How* does the text mean?" is the literary question. Earlier source, form, and redaction critics found Mark's rhetorical style rough and primitive. This judgment may be true at the level of the sentence. (English translations always smooth out Mark's Greek a bit.) But Mark's narrative rhetoric must be appreciated at the level of the scene. In the intriguing juxtaposition of scenes—with their characters, settings, and plot developments—the rhetoric of the Markan Gospel works its persuasive ways with the implied reader.

Narrative criticism compensates for the fragmentation of the text into smaller and smaller units by form and redaction criticism. Even redaction criticism, with its potential to be concerned for the Gospel as a whole, frequently bogs down in ever more meticulous divisions between "tradition" and "redaction"— what Mark received and what he added. Nevertheless, perhaps narrative criticism, in its holistic passion, overcompensates. Deconstructive criticism compensates for the totalizing effect of narrative criticism, creating a self-consistent unity of the text. Deconstructive criticism may overcompensate as well. But it is good for narrative criticism to be reminded of what it also knows, and often proclaims, of the tensions, gaps, and mysteries of the text itself—and even the text against itself.

Narrative criticism seeks to avoid the "intentional fallacy" of redaction criticism. The narrative critic does not pursue the quest for the real author's intention. Instead, the narrative critic seeks to analyze and appreciate the implied author's effect—that is, the text itself. But what is "the text itself"? Narrative critics affirm that it is the center of a communication process involving author, text, and reader. They (we) focus on the text, partly in reaction to redaction critics' focus on the author, but mostly because we find the text so intriguing.

Reader-response criticism seeks to avoid the objectivism of narrative criticism—viewing the text as an autonomous object. Reader-response criticism may overcompensate as well. Perhaps narrative criticism's appreciation for the role of the implied reader guards it from the extreme of objectivism. No doubt biblical criticism would benefit greatly from an approach that could—if not simultaneously, at least sequentially—keep in view all parts of the communication process: author, text, and reader. Then, "*What did* the text mean?" and "*How does* the text mean?" might contribute more fairly and more fully to the older and enduring question, "What does the text mean—to me? to us?"

Narrative Examples

We turn now to an extended example of narrative criticism at work in chapters 4–8 of the Gospel of Mark. Such an example should help clarify and integrate the narrative elements. Chapters 4–8 have been chosen because of their rhetorical richness, because they hold together as a subunit within the entire Gospel, and because what Mark does here with these smaller stories is quite distinctive from what Matthew and Luke do with many of the same stories in their Gospels. We could study each narrative element in turn; first characters, then settings, and so on. This type of analysis is often done by narrative critics. But here we will look at the interrelated narrative elements as the story unfolds from 4:1 through 8:26, a pattern increasingly frequent within narrative criticism. (Let the reader understand: my implied reader is reading Mark 4–8 along with this chapter.)

Parables on the Sea (4:1–34)

At the beginning of chapter 4, the Markan narrator takes considerable trouble to make sure the narratee locates Jesus at the sea. Within two verses the word *sea* occurs three times and the word *boat* once. The narratee knows from 1:16 that the Sea of Galilee is intended. The setting places Jesus opposite the crowd. Jesus is in the boat on the sea. (The Greek is even more dramatic: "he got into a boat and sat on the sea.") The crowd is beside the sea on the land. Spatial location underlines the differences between characters.

This setting represents a change from the previous scene. The action also changes. Jesus had been healing and exorcising demons; now he is teaching. The Markan Jesus is often said to be teaching or preaching, but few examples are given. Chapter 4, the parable chapter, is an important exception. The narrator's introductory comment, "He began to teach them many things in parables," is followed by Jesus' telling of one parable, that of the sower.

Verse 10 presents a change of characters and thus a new scene. It has proven very difficult for real readers to agree on which characters are now assumed by the narrator to be present. It becomes immediately clear that "when [Jesus] was alone" means when the large crowd had left, not when he was solitary. What does not become immediately clear is who are "those who were around him along with the twelve." If there are two groups (the twelve, the others), they speak as one, and Jesus so responds. It seems likely (although this observation is clear only from further analysis throughout the Gospel) that the implied author creates ambiguity about who is hearing Jesus in order to encourage the implied reader to read himself or herself into the story. The implied author, the narrator, and the Markan Jesus have a shared point of view, and they simultaneously address the characters, the narratee, and the implied reader. The would-be two groups who are really one (the twelve plus the others) are one over against "those outside."

To those inside has been given (the passive voice suggests "given by God") "the secret [or, better, "mystery"] of the kingdom of God." For those outside everything "comes in parables." Parables are comparisons or riddles. In understanding parables, those outside are no better off than those to whom the prophet Isaiah spoke: they may hear, but they do not understand. This ironic allusion to Isaiah 6:9–10, which is itself ironic, is an intertextual echo of the Septuagint.

This mysterious little scene about the mystery of the kingdom is followed by the Markan Jesus' allegorical explanation of the parable of the sower. Each element of the parable is taken to represent some element in the larger story of the growth of "the word." "The word" (*logos*) is an early Christian synonym for the gospel, the good news, the message by and about Jesus as the Christ. According to this explanation, the parable of the sower is about improper and proper ways of hearing the word. In its Markan narrative context (parable, insiders and outsiders, explanation), the story of the sower is symbolic of hearing parables as outsiders and as insiders. Insiders receive not only "the mystery" but also an additional explanation.

This twofold pattern, parable plus explanation, seems to be repeated. Verse 21 is a little parable about a lamp; verse 22 is a brief explanation. Verse 24 is a little parable about a measure; verse 25 is a brief explanation. Verse 23, right in the middle, is the echoing refrain: "Let anyone with ears to hear listen!" (cf. 4:9). Next the narrator presents Jesus presenting two slightly longer parables, both about seeds. Neither one is followed by an explanation, but verses 33–34 restate this pattern. To "them" (the outsiders) Jesus spoke the word in parables, "as they were able to hear it." To "his disciples" (and other insiders?) he explained everything privately. As other features in the Markan narrative make even more clear, who is inside and who is outside is not a matter of social status or role, but of response to Jesus. "Let anyone with ears to hear listen!"

The final two seed parables offer explicit comparisons to "the kingdom of God." The kingdom of God comes *from God*, not from human effort. It comes in God's time and thus, from a human point of view, it always comes as a surprise. All three seed parables suggest that the best predictor of the kingdom's fulfillment is not its beginning but God's power. But all of these implications are rhetorically shown, not told. Like the characters within the story, the implied readers of the narrative must have ears to hear and eyes to see. One becomes an insider by perceiving and understanding. The Markan Jesus and the Markan implied author recognize all such insight as a mysterious gift.

Mighty Deeds on and by the Sea (4:35–5:43)

The sea continues to be the dominant setting for Markan narrative events from 4:1 through 8:21. When the dominant setting switches to "the way" at 8:27, the plot also takes a turn. Narrative elements frequently echo each other in Mark's narrative. At 4:35 the narrator reports a dramatic event that occurs on the sea. Jesus is already in the boat; the disciples join him, as well as other people in other boats. A windstorm comes up, threatening to fill the boat with water from the waves. Yet Jesus is asleep in the stern. The desperate disciples wake him, saying, "Teacher, do you not care that we are perishing?" Apparently they assume Jesus *could* do something to help—if he just *would*. He does. He "rebukes" the wind, as he had earlier rebuked unclean spirits; and he tells the sea to become still. It does. Jesus also questions the disciples: "Why are you afraid? Have you still no faith?" The disciples—not too surprisingly, "filled with great awe"—question themselves: "Who then is this, that even the wind and the sea obey him?"

The sea scene ends there. No character answers this question. It is forwarded to the implied reader, who shares with the implied author knowledge of the Hebrew Bible in the form of the Septuagint. Psalm 107:23–32 is especially relevant.

> Some went down to the sea in ships,
>   doing business on the mighty waters;
> they saw the deeds of the LORD,
>   his wondrous works in the deep.
> For he commanded and raised the stormy wind,
>   which lifted up the waves of the sea.
> . . . .
> Then they cried to the LORD in their trouble,
>   and he brought them out from their distress;
> he made the storm be still,
>   and the waves of the sea were hushed.
>   —Psalm 107:23–25, 28–29

Who then is this, that even the wind and the sea obey him? The Lord God. The Lord Jesus Christ. The power of Jesus the Christ is the power of God. All these affirmations are shown, not told. The fact that the disciples do not explicitly answer their own rhetorical question has more to do with the discourse than with the story. The implied author has the disciples leave the question open for the implied reader. The implied author seems to know that a conclusion the implied reader must work to arrive at will be held more strongly. The narrative rhetoric is persuasive.

Despite the storm, Jesus and the disciples arrive on "the other side of the sea" at "the country of the Gerasenes." Historical interpreters, perhaps beginning with Matthew, who substitutes the name Gadarenes (Matt. 8:28), have had difficulty locating such a place. But from a narrative critical point of view, the country of the Gerasenes is Gentile territory opposite Jewish Galilee. If the implied reader does not know that narrative fact from the name, he or she will surely know it from the great herd of swine found there. Since Jewish law classifies the pig as an unclean animal, one unfit for humans or God, primarily Jewish areas do not support large herds of swine. The casting out of a legion of demons from the Gerasene man, who had lived as a wild man among the tombs, is the Markan Jesus' first healing of a Gentile. When the exorcised demons enter the swine, as they had requested, and the swine rush to their deaths in the sea, the Gentile region seems to be purged of evil and made ready for Jesus' preaching of the good news. Jesus tells the healed Gerasene to go home and tell how much "the Lord" has done for him. Instead, the man goes throughout the "ten [Greek] cities" of the region, the Decapolis, proclaiming "how much Jesus had done for him." Who then is the Lord? The scene ends with all marveling.

The sea, however, still orients the scenes and the movements of the plot. At 5:21 the narrator tells that Jesus crossed "again in the boat to the other side," where a great crowd gathered about him "by the sea." For any implied reader who might be confused about which side of the sea is now "the other side," the implied author again gives a second indication: Jairus, one of the rulers of the synagogue, appears. No synagogues are needed where herds of swine are kept. Back in Jewish Galilee, Jesus heals his own people again. Two healing stories are intercalated: the raising of Jairus's daughter and the healing of the hemorrhaging woman. A third indication of the Jewishness of the setting is the repeated number twelve: a twelve-year flow of blood, a twelve-year-old girl. As was mentioned above, twelve is symbolic of the twelve tribes and thus of Israel.

The intercalation is done very naturally. At times it has even been taken literally and historically rather than narratively and rhetorically. Because the woman interrupted Jesus on his way to Jairus's house, Jairus's daughter died. Here intercalation, the inserting of one story into another, is an integral part of the plot. But Markan intercalation is always for interpretive purposes. The framing story is to be interpreted in light of the inside story, and vice versa. Both suppliants have extreme needs. Jairus's daughter is "at the point of death," and then dead; the woman has spent everything she had on medical treatment, only to grow worse. In addition, both suppliants have extreme faith. The woman believes that Jesus' power is so great that merely touching the hem of his garment can heal her; Jairus, with Jesus' encouragement, believes that even if his daughter is dead Jesus' power can enable her to live again. According to Jewish law, the continual uncleanness of the hemorrhaging woman made her a social and religious outcast, as dead socially as Jairus's daughter was physically. The child becomes again a daughter to her father, and the woman becomes again a "daughter" (5:34) of Israel.

At the close of the raising of Jairus's daughter, and thus of the two intercalated healing stories, the narrator adds—not too surprisingly—"at this they were overcome with amazement." But the next addition is surprising: "[And] he strictly ordered them that no one should know this. . . ." Impossible! The commotion, weeping, and wailing mentioned in verse 38 were, in effect, the first phase of the girl's funeral. It would be more than a little difficult not to say something to the mourners. As is frequently the case, what cannot be taken literally can be meaningful at another level. Redaction critics labeled Jesus' command to secrecy here and elsewhere "the messianic secret" and interpreted it in terms of Mark's editing of tradition to meet the needs of his community. Narrative critics see it as a plot device that calls attention to the complexity of the image of Messiahship in the Markan Gospel. If Jairus told all that he knew about Jesus, he would tell *only* that Jesus was powerful beyond imagining. For the implied author of Mark that statement would be a half-truth; the other half, developed in the other half of Mark's Gospel and equally beyond imagining, is that Jesus is committed to using that power only for service, even in the face of suffering and death. At 5:43 the implied reader knows more than Jairus knows, but not yet the whole truth. Jesus' charge to keep quiet his powerful deed is another way for the implied author to raise the question of his identity. If Lord, if Messiah, what kind of Lord? what kind of Messiah?

Preaching/Rejection/Death (6:1–30)

The event that follows the raising of Jairus's daughter in the plotted narrative suggests another reason for the Markan Jesus' hesitancy in making his mighty deeds known: even a half-truth about his power can be misunderstood. Jesus is rejected in the synagogue in his hometown. His teaching results not only in the astonishment of the people, as it had done earlier, but also in their anger and offense at him. Who does he think he is, anyway? He's just Mary's son (probably a slur, since a male child was normally identified as his father's son). His brothers and sisters are not anything special. Jesus says, "A prophet is not without honor, except in his own country [hometown], and among his own kin, and in his own house" (6:4, RSV). The implied reader says, "Jesus is a prophet."

The Markan Jesus' response to this rejection is threefold: (1) to heal whomever he can, limited, it would seem, by the people's unbelief; (2) to move on to other villages and teach; (3) and to send out the twelve on a mission of their own. Jesus commissions the twelve, two by two, to go out to preach and exorcise unclean spirits, just as he has been doing. He charges them not to rely on their own provisions ("no bread, no bag, no money") but on the hospitality of others. He warns them that they will be rejected, just as he has been. They go and carry out their double mission of preaching and healing.

While the twelve are gone, as it were, the narrator tells another story, one about John the Baptizer. This is an intercalation, and it is arranged for interpretive purposes, not just for the convenience of the plot. The link is King Herod's learning about how Jesus' name had become known. What does Herod think about this famous Jesus? Others may think he is Elijah or a prophet, but Herod, apparently feeling the pangs of guilt, thinks Jesus is John the Baptizer raised to life again. For Herod, Jesus raises again the trauma of John's beheading.

In 1:14, passing reference is made by the narrator to the "handing over" (Greek, *paradidonai*) of John the Baptizer: "Now after John was arrested, Jesus came to Galilee, proclaiming the good news of God, . . ." John preached and was rejected. Jesus is preaching. Nothing more is said about John's arrest until 6:14–29, at which point Jesus has been rejected and the twelve are preaching. John's imprisonment and beheading at the command of Herod is told in a lively and detailed narrative flashback or analepsis. As this story within a story closes with John's death, Jesus' disciples return from a successful preaching tour. (They are sent out as "the twelve" [6:7], but they return as "the apostles" [6:30]. *Apostles* means the "ones sent out.") The Markan narrative rhetoric discloses a parallelism between the preaching, being rejected and "handed over," and death of John, Jesus, and the disciples. At chapter 6 John is dead, Jesus is rejected, and the disciples are preaching. What will happen to Jesus next? What will happen to the disciples?

Mighty Deeds by and on the Sea (6:31–56)

Jesus is concerned for his "apostles"; he takes them away from the crowd by boat to a wilderness place. But Jesus' attempt to find the leisure to eat with his disciples leads, ironically, to the work of teaching and feeding the crowd. Jesus teaches the great multitude that awaits him in the hoped-for deserted place because "they were like sheep without a shepherd." This echo of a common image of aimlessness from the Hebrew Bible (e.g., Num. 27:17; 1 Kings 22:17; Ezek. 34:5) alerts the implied reader to the Jewishness of the setting.

The story of the multiplication of the loaves and the fish and the feeding of the five thousand is filled with dialogue between Jesus and the disciples. "Send the crowd away to get food." "No, you feed them." "How can we feed them?" "Start with what you've got." The miraculous meal in the wilderness echoes God's provision of manna in the wilderness, but it also foreshadows for the implied reader the eucharistic meal. The four verbs *took*, *blessed*, *broke*, and *gave* (6:41) are repeated in the narration of the Last Supper (14:22), which models (actually is modeled after) the Eucharist. As is appropriate for meals that God hosts, everyone eats and is satisfied, *and* twelve baskets full of leftovers are collected. The number twelve reminds the implied reader (symbolically) that the recipients are Jews. The surplus of bread outshines the miracle of the manna, in which nothing extra could remain, except for use on the Sabbath (Ex. 16:13–30).

"Immediately" Jesus sends the disciples off by boat again, not to some nearby deserted place this time, but to Bethsaida, a city on the other (Gentile) side of the sea. Jesus dismisses the crowd and goes "up on the mountain" to pray. Which mountain? A mountain by the lakeshore in Galilee? No, the mountain where all of God's prophets communicate with God. The narrator's use of the contrast between land and sea to contrast characters at 6:47 is reminiscent of 4:1. "[And] when evening came, the boat was out on the sea, and he was alone on the land." The disciples are unable to complete their mission to "go on ahead" of Jesus to Gentile Bethsaida. The wind is against them. Then they think they see a ghost passing by them, walking on the water. The implied reader knows it is Jesus yet is able to understand their terror. Jesus' words are another intertextual echo from Exodus: "I am" (usually translated "It is I"). God said, "I am" to Moses from the burning bush (Ex. 3:14). Who then is this? It does not surprise the implied reader that the wind ceases.

The narrator's next comment, the conclusion to this scene, does surprise. "And they [the disciples] were utterly astounded, for they did not understand about the loaves, but their hearts were hardened" (6:51b–52). Why doesn't the narrator say, "They did not understand about the wind or the walking on water"? What do the loaves have to do with the sea? And why are so many images from Exodus being stacked up here? Bread in the wilderness, walking on (through) the sea, "I am"—and now hardened hearts. The passive voice ("their hearts were hardened") suggests that the disciples' hearts, like Pharaoh's, were hardened by God so that God's overall purpose for the people of God could be worked out. The implied reader must keep reading!

Surprising closings and openings of scenes are becoming the norm. From the cryptic reference to hardened hearts, the implied reader moves not to an anticipated arrival at Bethsaida on the east but to a surprising landing at Gennesaret, still on the west. In the midst of so many other amazing narrative events, one would not have been shocked to read of a successful, even miraculous, crossing to Bethsaida once Jesus entered the boat. But Jewish Gennesaret it is, where a narrative summary of Jesus' ministry of healing is presented. People bring the sick to him from everywhere; as many as touch even the fringe of his cloak are made well. The faith and healing of the hemorrhaging woman echoes for the implied reader. By the sea Jesus feeds five thousand; on the sea Jesus walks; by the sea Jesus heals many. Jesus has authority over the sea—and quite a bit more.

Conflict over Jewish Law (7:1–23)

Authority is the issue in the next series of scenes. Jesus' antagonists are "the Pharisees and some of the scribes who had come from Jerusalem" (7:1). Pharisees and scribes were the chief antagonists of the Markan Jesus in a series of five controversy stories narrated earlier (2:1–3:6). The "scribes who came down from Jerusalem" appeared earlier as ones accusing Jesus of being possessed by Beelzebul, the prince of demons (3:22–30). Jerusalem itself, which has a high positive connotation in traditional Judaism, has a negative connotation in the Gospel of Mark. So, when Pharisees and Jerusalem scribes gather together to Jesus, the implied reader anticipates conflict. And conflict there surely is.

The conflict is triggered by the failure of Jesus' disciples to observe the Jewish (and particularly Pharisaic) regulations about ritual handwashing before meals. The implied author finds it necessary in a parenthetical aside to explain this "tradition of the elders" for any implied reader who may be unfamiliar with it. Because at other times the implied author assumes the implied reader is quite familiar with the Hebrew Bible (in Greek translation), a mixed group of Jewish and Gentile implied readers may be indicated, or implied readers who are familiar with Jewish *Scripture* but not Jewish *tradition* may be assumed. In the explanatory aside, the Pharisees and all the Jews are "they."

The conflict is expressed more in monologue than in dialogue. The Markan narrator's telling is one-sided from the start. The Pharisees and scribes get one question, "Why do your disciples not live according to the tradition of the elders, but eat with defiled hands?" Even that question has been elaborately anticipated by the narrator (7:2–4). Jesus gets two paragraphs of direct defense and counterattack. Jesus turns a statement from the prophet Isaiah against his antagonists. The Isaiah passage underlines what is at stake here for the Markan Jesus: divine commandment versus human tradition. As an example of this opposition, Jesus suggests the disparity between one of the Ten Commandments, "Honor your father and your mother," and the traditional use (and abuse) of Corban. Corban refers to money or property that was verbally "offered" or "dedicated" to God, that is, withdrawn from ordinary use. Although the money was not handed over directly to the temple treasury, it was not required to be used for care of one's parents. The "tradition of the elders" that may momentarily sound honorable on the lips of the Pharisees and scribes is clearly condemned when it is reclassified by Jesus as "human tradition" in opposition to

"divine commandment." Jesus appeals to a higher authority—
Scripture—and one that his antagonists themselves profess to
honor. His antagonists are silenced.

A change of scene occurs with the entrance of a new group
of characters. Jesus calls the crowd to himself again and opens
with these words: "Listen to me, all of you, and understand."
The words echo similar uses of "listen" and "understand" in
chapter 4, the parable chapter, and, indeed, these words introduce a parable here. It is a very brief parable (comparison or
riddle) about defilement being caused by what comes out of
people, not by what goes into them. Because the previous
scene concerned the "defiled hands" of the disciples, the topic
continues despite the change of scene.

This pattern occurs again immediately (7:17): a change of
scene without a change of topic, a third scene concerned with
defilement. There is a spatial change: Jesus enters a house.
The narrator had not commented on his location earlier; it
was presumably out-of-doors. There is a shift in characters:
Jesus leaves the crowd. Then his disciples ask him about the
parable. The presence of the disciples was not mentioned at
the narration of the parable. The implied author does not
make everything explicit; thus what is made explicit becomes
all the more important.

The shift from Jesus' public teaching of the crowd to his
private teaching of the disciples occurs throughout the
Markan narrative. It occurs in chapter 4: parable to the crowd,
explanation of the parable to the disciples (and "those who
were around him"). Frequently, as in chapter 7, this character
shift is paralleled by a spatial shift: from out-of-doors or an
unspecified location to in "the house."

Chapter 7 also echoes chapter 4 in the introduction of Jesus'
explanation of the parable by questioning the disciples' lack of
understanding (7:18; 4:13). Only when characters to whom the
Markan Jesus is willing to give additional teaching misunderstand does the Markan implied author have an opportunity to

give additional teaching to the implied reader. And here the narrator goes beyond Jesus! Jesus says that persons are not defiled by anything that enters their stomachs and passes through their digestive systems. The immediate implication is that persons are not defiled by dirt from unwashed hands. But the narrator notes, parenthetically: "(Thus he declared all foods clean.)" (As the implied reader is aware, observing the rules concerning clean and unclean foods was one of the more obvious ways Jews were distinct from Gentiles.) Then Jesus says that persons are defiled by evil thoughts that come out of their hearts. The riddle is solved. The implicit is explicit.

Contact with Gentiles (7:24–8:10)

"[And] from there he set out and went away to. . . ." From where? Where have we been? the implied reader might well ask. The topic was defilement, and the antagonists were Pharisees and scribes, so the territory must have been Jewish; there is where they would be. In fact, the last landfall was Gennesaret. "[And] from there he set out and went away to the region of Tyre [and Sidon]" (7:24). These place names indicate quite a change. Tyre and Sidon are in the ancient land of Phoenicia, the Roman province of Syria, as far north as the Markan narrative reaches and definitely Gentile territory. But the Markan narrator likes to make sure the narratee follows. The second indication of the Gentile setting of the scene is the double description of the woman who seeks Jesus' help: "a Gentile [a Greek], of Syrophoenician origin."

The narrator tells that Jesus' intention in going north was not to seek out more crowds to heal. "[And] he entered a house and did not want anyone to know he was there. Yet he could not escape notice" (7:24b). The fact that the Syrophoenician woman seeks out the secluded Jesus is just the first indication of her persistence on behalf of her demon-possessed daughter. The Markan Jesus rebuffs her initial request, and he does so with a powerful and degrading metaphor. "Let the children be fed first, for it is not fair to take the children's food [bread] and throw it to the dogs." The children are Israel. She is the dog, and she yaps right back! Two can play at metaphors. "Sir, even the dogs under the table eat the children's crumbs." She has him. She has risked a second rebuke and won her daughter's health. "For this saying [word, *logos*]" (7:29, RSV), Jesus says, you may go home to a healed child, a healed Gentile child. (Jesus, too, seems to have experienced healing.)

The story of the Syrophoenician demoniac is not the first story of a Gentile healed by Jesus in Mark. (This interests form critics and bothers redaction critics, who say that it would make more sense if it were the first Gentile healing.) Even as the story echoes the healing of the Gerasene demoniac, it has a certain freshness. It explains more fully the outreach of Jesus' healing power. The Markan Jesus is not opposed to giving additional explanations—even in actions.

The next spatial shift is perhaps the most confusing one in the entire Markan narrative. "Then he returned from the region of Tyre, and went by way of Sidon towards the Sea of Galilee, in the region of the Decapolis" (7:31). Sidon is north of Tyre, and the region of the Decapolis is east of the Sea of Galilee. So Jesus went north to return south, through the east. The implied author seems less concerned with the logic of the travel route than with the nature of the destinations: Tyre, Sidon, the Decapolis. Gentile place names are accumulated for emphasis. The deaf-mute who is healed is also a Gentile.

The healing is, for Mark's Gospel, a particularly physical one (touching, spitting), but the techniques are common to healers in the Greco-Roman world. The man is healed privately, away from the multitude, and Jesus charges those who know of it to tell no one. But the charge backfires: "the more he ordered them, the more zealously they proclaimed it" (7:36). Astonishment beyond measure is the end result of this encounter with one who "makes the deaf to hear and the mute to speak."

Two stories of Gentile healings have followed the three-scene discussion of defilement. Maybe it is not just all *foods* that the Markan implied author thinks Jesus has declared clean. That possibility is strengthened by the next story: the feeding of the four thousand. The feeding stories resound with the loudest and clearest intratextual echoes of the Markan narrative. Their overall similarities set off their significant differences. The five thousand are fed somewhere on the west (Jewish) side of the sea. The four thousand are fed somewhere on the east (Gentile) side of the sea. (There have been no place references since the mention of the Decapolis.) In the former case, the Markan Jesus' compassion is linked to the people's being like sheep without a shepherd, an image from the Hebrew Bible. In the latter case, Jesus' compassion is linked to their hunger, a universal human problem. In the former case, twelve baskets of leftovers are collected; in the latter case, seven. As twelve is a number symbolic of the Jews, so seven is a number symbolic of "the nations," the Gentiles. (In Acts 6, at the instigation of the "Hellenists," seven deacons are chosen to assist the twelve apostles.)

The allusions—backward to the manna of the exodus and forward to the bread of the Last Supper and the Eucharist—remain constant between the two feeding stories. What is added is that such bread is for Gentiles as well as for Jews. Jesus heals and feeds his own; that would be story enough. But Jesus also heals and feeds outsiders. That action takes some explaining; it is harder to understand.

Signs and Seeing (8:11–26)

After dismissing the four thousand, Jesus "immediately" gets into a boat with his disciples and goes to the district of Dalmanutha. The location of such a place is no longer known, although it is generally thought to be in Galilee on the sea. Will the Markan narrator give a second clue about the setting? Yes! "The Pharisees came and began to argue with him . . ."

(8:11). The implied reader knows the journey has returned to Galilee. Just before his departure from Galilee to Gentile Tyre and Sidon, Jesus was arguing with the Pharisees. Now on his return from the Gentile Decapolis, Jesus and the Pharisees pick up where they left off. If Jesus has so much authority, surely he can produce a sign from heaven, that is, from God, for the Pharisees. Something clear and explicit would be nice. Jesus sighs. No such sign will be given—to them or to "this generation." In Mark's Gospel Jesus performs mighty deeds (*dynameis*) but not signs (*sēmeia*). (Contrast John's Gospel.) To ask for a sign is to demand that divine power be present on one's own terms rather than to perceive it wherever it manifests itself. So Jesus leaves the Pharisees. He gets into the boat again and departs "to the other side."

Yet the next scene is not on "the other side" but on the sea itself. It is the third scene carried out on the sea in Mark's narrative: first, calming the sea; second, walking on the sea; third, a conversation in the boat on the sea. This dialogue is not just another conversation between Jesus and the disciples. It is a careful, symbolic drawing together of themes that have been developed since 4:1. The implied reader's ears ring with echoes: the sea, the boat, loaves of bread, hardened hearts, eyes that do not see, ears that do not hear, five thousand, twelve baskets, four thousand, seven baskets, understand? So many things have happened, and then happened again in a different setting. Jesus tells a parable to all, and then explains it to some. Jesus heals and feeds at home, and then far beyond. There is much to hear and see, to perceive and understand.

As the disciples did not answer their own rhetorical question at 4:41 ("Who then is this, that even the wind and the sea obey him?"), so they do not answer Jesus' rhetorical question at 8:21 ("Do you not yet understand?"). The beneficiary of both silences is the implied reader, the one for whom the story is being told. To hear only the silence of the disciples and not also the rhetoric of the implied author is to try to read the story without the discourse. Narrative is always story-as-discoursed. Markan rhetorical discourse relies on juxtaposition: item, item, item; comparison, contrast, insight. The implied reader must make the connections—and *may*—because neither the characters nor the narrator make them explicit. Sea, boat, bread, twelve, seven. Do *you* not yet understand?

The conclusion of a large section of Mark (4:1–8:21) with Jesus' questioning of the disciples (8:14–21) suggests that Jesus' disciples are distinguished from his opponents not by possessing the right answers but by being possessed by the right question: not "Why does he not perform a sign from heaven?" (see 8:11), but "Who then is this . . . ?" (4:41). Jesus responds to opponents and followers with both questions and answers: "Why does this generation ask for a sign?" (8:12). "Truly I tell you, no sign will be given to this generation" (8:12). "Do you not yet understand?" (8:21). "I am" (the literal meaning of the Greek, 6:50). "I will go before you to Galilee" (14:28; cf. 16:7). Some interpreters—including redaction, narrative, and reader-response critics—see the misunderstanding (or incomprehension) of the disciples as central to Mark 4–8. Others, including the present author, see as a central thrust of these chapters the search for understanding—understanding of who Jesus is and thus of what following him entails. The disciples embody that search, that ongoing process. Like Mark's Gospel itself (its opening line is "The beginning of the good news . . ."), the search for understanding does not come to a decisive end in the Markan narrative. But neither the Markan narrator nor the Markan Jesus (nor his messenger at the empty tomb) gives up on the disciples. In this action, too, the implied reader is asked to follow.

"[And] they came to Bethsaida" (8:22). Bethsaida! Because of the significance of the sea conversation, a real reader, at least, and perhaps the implied reader as well, could almost forget about crossing the sea and surely about Bethsaida. Many scenes back—after feeding the five thousand and before walking on the sea—Jesus had tried to send the disciples across the sea before him to Gentile Bethsaida. They never made it on their own. And now Jesus has led them there, led them to the Gentiles by an elaborate detour, through an additional explanation, as a second chance to see and hear the given mystery. The detour involved starting from the familiar (healings at Gennesaret, 6:53–56), arguing against the conventional (the tradition of the elders, 7:1–23), responding to the "other" (Syrophoenician woman and deaf-mute in the Decapolis, 7:24–37), feeding all who are hungry (feeding the four thousand, 8:1–10), departing from those who demand divine presence on their own terms (Pharisees requesting a sign, 8:11–13), and questioning those who travel alongside (conversation with the disciples on the sea, 8:14–21). So they came at last to Bethsaida, and at Bethsaida the blind see, even if by stages.

Several echoes of the healing of the deaf-mute in the Decapolis are heard in the story of the healing of the blind man of Bethsaida. Both suppliants are Gentiles and suffer from communicative disorders. Both persons are healed away from the crowd. Jesus even leads the blind man out of the village. Both stories involve physical healing techniques: applying spittle or saliva to the affected body part and touching with the fingers or hands. Both accounts conclude with Jesus' admonition not to make the healing known. Jesus tells the once-blind man not even to go into the village. The distinctive aspect of the healing of the blind man of Bethsaida—not only in Mark but in all the Gospels—is a healing process of two stages. Blindness and sight are frequently used symbolically in the ancient (and contemporary!) world. The two-stage transition from one to the other increases the symbolic possibilities.

The two-stage healing.of.the blind man outside Bethsaida is almost universally recognized as a pivotal scene in the Markan Gospel. It is generally linked symbolically with the two scenes that follow it: the "confession" of Peter (8:27–30) and Jesus' first passion prediction (8:31–33). Peter "sees" that

Jesus is the Messiah, the Christ. But he fails to "see" that, as the Christ, Jesus must suffer. To heal Peter (and perhaps the implied reader) of that blindness will require a second stage, the second half of Mark's Gospel. The narrative clearly supports this reading.

But the two-stage healing of blindness is a transitional scene, and it also has symbolic links with the scenes that precede it. Jesus has been working in two stages all along: parables and explanations, Jewish healings and Gentile healings, Jewish feeding and Gentile feeding. The duality of the Markan Jesus' technique reflects the twofoldness of the Markan implied author's convictions: Jesus is Messiah for both Jews and Gentiles; Jesus is Messiah of power and suffering service. To see that is to see everything clearly.

Conclusion

The implied author of Mark is a storyteller—and a masterful one. For this reason, narrative criticism seems an especially appropriate approach to reading and interpreting the Gospel of Mark. Narrative critics seek to learn more about *how* the story means, that is, how the implied author uses characters, settings, plot, and rhetoric to communicate meaning. If such study can help us align ourselves with the implied reader, our own roles as real readers—and rereaders—of Mark will surely be enriched. We will look intently—and see.

2

Fallible Followers

Women and Men in the Gospel of Mark

Discipleship—that is, following Jesus—has been recognized as a central theme or motif in the Gospel of Mark.[1] Understandably enough, the portrayal of the disciples in Mark has often been the focus of scholarly investigation of the theme of discipleship. Ernest Best's study, *Following Jesus: Discipleship in the Gospel of Mark*,[2] serves as an excellent example. Best also exemplifies a certain overschematization of the Markan relation of disciples and discipleship. "If a writer wishes to talk about discipleship using men as examples," proposes Best, "there are two obvious approaches."

> He may either set forward a series of examples of good discipleship with the implication that these examples

1. I am pleased to acknowledge the support of the Center for Programs in the Humanities at Virginia Polytechnic Institute and State University for research conducted during summer 1982 and reflected here.

2. Ernest Best, *Following Jesus: Discipleship in the Gospel of Mark*, JSNTSup 4 (Sheffield: JSOT Press, 1981). See also Best, "The Role of the Disciples in Mark," *NTS* 23 (1977): 377–401, and Best, "Mark's Use of the Twelve," *ZNW* 69 (1978): 11–35.

> should be followed (so Daniel 1–6; 2 Maccabees; 4
> Maccabees) or he may instruct through the failures of
> his examples (so many of the stories about the patri-
> archs and David). Mark chose the latter course.[3]

I agree with Best, against Weeden,[4] that the "failure" of the disciples contributes to a characterization of discipleship rather than to a polemic against the historical opponents of the author of Mark's Gospel. Yet I disagree with Best on two important points. I affirm that: (1) what Mark has to say about discipleship is understood not only from the failure of the disciples but also from their success, and especially from the tension between their success and their failure; and (2) what Mark has to say about discipleship is understood in reference not only to the disciples but also to other Markan characters who meet the demands of following Jesus. Followers and followership might be better keys to our investigation than disciples and discipleship.

Fallible Followers

Certainly the disciples are chief among the followers of the Markan Jesus. And, equally certainly, the disciples are fallible followers. The reason for this portrayal is to be sought in the author's approach to the reader, as both Robert Tannehill and Joanna Dewey have persuasively argued. According to Tannehill:

> a reader will identify most easily and immediately
> with characters who seem to share the reader's situa-
> tion. . . . [The author] composed his story so as to

---

3. Best, *Following Jesus*, 12. But see ibid., 205–6, on the role of "the Twelve," according to Best a group to be distinguished from the disciples.

4. Theodore J. Weeden, "The Heresy That Necessitated Mark's Gospel," *ZNW* 59 (1968): 145–58; Weeden, *Mark—Traditions in Conflict* (Philadelphia: Fortress, 1971).

make use of this initial tendency to identify with the disciples in order to speak indirectly to the reader through the disciples' story. In doing so, he first reinforces the positive view of the disciples which he anticipates from his readers, thus strengthening the tendency to identify with them. Then he reveals the inadequacy of the disciples' response to Jesus . . . [which] requires the reader to distance himself from them and their behavior. But something of the initial identification remains, for there are similarities between the problems of the disciples and the problems which the first readers faced. This tension between identification and repulsion can lead the sensitive reader beyond a naively positive view of himself to self-criticism and repentance. The composition of Mark strongly suggests that the author, by the way in which he tells the disciples' story, intended to awaken his readers to their failures as disciples and call them to repentance.[5]

Dewey adds to this view by noting that the implied reader identifies both with the disciples and with Jesus: the implied reader's situation is that of the disciples, but his or her values are those of Jesus; "both the disciples and the implied reader are to live according to the behavior demanded by Jesus."[6] The ups and downs of the Markan disciples, then, suggest the demands of discipleship. Followership is not easy.

Nor is followership exclusive. The disciples are not the only Markan characters who follow Jesus. Throughout the narrative, exceptional individuals believe in Jesus (Jairus, 5:22–24a, 35–43); follow Jesus (Bartimaeus, 10:46–52); agree with Jesus (one of the scribes, 12:28–34); recognize Jesus (centurion, 15:39); honor Jesus (Joseph of Arimathea, 15:42–46)—and thus exemplify to

---

5. Robert Tannehill, "The Disciples in Mark: The Function of a Narrative Role," *JR* 57 (1977): 392–93.
6. Joanna Dewey, "Point of View and the Disciples in Mark," *SBLSP* 21 (1982): 103.

the reader, in at least one special action, what following Jesus entails.[7] In his response to Jesus, the centurion is the exceptional soldier, Jairus the exceptional synagogue ruler, Joseph the exceptional council member, and the scribe who is "not far from the kingdom of God" (12:34; contrast 12:38–40) the exceptional scribe. Perhaps Bartimaeus, whose only group membership seems to be the crowd, is less exceptional in this sense.

The crowd, I have argued elsewhere,[8] is portrayed in the Gospel of Mark—as the disciples are portrayed—in both positive and negative ways in relation to Jesus; and the crowd serves to complement the disciples in a composite portrait of the followers of Jesus. Jesus calls to himself both the disciples and the crowd (disciples: 1:16–20; 3:13–19; 6:7; 8:1, 34; 9:35; 10:42; 12:43; crowd: 7:14; 8:34). And both the disciples and the crowd follow Jesus (disciples: 1:18, 20; 6:1; 10:28; crowd: 2:15; 3:7; 5:24; 10:32?; 11:9). Jesus teaches and feeds both the disciples and the crowd (teaching disciples: esp. 8:31; 9:31; teaching crowd: esp. 2:13; 4:1–2; 6:34; 10:1; feeding disciples: 14:22–25; feeding crowd: 6:39, 41, 42; 8:2, 6)—and also heals the crowd (esp. 1:33–34; 3:10; 6:56). And both the disciples and the crowd are amazed or astonished at Jesus (disciples: 4:41; 6:50, 51; 9:6, 32; 10:24, 26, 32; crowd: 1:22, 27; 2:12; 5:15, 20; 6:2; 7:37; 9:15; 10:32?; 11:18). Again and again the crowd comes to Jesus, time after time the disciples go with

---

7. Tannehill also makes note of characters such as these in relation to Jesus and the disciples, but in Tannehill's interpretation these characters "replace the disciples in the roles which they fail to fill"; they "point to the way which contrasts with the disciples' failure" ("Disciples in Mark," 405).

8. Elizabeth Struthers Malbon, "Disciples/Crowds/Whoever: A Markan Narrative Pattern" (paper circulated for the Literary Aspects of the Gospels and Acts Group at the annual meeting of the SBL, 1982). The citations given below are but a partial listing of the references discussed in "Disciples/Crowds/Whoever" [here, revised, chapter 3].

Jesus. Jesus spends more time with the disciples and asks more assistance from them—in teaching (3:14; 6:12, 30), healing (3:15; 6:7, 13), feeding (6:41; 8:6), and other tasks (1:17; 3:9, 14–15; 6:7, 37, 41, 45; 8:6; 11:1; 14:13, 32, 33–41). Yet the crowd crowds Jesus (2:4; 3:9, 20; 6:31), and the disciples misunderstand discipleship (e.g., 9:33–37, 38–41; 10:35–45). Although both the disciples and the crowd find themselves in opposition to Jewish leaders because they follow Jesus (disciples: 2:15–17, 18, 23–27; 7:1–13; 8:15; 9:14; crowd: 11:18, 32; 12:2; 14:2), in the end both abandon Jesus, who must then face the opposition of Jewish leaders alone (disciples: 14:10, 43, 50, 66–72; crowd: 14:43, 56?; 15:8, 11, 15). Both the disciples and the crowd are fallible followers.

The Gospel of Mark is not an allegory in which a group of characters in the story may be equated with a group of persons beyond the narrative. The disciples are equivalent to neither Mark's supposed opponents nor Mark's imagined readers. The Gospel of Mark, however, is metaphoric and imagistic, and the disciples and the crowd—especially taken together—do evoke a composite image of the followers, the fallible followers, of Jesus. Were only the disciples depicted as followers, the demands of discipleship would be clear, but discipleship might appear restrictive. Were only the crowd depicted as followers, the outreach entailed in following Jesus would be clear, but followership might appear permissive. With both disciples and the crowd depicted as fallible followers, the Markan narrative message is plain: discipleship is both open-ended and demanding; followership is neither exclusive nor easy.

Besides the disciples and the crowd in general and a handful of individuals (such as Jairus, Bartimaeus, and Joseph) in particular, are there other followers of Jesus in the Gospel of Mark? Are there other Markan characters whose actions and whose relations to Jesus present to the readers an image of followership? I believe the women of the Markan Gospel are just such characters.

Women as Fallible Followers

Other commentators have suggested that the women characters of Mark are to be viewed as models of discipleship, but
these suggestions are linked with views of the overall pattern
of characterization in Mark that I find untenable. On the one
hand, both Marla Schierling[9] and John Schmitt[10] posit that the
women characters provide a positive model of discipleship
over against the negative model presented by the twelve male
disciples. On the other hand, Winsome Munro argues that,
although a strong and positive image of women as disciples is
alluded to or presupposed by the Markan text, the Markan
author has suppressed this image as much as possible—its
probable historical reality posing an insurmountable obstacle
to its total suppression.[11] Furthermore, Munro suggests, the
Markan author's "suppression" of a more positive image of
women as disciples parallels his negative portrayal of the disciples (and the family of Jesus)—not as *theios anēr* advocates à
la Weeden, but as representatives of the Jerusalem church
hierarchy à la Schreiber and Tyson.[12] Thus, while Schierling
and Schmitt and Munro disagree on whether or not Mark evi-
dences a positive attitude toward the women characters, they
agree that Mark depicts the disciples negatively. This latter

9. Marla Schierling, "Women as Leaders in the Marcan Communities," *Listening* 15 (1980): 250–56. See also "Women, Cult, and
Miracle Recital: Mark 5:24–34" (Ph.D. diss., Saint Louis University,
1980), esp. chaps. 2 and 5.

10. John Schmitt, "Women in Mark's Gospel: An Early Christian
View of Woman's Role," *TBT* 19 (1981): 228–33.

11. Winsome Munro, "Women Disciples in Mark?" *CBQ* 44
(1982): 225–41.

12. Munro, "Women Disciples in Mark?" 237–41. As Munro
notes (238 n. 28), J. Schreiber ("Die Christologie des Markusevangeliums," *ZTK* 58 [1961]: 175–83) sees the family of Jesus as the
focus of the Markan polemic, whereas J. B. Tyson ("The Blindness of
the Disciples in Mark," *JBL* 80 [1961]: 261–68) sees the focus of this
polemic as Peter, James, and John, represented by the disciples.

view, I have suggested above, is a half-truth—with all the dangers thereof.

The entire Markan pattern of characterization is, I believe, more complex. The disciples are not simply the "bad guys"; and the women do not simply oppose them or parallel them. Rather, the women characters (along with the crowd and several exceptional male characters) supplement and complement the Markan portrayal of the disciples, together forming, as it were, a composite portrait of the fallible followers of Jesus. Thus, two questions will be central to our consideration of the women characters in Mark: (1) How do the women characters shed light on what it means to follow Jesus? and (2) Why are women characters especially appropriate for the role of illuminating followership?

A *quantitative* analysis of the Markan women characters establishes a useful baseline for comparing Mark with the other Gospels. Winsome Munro enumerates the female and male characters in each of the Gospel sources—"excluding genealogies, lists of authorities, undifferentiated groups, and characters in parabolic and other teaching material"—and concludes that Mark and John include about the same proportion of women characters (roughly one-fourth), while "L," the material unique to Luke, features the greatest proportion (three-eighths), and "M," the material unique to Matthew, and "Q," the material shared by Matthew and Luke, include the smallest—and nearly negligible—proportion. In addition, Munro notes that "more actual women appear in Markan material than in any other source, though this is to be expected since Mark contains more narration than any other."[13]

---

13. Munro, "Women Disciples in Mark?" 226. Leonard Swidler calculates not the women characters but all the passages "that deal with one or more women, or with the feminine" (*Biblical Affirmations of Women* [Philadelphia: Westminster, 1979], 224) and concludes (234) that: "Mark's Gospel has the least number of passages dealing with women of the three Synoptic Gospels (20 to Matthew's 36 and Luke's 42) and the smallest number of verses concerning women of all four Gospels (114 to John's 119, Matthew's 180, and Luke's 220)."

A *quantitative* analysis has its limits, of course; and *qualitative* analysis of the passages enumerated is more essential to our understanding of them in their Markan context, as Munro recognizes.[14] In her analysis Munro makes a distinction between the Markan women characters before 15:40 and those in 15:40–16:8. Although I do not agree with Munro's conclusions, I share with her (and also with Schmitt) the desire to investigate a possible *pattern* in the Markan presentation of women characters.

Munro seems to underestimate the importance of the women characters prior to Mark 15:40, yet she is surely correct in observing that not all references to women characters are equally significant within the Markan narrative. Munro also correctly notes that "the anonymity and relative invisibility of women in Mark is due in part to the androcentric bias of his culture which viewed women only in terms of their relations to men, usually as their mothers, wives, or daughters, except in instances of extraordinary importance."[15] I would add that those women or girls who are visible in the Markan narrative as daughters, mothers, or mothers-in-law seem *almost* incidental to it.[16]

---

14. And, I suppose, as Swidler recognizes. Swidler's qualitative analysis, however, involves only commenting on each Markan passage involving women or the feminine in the order of its occurrence in the Gospel, and his comments are not particularly helpful. His goal seems to be a simple (or simplistic? see the review by Wayne A. Meeks in *JBL* 100 [1981]: 466–67) rating: positive, ambivalent, or negative toward women.

15. Munro, "Women Disciples in Mark?" 226.

16. No wives are present as characters in Mark, although Jesus discusses wives and husbands on two occasions: (1) a discussion about divorce, first with Pharisees and then with his disciples (10:2–12); and (2) a discussion with Sadducees about marriage bonds in the resurrection (12:18–27). In both cases Jesus responds by quoting Torah. Jesus also quotes Torah concerning mothers and fathers (7:9; 10:19).

n Jesus heals the daughter of a Jewish father
ɔ–43),[17] the daughter of a Gentile mother (7:24–30),
ᴧe mother-in-law of a disciple (1:30–31). The healings of
remales naturally suggest that Jesus did not limit his healing
power to one sex; however, the two healed daughters contribute little else to the narrative. (The same cannot be said, of
course, of the healed daughter's mother, the Syrophoenician
woman.) Upon being healed, Simon's mother-in-law does contribute to the narrative and to Jesus and his first four disciples—
in serving (*diēkonei*, 1:31) them, although it is not clear at this
early point in the narrative whether her service, her ministry,
shares—and foreshadows—the theological connotations that
the ministry of Mary Magdalene, Mary the mother of James
and Joses, and Salome manifests later (*diēkonoun*, 15:41).

The presence and action of Jesus' mother (and brothers) elic-
its not a healing but an important saying from Jesus (3:31–35).
In fact, Jesus' mother and brothers seem to appear in the narrative—not by name (for which see 6:3) but as "mother" and
"brothers"—for the sake of the saying:[18] "Whoever does the will
of God is my brother, and sister, and mother" (3:35).[19] It is generally argued that Jesus' mother is implicitly included among *hoi
par' autou* (those around him) at 3:21, and that—since 3:21 and
3:31–35 frame the Beelzebul argument of Jesus and the scribes—
Jesus' family is linked with the scribes in misunderstanding
Jesus.[20] While this seems reasonable in a text so fond of framing

---

17. The child's "father and mother" are mentioned together in
5:40.

18. Rudolf Bultmann, *History of the Synoptic Tradition*, rev. ed. (New
York: Harper & Row, 1963), 29–30.

19. Although the Markan narrative later refers to the sisters of
Jesus (6:3), no sisters appear as characters in 3:31–35. The inclusion
of "sister" in the saying at 3:35 serves to broaden its metaphorical
application (cf. 10:29–30).

20. E.g., John Dominic Crossan, "Mark and the Relatives of
Jesus," *NovT* 15 (1973): 85–87.

and intercalation, Jesus' mother is no more central to the action than Jesus' brothers, and no more—or less—fleshed out as a character. Yet the saying elicited by the presence of Jesus' mother and brothers is central to the breakdown of status criteria for followers of Jesus (family membership, selection as one of the twelve disciples, etc.) and the insistence upon action criteria ("whoever does . . .").[21] Women characters who are more involved in the Markan narrative than Jesus' mother continue to be involved in this shift of criteria for followership.

Jesus' mother Mary provides the occasion for Jesus' designation of his family as "whoever does the will of God." Two other Marys and Salome (15:40) observe the occasion on which Jesus most clearly embodies doing the will of God (see 14:36). Between the appearance of Jesus' mother at 3:31–35 and the appearance of the women at the crucifixion at 15:40–41, two women characters are the beneficiaries of Jesus' healing power (one for herself and one for her daughter) by virtue of their bold and active faith; and two women characters are examples of the self-denying service following Jesus entails. Furthermore, in each of the four cases the woman initiates the action in a striking way; Jesus responds or observes.

Bold and Faithful Women

The hemorrhaging woman emerges from the great crowd (*ochlos*, 5:24, 27, 30, 31) that followed Jesus, giving evidence of the presence of women in the crowd, a presence generally "obscured by the androcentric nature of the language which uses masculine forms for common gender."[22] Yet by her

---

21. Munro's conclusion concerning 3:31–35 seems overdrawn: "The question of women among his [Jesus'] following is not only beside the point for Mark, but even something which he perhaps seeks to avoid" ("Women Disciples in Mark?" 228).

22. Ibid., 226.

emerging, the hemorrhaging woman distinguishes herself from the other women and men of the crowd; she is bold, for her faith is strong. The account of the hemorrhaging woman emerges from the account of Jairus and his daughter; the woman's faith is a model for the faith Jairus will need. In addition, the intercalated healings of Jairus's daughter and the hemorrhaging woman (both Jews) seem paired with the immediately prior healing of the Gerasene demoniac (a Gentile).[23] All three are severe cases: the illnesses of the Gerasene and the woman have proven intractable (5:2–5, 25–26); Jairus's daughter dies before Jesus arrives (5:35).

The healing of the hemorrhaging woman is unique in the Markan Gospel, however, in taking place solely at the woman's initiative (5:28–29). Jesus feels his flow of power that stops her flow of blood (5:30) and confirms what she has already experienced: "Daughter, your faith has made you well; go in peace . . ." (5:34; cf. 10:52, to Bartimaeus). As Schierling points out, the hemorrhaging woman has suffered as Jesus: "Only here and in relation to Jesus is the word 'suffering' [*paschō*, 5:26; 8:31; 9:12] ever mentioned. . . . Mark recognizes the suffering of this woman in society as similar to that which Jesus experienced before his death."[24] Moreover, the Markan Jesus brings an end to the hemorrhaging woman's physical and social suffering with no reference to ritual "contamination" from her touch (see Lev. 5:3);[25] bold faith, not bodily purity, is a criterion of followership.

Bold faith characterizes the Syrophoenician woman as well. The hemorrhaging woman reasoned with herself that Jesus'

---

23. For a list of narrative contrasts see Frank Kermode, *The Genesis of Secrecy: On the Interpretation of Narrative* (Cambridge, Mass.: Harvard University Press, 1979), 135.

24. Schierling, "Women as Leaders," 254.

25. See Marla J. Selvidge [formerly Schierling], "Mark 5:24–34 and Leviticus 15:19–20: A Reaction to Restrictive Purity Regulations," *JBL* 103 (1984): 619–23; a correction appeared in *JBL* 104 (1985): 300.

power was such that touching his garments would provide healing (5:28); she proved to be right. The Syrophoenician woman reasons with Jesus (metaphorically) that Gentiles can be served with no loss to Jews (7:28); the Markan Jesus decides that she too is right. The healings these daring women seek are dramatic: the healing of the hemorrhaging woman is the only Markan healing that occurs without the expressed intent of Jesus; the healing of the Syrophoenician woman's daughter is the only Markan healing that occurs at a distance from Jesus. And, as the intercalated healings of Jairus's daughter and the hemorrhaging woman are paired with the immediately preceding healing of the Gerasene demoniac, so the healing of the Syrophoenician woman's daughter is paired with the immediately succeeding healing of the deaf-mute in the Decapolis.[26] Perhaps Luke was not the only evangelist to establish male-female pairings.

The focal point of the encounter between Jesus and the Syrophoenician woman, however, is the question of the scope of Jesus' healing power: Is it to be offered to Gentiles as well as Jews, to outsiders as well as insiders? Although at this point in the narrative the Markan Jesus has already healed the (Gentile) Gerasene demoniac, and although Jesus' presence in the Gentile region of Tyre (7:24) undermines his statement that "it is not right to take the children's bread and throw it to the dogs" (7:27),[27] the Syrophoenician woman's clever reply to Jesus' saying is presented as convincing him to change his mind (7:29). The Syrophoenician woman, an outsider as a Gentile and an outsider as a woman, achieves her goal because

---

26. These parallel pairings are disguised by the intriguing, if somewhat problematic, outline of the compositional structure of 4:1–8:26 presented by Norman Petersen ("The Composition of Mark 4:1–8:26," *HTR* 73 [1980]: 85–217).

27. See Paul J. Achtemeier, "Toward the Isolation of Pre-Markan Miracle Catenae," *JBL* 89 (1970): 287.

of her "saying" (*logos*, 7:29)—not because of her faith alone or her reasoning alone, but because of her speaking up and speaking out—because of her action.

Active faith characterizes both the Syrophoenician woman and the hemorrhaging woman and involves them both in the life-giving power manifest in Jesus. Active faith is a signal of followership (e.g., 11:22–24), life-giving power a sign (e.g., 10:29–31). Self-denying service is a further signal of followership (e.g., 8:34); a further sign is death-defying life (e.g., 8:35–37). Self-denying service characterizes both the poor widow and the anointing woman, who appear near the close of the Markan Jesus' death-defying life.

Self-denying, Serving Women

The poor widow who gives away her last two coins does not encounter Jesus; Jesus observes her. And Jesus calls her action to the attention of his disciples as his final act in the temple. The Markan Jesus' initial act in the temple was the driving out of those who bought and sold there (11:15–19), an account intercalated with the cursing and withering of the fig tree (11:12–14, 20–26). The episode of the poor widow's gift might well be understood as an enacted parable parallel to the fig tree incident[28] or parallel to the intercalated fig tree/temple incident as a whole. The fig tree episode introduces a series of controversies between Jesus and Jewish religious authorities in the temple; the account of the poor widow's gift closes the series. As the withering of the fig tree alludes to the destruction of the temple cult and the temple itself (see chapter 13), so the widow's gift of "her whole living" (*holon ton bion autēs*, 12:44) alludes to Jesus' gift of his life (see chapters 14–15). And Jesus' death is related to the temple's downfall (see 15:37–38).

---

28. L. Simon, "Le sou de la veuve: Marc 12/41–44," *ETR* 44 (1969): 115–26.

The poor widow who gives all (12:41–44) is in striking contrast to the scribes who take all (12:38–40), who "devour widows' houses" (12:40), that is, their means of living. From beginning to end Jesus' ministry is in striking contrast to the scribes' activities and attitudes (1:22; 2:6, 16; 3:22; 7:1, 5; 8:31; 9:11, 14; 10:33; 11:18, 27; [12:28, 32 refer to the exceptional scribe]; 12:35, 38; 14:1, 43, 53; 15:1, 31). Thus Jesus is unlike the self-centered scribes and like the self-denying widow in being one who gives. Addison Wright's argument to the contrary seems more ingenious than convincing. Stressing the immediate context of the account of the widow's gift (esp. 12:40 and 13:2), Wright concludes that one must

> see Jesus' attitude to the widow's gift as a downright disapproval and not as an approbation. The story does not provide a pious contrast to the conduct of the scribes in the preceding section (as is the customary view); rather it provides a further illustration of the ills of official devotion. . . . She has been taught and encouraged by religious leaders to donate as she does, and Jesus condemns the value system that motivates her action, and he condemns the people who conditioned her to do it.[29]

Wright correctly insists that we must not ignore the context of the account of the widow's gift, yet that context includes the episode's place in a whole series of events. As Jesus' first action in the temple, the driving out of buyers and sellers, points to the temple's end, so Jesus' final action in the temple,

---

29. Addison Wright, "The Widow's Mites: Praise or Lament?" *CBQ* 44 (1982): 262. Strangely enough, the moralizing (and unconvincing) interpretation of 12:41–44 offered by Ernest Best (*Following Jesus*, 155–56), while the very type of thing against which Wright argues, is based not on a link back to 12:40 (widow's houses) but on "a better link forwards" to 13:2 (and chap. 13 as a whole), the very thing for which Wright argues.

or rather his reaction to the poor widow's action, points to his own end. Moreover, the temple's end and Jesus' end are carefully interrelated in the Markan Gospel, not only in the juxtaposition of Jesus' death on the cross (15:37) and the rending of the temple curtain (15:38), but also in the intercalation (admittedly in the broadest sense) of the accounts of the passion of Jesus (chapters 11–12, 14–16) and the passion of the community (chapter 13).[30] The crises the community of Jesus' future followers (Mark's readers; see 13:14) will face are to be interpreted in light of the crises Jesus does face in Jerusalem.[31]

Even though the frame and middle of this large-scale intercalation are to be interpreted together, one can skip from 12:44 to 14:1 with no noticeable gap in the story line. Chapter 13, the eschatological discourse, is intrusive. And the intrusion is framed by two stories about exemplary women in contrast to villainous men. Jesus' condemnation of the scribes'

---

30. The phrase "the passion of Jesus and the passion of the community" comes from John R. Donahue, S. J. (lectures given at the Vanderbilt Divinity School, fall 1977). But see Norman Perrin, *The New Testament: An Introduction* (New York: Harcourt, Brace, Jovanovich, 1974), 148, 159. The positions of Perrin and Donahue represent developments, based on more detailed literary analysis, of the more historically oriented positions of Etienne Trocmé and Rudolf Pesch. My designation of chaps. 11–12/13/14–16 as an intercalation is in line with the literary analysis of Perrin and Donahue and does not judge the issue of the historical creation of the Gospel of Mark. Kermode also recognizes chap. 13 as "the largest of his [Mark's] intercalations," but in Kermode's view the insertion is not between chaps. 11–12 and 14–16 but between chaps. 1–12, Jesus' ministry, and 14–16, Jesus' passion (*The Genesis of Secrecy*, 127–28).

31. See also Tannehill, "The Disciples in Mark," 404, and R. H. Lightfoot, *The Gospel Message of St. Mark* (Oxford: Clarendon, 1950), 48–59. Kermode's further expansion of the concept of intercalation is well taken: "Should we think of the whole gospel as an intercalated story? . . . It stands at the moment of transition between the main body of history and the end of history; and what it says has a powerful effect on both" (*The Genesis of Secrecy*, 133–34).

typical actions and his commendation of the poor widow's exceptional action immediately precede chapter 13; the accounts of the chief priests' and scribes' plot against Jesus and the woman's anointing of Jesus immediately succeed chapter 13.[32] One woman gives what little she has, two copper coins; the other woman gives a great deal, ointment of pure nard worth three hundred denarii; but each gift represents self-denial.

It is perhaps ironic that the poor widow's gift occurs in the doomed temple;[33] it is surely ironic that the anointing of Jesus Christ, Jesus Messiah, Jesus the anointed one, takes place not in the temple but in a leper's house (14:3), and not at the hands of the high priest but at the hands of an unnamed woman. Munro considers "the seclusion of the home" simply the characteristic place of appearance of the women characters in Mark's Gospel, since for Mark "women do not seem properly to belong in the public ministry of Jesus."[34] This interpretation misses the irony of the anointing scene—and the significant connotation of the house as the place of gathering of Jesus' followers as opposed to

---

32. Interestingly enough, if the three criteria John R. Donahue, S.J., established for a Markan insertion (*Are You the Christ? The Trial Narrative in the Gospel of Mark*, SBLDS 10 [Missoula, Mont.: Scholars Press, 1973], 241) were to be expanded from the level of the phrase to the narrative level, at least two of the three would be met in the case of chaps. 11–12/13/14–16. First, "close verbal agreement" would become "close narrative agreement" and would be satisfied by the two stories about self-denying women, each following a reference to devious and self-centered men in official religious positions. Second, "synoptic alteration" at the narrative level is clear: both Matthew and Luke parallel Mark 13, but Matthew drops the preceding account of the poor widow, and Luke drops (or moves and significantly alters) the succeeding account of the anointing woman.

33. Wright's argument ("The Widow's Mites," 263, 264) that the destruction of the temple (foretold at 13:2) indicates the absurdity of the poor widow's gift serves, ironically, to call attention to this irony.

34. Munro, "Women Disciples in Mark?" 227.

the synagogue and the temple.[35] A further irony is manifest in the juxtaposition of the unnamed woman, who gives up money for Jesus and enters the house to honor him (14:3–9), and Judas, the man who gives up Jesus for money and leaves the house to betray him (14:10–11).

Whatever the woman's reason for the bold yet gracious anointing she initiates, Jesus graciously accepts it as an anointing "beforehand for burying" (14:8). To this interpretation Jesus adds an equally significant comment: "And truly, I say to you, wherever the gospel is preached in the whole world, what she has done will be told in memory of her" (14:9). This woman's gracious self-denial is forever linked with the good news of Jesus' gracious self-denial. No other Markan character is given this distinction. Whoever would follow Jesus must deny himself or herself (8:34). The anointing woman, like the poor widow, embodies the self-denial of followership. The Markan Jesus presents the demand for self-denial in a striking statement (8:34); two Markan women characters enact the demand in equally striking actions. Thus their actions are to be followed by those who would follow Jesus' words and follow Jesus.

Women as Followers from Beginning to End

At 15:40–41 we learn that not only do women characters exemplify (or even symbolize) followership, but women characters have been followers of Jesus throughout his ministry, from its beginning in Galilee to its end in Jerusalem. After Jesus' death on the cross (15:37), after the rending of the temple curtain (15:38), after the centurion's "confession" of Jesus as "Son of God" (15:39), the narrator informs the reader that "there

---

35. Elizabeth Struthers Malbon, "*Tē Oikia Autou:* Mark 2:15 in Context," *NTS* 31 (1985): 282–92. See also Best, *Following Jesus,* 226–29.

were also women looking on from afar, among whom were
Mary Magdalene, and Mary the mother of James the younger
and of Joses, and Salome, who, when he was in Galilee, followed
him, and ministered to him; and also many other women who
came up with him to Jerusalem" (15:40–41). Although, in my
view, Munro distinguishes too sharply between the Markan
women characters prior to and subsequent to 15:40–41, she is
surely right in observing a significant shift at this point. While
there may be "little preparation for the women who appear at
the death and burial of Jesus and at the empty tomb"[36] in the
sense of literal and straightforward narrative anticipation, the
same cannot be said in terms of metaphorical and allusive narrative dimensions.[37] Individual women characters have previously exhibited in particular actions the active faith and
self-denying service of followership, but at 15:40–41 we learn
that many (*pollai*, 15:41) women, and especially three named
women (Mary Magdalene, Mary the mother of James and Joses,
and Salome, 15:40), have continuously followed (*ēkolouthoun*,
15:41) Jesus and ministered to (*diēkonoun*, 15:41) him.

Munro argues persuasively and on several grounds that
these women are to be identified as disciples: (1) The verb
akoloutheō (cf. 1:18; 2:14) "always denotes commitment to
some degree and never mere physical following when it is
applied to Jesus";[38] (2) the parallel verb *diakoneō* (cf. [and contrast?] 1:31; cf. 1:13; 10:45) must be related to Jesus' saying at
10:45 where *diakoneō* is "of the essence of the messianic ministry in which disciples are called upon to participate—which
is to say, it is of the essence of discipleship";[39] and especially
(3) the pattern of "a nucleus of three within an inner circle or

---

36. Munro, "Women Disciples in Mark?" 230.
37. Cf. Marla J. Selvidge, "Mark and Woman: Reflections on
Serving," *Explorations* 1 (1982): 23–32.
38. Munro, "Women Disciples in Mark?" 231.
39. Ibid., 234.

crowd"[40] links the *pollai* with the disciples and Mary, Mary, and Salome with Peter, James, and John. Yet the fact that the narrator has delayed this reference to women as disciples until nearly the end of the Gospel, together with "the overall invisibility of women in the Second Gospel,"[41] suggests to Munro that "Mark is aware of a female presence in Jesus' ministry but obscures it."[42] It suggests a different reading to me.

In terms of the narrative theory of Gérard Genette, 15:40–41 is a repeating analepsis, an "analepsis on paralipses," that is, a retrospective section that fills in an earlier missing element (or paralipsis).[43] The missing element that a repeating analepsis fills in, however, is "created not by the elision of a diachronic section but by the omission of one of the constituent elements of a situation in a period that the narrative does generally cover."[44] Something that happened earlier is told only later—and perhaps not to obscure but to clarify.[45] That 15:40–41 appears to be the only repeating analepsis in the Gospel increases its significance; its narrative role and content, however, are not without parallel. It is frequently argued that the Markan narrator delays the recognition of Jesus as "Son of God" by a human character (not the narrator [1:1] or unclean spirits [3:11]) until that moment when the true meaning of Jesus' sonship can be understood—the moment of Jesus' death on the cross (15:37, 39). Could it not also be argued that the Markan narrator delays explicit reference to the women disciples or followers until that moment when the

---

40. Ibid., 231.

41. Ibid., 241.

42. Ibid., 234.

43. Gérard Genette, *Narrative Discourse: An Essay in Method*, trans. Jane E. Lewin (Ithaca, N.Y.: Cornell University Press, 1980), 51–54.

44. Ibid., 51–52.

45. Cf. Schmitt, "Women in Mark's Gospel," 232: "That Mark leaves these women for this late moment in his narrative might show that he was careless, or more probably, it indicates a deliberate plan to save them for the culminating irony."

true meaning of discipleship, followership, can be understood—again, the moment of Jesus' death on the cross?

The effect of this delay with regard to *women* disciples/followers only is to compound the surprising reality of Jesus' crucifixion with the surprising reality of the women's discipleship. Within the Markan story, only the women follow Jesus to the end. At Gethsemane one of the twelve betrays Jesus (14:43–45) and the remaining eleven forsake him (14:50). The women, on the other hand, witness the crucifixion—though "from afar" (15:40–41)—and the empty tomb (16:1–8). Experience of the crucifixion and resurrection is central to followership. Again, it is frequently argued that the fact that it is a Roman centurion who recognizes the crucified Jesus as "Son of God" suggests the surprising openness of the Christian faith to the Gentile world. Could it not also be argued that the fact that it is the women disciples/followers who follow to the end suggests the surprising openness of Christian discipleship/followership to all people?[46]

From the first-century Jewish and Jewish-Christian point of view, one could hardly be more of an outsider to the central dramas of religious faith and practice than a Roman centurion—or a woman! But the reversal of outsiders and insiders is basic to the good news of Jesus according to the good news of Mark. For example, being family (expected insider status) does not necessarily make one a follower (true insider status; see 3:31–35); instead, being a follower makes one family (see 10:28–31). And, for example, "many that are first will be last, and the last first" (10:31). In the first-century Jewish world, Roman centurions were surely among "the last"; and in the first-century Jewish, Christian, and Roman worlds, women were surely among "the last."[47] But "the beginning of the

---

46. Munro ("Women Disciples in Mark?" 235–36) argues *against* a similar view.

47. See Krister Stendahl, *The Bible and the Role of Women*, FBBS 15 (Philadelphia: Fortress, 1966), 25–28.

gospel of Jesus Christ, the Son of God" (1:1) is, according to Mark, the beginning of the end of that old order.

Munro sees Mark as so caught up in the old order that he suppresses (narratively) the discipleship of women that was part (historically) of the new order inaugurated by Jesus' ministry and the early Christian response to it.[48] By contrast, I find Mark's Gospel permeated (narratively) by the reversal of expectations—historically conditioned expectations.[49] It would seem that the historical reality of women's lower status and the historical reality of women's discipleship[50] together support in Mark's Gospel the surprising narrative reality of women characters who exemplify the demands of followership. How do the women characters shed light on what it means to follow Jesus? By following and ministering, by bold and active faith and self-denying service. Why are women characters especially appropriate for the role of illuminating followership? Perhaps because, in the community of the author, women were in a position to bear most poignantly the message that among followers the "first will be last, and the last first."

---

48. Munro, "Women Disciples in Mark?" 234–41. Apparently, Munro would argue that women characters are virtually invisible before 15:40 because they are "embarrassing" or "problematic" (235) as women, whereas after 15:40 women characters are suppressed or discredited because they "represent a reality in the ecclesiastical politics of Mark's time" (239).

49. For an independent critique of Munro's thesis see Marla J. Selvidge, "'And Those Who Followed Feared' (Mark 10:32)," *CBQ* 45 (1983): 396–400. For a discussion of the reversal of expectations concerning Galilee and Jerusalem, see my "Galilee and Jerusalem: History and Literature in Marcan Interpretation," *CBQ* 44 (1982): 242–55; reprinted in *The Interpretation of Mark*, ed. William R. Telford (London: T. & T. Clark, 1995), 253–68. See also Tannehill's "The Disciples in Mark" and especially Tannehill's reference (395) to Wolfgang Iser's discussion of the role of "negation" in the novel.

50. See Constance F. Parvey, "The Theology and Leadership of Women in the New Testament," in *Religion and Sexism*, ed. Rosemary Radford Ruether (New York: Simon & Schuster, 1974), 117–49.

At 15:40–41 women characters are most clearly depicted as followers of Jesus. Many women follow even when the twelve disciples flee. I have argued that fleeing indicates that the disciples are fallible, not that they are nonfollowers. Are the women followers fallible as well? Certainly the fact that the women followers at Jesus' crucifixion looked on "at a distance" (*apo makrothen*, 15:40) reminds the reader that upon Jesus' arrest Peter followed "at a distance" (*apo makrothen*, 14:54).[51] Presumably a stronger disciple or stronger followers would have drawn nearer to Jesus at these critical moments of trial and crucifixion. To be present at all is a mark of followership, but remaining "at a distance" is a mark of fallibility—for Peter and for the women.

After Jesus' death only Joseph of Arimathea and Mary Magdalene, Mary the mother of James and Joses, and Salome are present. When Joseph lays Jesus' body in the tomb just before the Sabbath, the two Marys are there to observe (15:47); and just after the Sabbath the two Marys and Salome (16:1)[52] go there to anoint Jesus' body.[53] Some interpreters fault the three women characters for this move; the women should have

---

51. Munro, "Women Disciples in Mark?" 235: "The phrase *apo makrothen* has even stronger impact if Mark intends an allusion to the innocent sufferer of the psalms from whom friends, companions, and kinsfolk stand aloof and far off (Ps. 38:11; 87:9 [LXX; in the English text 88:8]), which is quite explicit in Luke 23:49." On the contrary, Selvidge ("'And Those Who Followed Feared'") suggests translating 15:40 not as "women watching from afar" but as "women from afar watching," stressing not the spatial and psychological distance of the women but their geographical origin.

52. I am assuming that the second Mary named at 15:40, 15:47, and 16:1 is the same person and that the references to her in 15:47 and 16:1 are shortened versions of the reference in 15:40. Cf. Munro, "Women Disciples in Mark?" 226 n. 1.

53. The narrative rhythm of women/Joseph/women at 15:40–41/15:42–46/15:47–16:8 might be compared and contrasted with the narrative rhythm of Jairus/woman/Jairus at 5:21–24/5:24–34/5:35–43.

known, they argue, that Jesus would be resurrected, that Jesus'
anointing for burial had already taken place at the hands of the
unnamed woman in the house of Simon the leper.[54] But the
Markan narrative makes no mention of the presence of the
women followers at Simon the leper's house and explicitly
states that the predictions of Jesus' passion and resurrection
are presented to the disciples, the twelve (8:31; 9:31; 10:33–34;
cf. 9:9; contrast Luke 24:5–8). Those at Simon the leper's
house do not understand the implications of the anointing
(14:4–5; *tines* [some] at 14:4 is ambiguous), and the twelve do
not understand the reference to the resurrection (9:32; cf.
9:10). It seems unlikely, then, that the Markan narrator and
implied reader would expect the women followers to anticipate or understand the resurrection with no forewarning.

More often, however, the three women are faulted not for
coming to the tomb with the intention of anointing Jesus'
body but for going out from the tomb in silence. Some interpreters emphasize that the women's presence at the tomb at all
is a positive sign of their followership in contrast to the disciples' absence as a sign of their fallibility or failure.[55] Yet other
interpreters focus on the women's silence—either as an element that seals the disciples' failure (the disciples never hear
the news)[56] or as a parallel to the disciples' fallibility (the

---

54. Munro's argument is related: "Even the intended role of
anointers of Jesus' body for burial is denied them, for contrary to
their expectation they find the tomb empty. The one they seek eludes
them, but even so their task is redundant, for it has been performed
beforehand by the anointing woman of Mark 14:3–9 (see v. 8)"
("Women Disciples in Mark?" 239).

55. Schierling, "Women as Leaders," 251–53; Schmitt, "Women
in Mark's Gospel," 232–33.

56. Munro, "Women Disciples in Mark?" 237–38; Weeden,
Mark—Traditions in Conflict, 50, 117; John Dominic Crossan,
"Empty Tomb and Absent Lord (Mark 16:1–8)," in *The Passion in
Mark,* ed. Werner H. Kelber (Philadelphia: Fortress, 1976), 135–52,
esp. 149.

women never tell the news).[57] I find convincing David Catchpole's argument concerning 16:8b. Based on an analysis of the redactional context of 16:8b (especially the silence) and of the textual parallels to fear in Mark, the Pauline corpus, and Jewish tradition, Catchpole concludes "that Mark 16:8b can be interpreted within an established and continuing tradition. The fear and silence of the women belong to the structure of epiphany."[58] Thus the women's fear and silence are as much signs of the limits of humanity in the presence of divinity as signs of fallibility as followers in the usual sense. Yet the fear and silence are sure signs of distinction between the silent followers and the one they follow, and all followers are fallible in this sense.

Perhaps one's initial impression is of a certain irony to the women's silence: throughout the narrative Jesus asks various characters to be silent and they rarely are; here the "young man" who speaks for Jesus asks the women not to be silent and they are. But the closest Markan comparison with *oudeni ouden eipan* at 16:8 is *mēdeni mēden eipēs* at 1:44, and the earlier passage may help clarify the later one. At 1:44 Jesus charges the healed leper to "say nothing to any one (*mēdeni mēden eipēs*); but go, show yourself to the priest, and offer for your cleansing what Moses commanded, for a proof to the people." Surely in showing himself to the priest the former leper would say something to the priest; the priest, however, would not be just

---

57. Joanna Dewey, *Disciples of the Way: Mark on Discipleship* (Women's Division, Board of Global Ministries, The United Methodist Church, 1976), 134. See also, but in quite a different sense from Dewey, Munro, "Women Disciples in Mark," 238–39. In my terminology, Dewey's reading suggests that Mark portrays both the disciples and the women as fallible followers, whereas Munro's reading suggests that Mark discredits both the disciples and the women as opponents.

58. David Catchpole, "The Fearful Silence of the Women at the Tomb: A Study in Markan Theology," *JTSA* 18 (1977): 9.

any one, but the very one the leper was instructed to inform. At the close of Mark, the disciples and Peter are not just "any one," but the very ones the women are instructed to tell. Thus *oudeni ouden eipan*, like *mēdeni mēden eipēs*, may mean "said nothing to any one else" or "to any one in general."[59] Who but a disciple, a follower, of Jesus would be able to accept and understand the women's story? And the story of Jesus' resurrection, like the story of Jesus' healing of the leper (1:45), does seem to have gotten out.

As Tannehill and Dewey have sought the reason for the mixed portrayal of the twelve disciples in the author's approach to the reader,[60] so I suggest that the significance of the women's silence is to be found in the outward movement of the text from author to reader. It would appear that the narrator assumes that the hearer/reader assumes that the women did tell the disciples about the resurrection, because later someone surely told the narrator who now tells the hearer/reader! In addition, at the close of the Markan Gospel the narrator's story and that of his characters comes to an end—it reaches the point of silence, but the hearer/reader's story is at a new beginning—it is the hearer/reader's turn to speak now.[61] The women characters follow Jesus after the disciples flee; the narrator tells Jesus' story after the women's silence; it remains for the hearer/reader to continue this line of followers.

Thus, although women characters are portrayed as followers in the Markan Gospel, minimal emphasis is placed on their fallibility as followers in comparison with the crowd and especially the disciples. In interpreting this observation we do well

---

59. Ibid., 6.

60. See the section on "Fallible Followers" above.

61. Cf. Tannehill, "Disciples in Mark," 404: "The Gospel is open ended, for the outcome of the story depends on decisions which the church, including the reader, must still make."

to remember the tendency of the Markan Gospel to overturn expectations. Apparently Mark's implied reader expects disciples to be exemplary; their fallibility is surprising. The implied reader expects little from the crowd—and even less from women; their followership is surprising. Perhaps the Markan accenting of both the fallibility of the twelve male disciples and the followership of the women serves to counter stereotyping of the followers and potential followers of Jesus. It would be a sad irony to respond to Mark's refusal to absolutize the twelve as models of discipleship by absolutizing the women as disciples.

Women characters of Mark are "good" or "positive" because they are followers or exemplify followership—not because they are women. Women can be villains as well as heroes in the Gospel of Mark. Herodias instigates actions that result in the death of John the Baptist by using a person of lower status and authority than herself, her daughter, to influence a person of higher status and authority than herself, her husband, King Herod (6:17–29).[62] Similarly the chief priests instigate actions that result in the death of Jesus by using the lower status crowd to influence the higher status Pilate (15:6–15). In an additional parallel of male and female opponents of Jesus, the high priest's maid twice questions Peter (15:66–72) as the high priest twice questions Jesus (15:53–65), marking Peter's denial in the courtyard as an ironic transformation of Jesus' trial in the house. The high priest and the chief priests are the archenemies of the Markan Jesus, and two women characters function in comparable roles in relation to John the Baptist who comes before Jesus and Peter who follows after him.

Thus not all women in Mark are followers of Jesus, just as not all followers of Jesus in Mark are women. Women characters are not as numerous as men in Mark, nor are their names

---

62. Munro ("Women Disciples in Mark?" 226) notes that Herodias "receives more attention than any other particular woman in the Gospel."

as frequently given,[63] but their connotative value, like that of the men, is determined not by their sex or their numbers but by their relation to Jesus and their actions—either toward Jesus himself or in light of Jesus' demands for followership. No one is excluded from followership; no one is protected from fallibility.

The Markan portrait of fallible followers is a composite one; it includes the disciples, the crowd, women, certain exceptional individuals like Bartimaeus and Joseph of Arimathea, whoever takes up his or her cross, whoever does the will of God. Only by such a composite and complex image of followers is the author of the Markan Gospel able to communicate clearly and powerfully to the reader the twofold message: anyone can be a follower, no one finds it easy.

Postscript

My observations about women and men in the Gospel of Mark have been literary. But one might well ask: What are the implications of these literary observations for historical reconstructions of the relations of Christian women and men in the first century and for ethical guidelines for Christian women and men in the twentieth—and twenty-first—century? How is one to relate the Markan narrative to early church history and to contemporary church policy? Weeden, for example, interprets the Markan disciples of Jesus as representatives of the historical opponents of Mark, and Munro understands the Markan women followers in a similar way. An increasing number of articles and books for laity suggest correlations between Jesus' relation to women and men as portrayed in

---

63. Munro (ibid.) records five named and eight anonymous female characters to twenty-five named and sixteen anonymous male characters in Mark.

Mark and other biblical texts and appropriate responses of churchwomen and churchmen today.[64]

And yet, even though both the relation of the Markan narrative to early Christianity and its relation to contemporary Christianity represent valid movements outward from the text, neither is given directly and unambiguously within the text. A danger common to movement outward in either temporal direction is allegorization of the Markan text in terms of something beyond the text: equating, for example, the disciples (and/or the women) with the opponents of Mark's church, or the women followers of Jesus with ordained clergywomen.[65] Without doubt the Gospel of Mark is not simply a literal narrative; it moves and means by metaphors, but it is not an allegory. By its internal subtlety and complexity the text defies fragmentation and resists allegorization. Women and men, disciples and crowds, all contribute to the development of a composite and complex image of what it means to be a follower of Jesus. The women characters themselves are presented in an interwoven pattern that resists reduction to "what

---

64. In addition to Dewey (*Disciples of the Way*), Schierling ("Women as Leaders"), Schmitt ("Women in Mark's Gospel"), Stendahl (*The Bible and the Role of Women*), and Swidler (*Biblical Affirmations of Women*) cited above, see: Bruce Chilton, "The Gospel of Jesus and the Ministry of Women," *The Modern Churchman* 22 (1978–1979), 18–21; Elizabeth E. Platt, "The Ministry of Mary of Bethany," *ThTo* 34 (1977): 29–39; Letty M. Russell, ed., *The Liberating Word: A Guide to Nonsexist Interpretation of the Bible* (Philadelphia: Westminster, 1976); Leonard Swidler, "Jesus Was a Feminist," *Catholic World* 212 (1971): 177–83; Rachel Conrad Wahlberg, *Jesus according to a Woman* (New York: Paulist Press, 1975) and *Jesus and the Freed Woman* (New York: Paulist Press, 1978). Concern for early church history and contemporary church life may be combined, of course; Schierling's "Women as Leaders in the Marcan Communities" serves as a good example.

65. Schierling's easy movement from "women within the Marcan complex" to "woman" seems problematic at this point ("Women as Leaders").

the women stand for." Perhaps the complex relations of characters within the text should prepare us for the complex relations of the text to realities beyond it.[66] Perhaps Markan fallible followers have something to say to Markan historians and hermeneuts: interpretation, like followership, is never easy, and never perfect, and never ending.

66. Frank Kermode's discussion of history and history-likeness, of truth and meaning (*The Genesis of Secrecy*, 101–23), is interesting at this point.

3

Disciples/Crowds/Whoever

Markan Characters and Readers

In recent years the portrayal of the disciples in Mark has received considerable scholarly attention.* Conclusions have ranged from Theodore Weeden's view that the disciples are representatives of Mark's historical opponents and thus negative in value[1] to Robert Tannehill's view that the disciples are, if one may put it thus, representatives of Mark's parishioners, the readers, and basically positive in value—not perfect, in fact problematic, but potential models nonetheless.[2] I find Tannehill's view more convincing, and I wish to extend it in two ways: by examining the relation between the disciples and the crowd within the Markan narrative and by considering the relation of these Markan characters to the hearers or readers of the Markan narrative. It is my threefold thesis that: (1) the dis-

---

* I am pleased to thank the American Council of Learned Societies for a Research Fellowship in support of this research.

1. Theodore J. Weeden, "The Heresy That Necessitated Mark's Gospel," *ZNW* 59 (1968): 145–58; *Mark—Traditions in Conflict* (Philadelphia: Fortress, 1971).

2. Robert Tannehill, "The Disciples in Mark: The Function of a Narrative Role," *JR* 57 (1977): 386–405.

ciples of Jesus are portrayed in the Gospel of Mark with both strong points and weak points in order to serve as realistic and encouraging models for hearers/readers who experience both strength and weakness in their Christian discipleship; (2) the crowd is also portrayed in the Gospel of Mark in both positive and negative ways in relation to Jesus and serves to complement the disciples in a composite portrait of followers of Jesus; (3) both separately and together, the disciples and the crowd serve to open the story of Jesus and the narrative of Mark outward to a larger group—whoever hears or reads the Gospel of Mark. My focus will be on part two of my thesis, part one having been argued persuasively by others,[3] and part three being offered here more as a suggestion than as a conclusion.

Two questions will orient my presentation. First: What parallels and distinctions between the disciples and the crowd does the Markan narrative manifest? Second: In light of these parallels and distinctions, are the disciples and the crowd presented as basically competing or basically complementary character groups in the Markan narrative? In order to answer these questions, I wish to classify, compare, and contrast the kinds of activities that characterize each group's relationship with Jesus.[4] (Specific Markan references to the two groups are

---

3. In addition to Tannehill, see Joanna Dewey, "Point of View and the Disciples in Mark," *SBLSP* 21 (1982): 97–106.

4. Ernest Best also compares and contrasts the kinds of activities that characterize the disciples' and the crowd's relationship with Jesus ("The Role of the Disciples in Mark," *NTS* 23 [1977]: 390–93)—but with very different motives and conclusions. The crowd is examined as the "only possible candidate" for the "position as background 'good' group" against which the disciples as "bad" group could be set (390). But it is concluded that "the crowd possesses no unitary role in the gospel" (392), that the disciples and the crowd are two separate groups, not "one group which is a sub-group of another" (392), and that "Mark's crowd is not 'religious' but the group from which those who will be religious are called" (393). See also n. 35 below.

listed in the Appendix to Chapter 3.[5]) Whom does Jesus call, teach, heal, feed, command? Who follows Jesus, comes to Jesus, goes with Jesus, is amazed at Jesus, assists Jesus, hinders Jesus, abandons Jesus?

Calling and Following

Although we are accustomed to associating Jesus' activity of calling with the disciples, in fact the Markan Jesus calls to himself both the disciples and the crowd. After the inaugural statement of 1:14–15, the initial action of the Markan Jesus' ministry in Galilee is the calling of Simon and Andrew (1:16–18; 17, *deute opisō mou*, come after me) and James and John (1:19–20; 20, *kalein*, call). Ernest Best limits the references in his category "They are called by Jesus" to 1:16–20.[6] Additional references to calling, although certainly not "call narratives" in the technical sense, might be investigated under the broader category of Jesus called them to himself, Jesus summoned them.[7]

---

5. *Mathētes* (disciple) always occurs in the plural, *mathētai*, and usually with a possessive (and J. Keith Elliot argues that other possessives have been dropped by copyists ["*Mathētes* with a Possessive in the New Testament," *TZ* 35 (1979): 300]). (Three references to *mathētai* are marked as the disciples of John, one as the disciples of the Pharisees.) Except at 10:1, *ochlos* (crowd) always occurs in the singular, indicating that the Markan author thinks of the crowd as, in Ernest Best's words, "a unified sociological entity," or, as I would rather say, a unified narrative entity, a "character." However, the frequent Markan reliance on pronouns used alone, and on verb endings to indicate person, limits the usefulness of a listing such as the Appendix to Chapter 3.

6. Best, "Role of the Disciples," 385.

7. On the literary function of *proskaleomai*, *kaleō*, and *phōneō* in relation to the Markan disciples of Jesus, see Vernon K. Robbins, "Summons and Outline in Mark: The Three-Step Progression," *NovT* 23 (1981): 97–114.

At 3:13–19 Jesus "called to him (3:13, *proskaleisthai*) those whom he desired" and appointed "twelve" (3:14, *dōdeka*), "whom also he named apostles" (3:14, *apostolos*).[8] At 6:7 Jesus "called to him (*proskaleisthai*) the twelve (*dōdeka*)" in order to send them out on a mission of healing and teaching. The account of the feeding of the four thousand opens with the notice (8:1) that Jesus "called his disciples (*mathētai*) to him (*proskaleisthai*)"; and on four additional occasions the reader learns that Jesus called his disciples (or the twelve) to himself, and then said something to them concerning the demands of discipleship: 8:34, *mathētai, proskaleisthai*; 9:35, *dōdeka, phōnein* (call out); 10:42, them (the ten? the twelve?), *proskaleisthai*; 12:43, *mathētai, proskaleisthai*.

Twice in the Markan narrative Jesus is reported to have called the crowd to himself: at 7:14 (*ochlos* [crowd], *proskaleisthai*) for the saying ("parable") on defilement, and at 8:34 (*ochlos, proskaleisthai*)—together with his disciples—for the saying on taking up one's cross and following Jesus. At 10:46–52, Jesus, through the agency of the many (10:48, *polloi*) calls (*phōnein*) Bartimaeus, who emerges from the many, is healed of his blindness, and follows Jesus on the way. One additional episode is clearly a calling but not so clearly a calling of either a disciple or one from the crowd. Jesus' interaction with Levi, the tax collector, at 2:14 parallels Jesus' interaction with Simon and Andrew and James and John, the fishermen, at 1:16–20: Jesus calls (2:14, *Akolouthei moi*; Follow me), Levi follows. Levi, however, is not listed by Mark as one of the twelve disciples or apostles (3:13–19). Perhaps Levi, like Bartimaeus, is

---

8. There is, according to Kurt Aland et al., eds. (*The Greek New Testament*, 3d. ed. [United Bible Societies, 1975]), a "considerable degree of doubt" whether the phrase *ous kai apostolous ōnomasen* is the superior reading. Ernest Best regards the phrase as "not original" but coming from Luke 6:13 (*Following Jesus: Discipleship in the Gospel of Mark*, JSNTSup 4 [Sheffield: JSOT Press, 1981], 187 n. 18).

to be understood as emerging from the crowd as a ˌ
tive of the crowd or at least of the potential of the cɩ
reading 2:13–15 we note that the reference to Levi (2:14ˌ
lows immediately a reference to Jesus teaching the crowd
(2:13) and is in turn followed by a reference to the many (2:15,
polloi) who followed Jesus.

Thus the Markan Jesus called to himself both the disciples
(or the twelve[9]) as a group (3:13–19; 6:7; 8:1; 8:34; 9:35; 10:42;

---

9. I find Best's reading of a distinction between "the twelve" and
"the disciples" in Mark confusing. Best, whose basic concern is to
separate tradition and redaction, concludes: "Mark distinguishes to
some extent between the twelve [basically traditional] and the disciples [basically redactional], the latter being the wider group . . . . Yet
Mark makes little distinction in the way in which he uses the twelve
and the disciples . . ." ("Mark's Use of the Twelve," *ZNW* 69 [1978]:
32). Mark "is not concerned to identify the Twelve and the disciples
in such a way that when the disciples are mentioned we are to understand him to mean the Twelve and only the Twelve. It is, rather, the
other way round: the Twelve is normally to be understood as signify-
ing the wider group, the 'disciples'" ("Role of the Disciples," 380; cf.
Following Jesus, 183, 188 n. 23, 204; cf. Heber F. Peacock, "Discipleship in the Gospel of Mark," *RevExp* 75 [1978]: 556). Perhaps Gérard
Genette's discrimination of three narrative levels is helpful at this
point (*Narrative Discourse: An Essay in Method*, trans. Jane E. Lewin
[Ithaca, N.Y.: Cornell University Press, 1980]). I judge that, *at the
level of story*, "the twelve" and "the disciples" (and the "apostles") refer
to the same group of characters. At the levels of the relation of story
and narration and story and narrating, however, there is an expansive
movement from this group, to additional characters (see esp. 4:10 and
10:32), to the implied readers; and at these levels "disciples" is a more
flexible term than "the twelve." With my view, compare Edward
Lynn Taylor, Jr., "The Disciples of Jesus in the Gospel of Mark"
(Ph.D. diss., Southern Baptist Theological Seminary, 1979), 91–93.
R. P. Meye ("Messianic Secret and Messianic *Didachē* in Mark's
Gospel," in *Oikonomia: Heilsgeschichte als Thema der Theologie*, ed. F.
Christ [Hamburg: Herbert Reich, 1967], 63–65) and S. Freyne (*The
Twelve: Disciples and Apostles: A Study in the Theology of the First Three
Gospels* [London: Sheed & Ward, 1968], 107–19) also view "the
twelve" and "the disciples" as identical.

12:43) and individual disciples by name—Simon and Andrew and James and John (1:16–18; 1:19–20); and the crowd as a group (7:14; 8:34) and individuals from the crowd by name— Levi (2:13–14) and Bartimaeus (10:46–52). We will return later to the one occasion on which Jesus called to himself the crowd *with* his disciples and spoke to both groups concerning those who would follow him, whoever would save his life by losing it (8:34–9:1).

Directly related to Jesus' calling to himself both the disciples and the crowd is the following of Jesus by both the disciples and the crowd. A careful examination of who is said to follow Jesus is revealing. Simon and Andrew follow him (1:18, *akoloutheō*); James and John come after him (1:20, *aperchomai opisō*); the disciples as a group follow him (6:1, *mathētai, akoloutheō*), as Peter later points out they have done (10:28, *akoloutheō*). None of this surprises. But Jesus is also followed by many (2:15, *polloi, akoloutheō*), a great multitude (3:7, *polu plēthos, akoloutheō*), a great crowd (5:24, *ochlos polus, akoloutheō*), and by one who emerges from the crowd, Bartimaeus (10:48, *polloi*; 10:52, *akoloutheō*).

In some cases, however, it is not possible to identify clearly the persons who are said to follow Jesus. At 10:32 those "on the road, going up to Jerusalem," those whom "Jesus was walking ahead of," appear to be Jesus' disciples (see 10:23, 24, *mathētai*). But "those who followed" appear to be an additional group because 10:32b seems to differentiate "the twelve" from the larger traveling group.[10] Are these additional followers drawn from the crowd? (At 10:46 Jesus leaves Jericho, still on the way to Jerusalem, "with his disciples and a great multitude.") At the entry into Jerusalem "those who went before

---

10. I find unconvincing Best's argument that "it is probable that Mark does not intend to depict separate groups" at 10:32 and his translation of the second clause as "and as they were following they were afraid" ("Twelve," 23, 24; cf. *Following Jesus*, 120).

and those who followed cried out, 'Hosanna! Blessed is he who comes in the name of the Lord!'" (11:9–10). Are these followers from the crowd? (At 11:8 "many [*polloi*] spread their garments on the road.")

In other cases, while individual followers are identified by name, it is not possible to determine clearly to which group (if any) they may belong. At 2:14 Jesus says to Levi, "Follow me" (*Akolouthei moi*) as he had earlier said to Simon and Andrew, "Follow me" (1:17, *deute opisō mou*); and Levi leaves his tax office and follows Jesus as the four fishermen had left their nets and followed him. But Levi, unlike Simon and Andrew and James and John, is not listed as one of the twelve (3:13–19).[11] Immediately after the call of Levi, "Jesus and his disciples" are at table with "many tax collectors and sinners"— "for there were many (*polloi*) who followed him" (2:15). Presumably Levi is one of the tax collectors rather than one of the disciples. But since Levi did follow Jesus, he is presumably one of the "many (*polloi*) who followed him." Just before calling Levi (2:14), Jesus had been teaching the crowd (2:13, *ochlos*). Thus Levi seems to emerge from the crowd as a follower.[12]

A second case of uncertain group identification of followers occurs at 15:40–41. Many women are said to have observed Jesus' crucifixion; three are named: "Mary Magdalene, and Mary the mother of James the younger and of Joses, and

---

11. In Matthew's Gospel the follower from the tax office is "Matthew" (9:9), who is listed among the "twelve apostles" (10:2) as "Matthew the tax collector" (10:3).

12. Cf. Best: "The association of v. 13 with v. 14 implies that before he responded to the call Levi was a member of the crowd, i.e., the unevangelised" (*Following Jesus*, 177). In Best's schema, however, Levi's response to Jesus breaks Levi's link with the crowd. When one from the crowd follows Jesus, so Best seems to assume, he or she relinquishes membership in the crowd; no matter how many of the crowd follow Jesus, the crowd as crowd is—by definition—never to be recognized in the category of followers.

Salome, who, when he [Jesus] was in Galilee, followed (*akoloutheō*) him, and ministered to (*diakoneō*) him" (15:40b–41a). (*Akoloutheō* and *diakoneō* are generally recognized as "discipleship" words in Mark.) These three women are part of a larger group since "also many other women (*kai allai pollai*) . . . came up with him to Jerusalem" (15:41b). Have the three named women, then, emerged from the many, from the crowd?[13]

It would appear that following, while central to discipleship, is not limited to "disciples." The category of "followers" over-laps with the categories of "the disciples" and "the crowd." Additional references to *akoloutheō* suggest a similar conclusion. At 9:38, John, speaking for the twelve (9:35), the disciples (9:31), reports to Jesus that they forbade a man casting out demons in Jesus' name "because he was not following us." John apparently expects Jesus' approval; Jesus, however, disapproves, stating that "no one who does a mighty work in my name will be able soon after to speak evil of me. For he that is not against us is for us" (9:39–40). Being "for" Jesus is not defined by membership among the twelve disciples; and followers of Jesus are charac-terized by action on behalf of others—whether a mighty work or the giving of a cup of water (9:41). At 10:17–22, action on behalf of others is again presented as a characteristic of follow-ership. In the absence of his willingness to sell his possessions and give to the poor, neither the rich man's knowledge and observance of the law nor Jesus' love for him enables the rich man to follow (10:21, *akoloutheō*) Jesus.

---

13. Based on the significance of *akoloutheō* and *diakoneō* and espe-cially on the pattern of "a nucleus of three within an inner circle dis-tinguished from the outer circle or crowd" (231), Winsome Munro regards the women mentioned at 15:40–41 as women disciples—the existence of whom, Munro argues further, Mark intentionally obscured ("Women Disciples in Mark?" *CBQ* 44 [1982]: 225–41).

Mark 8:34 is a pivotal verse concerning disciples, the crowd, and followers: "And, calling to himself the crowd with his disciples, he said to them, 'If anyone wishes to follow after me, let that one deny himself and take up his cross and follow me'" (author's translation). "Anyone" can be a follower—one of the disciples, one of the crowd, one of the hearers or readers—as long as one is willing to deny oneself and take up one's cross.[14] Disciples, crowds, whoever—everyone is a potential follower. The demands of followership, however, make for a different actuality.

Not everyone is able to be a follower. And no followers, whether disciples or the crowd, find following easy. There is a profound irony in Peter's following (14:54, *akoloutheō*) Jesus at a distance into the courtyard of the high priest, for while the house of the high priest is the scene of Jesus' trial, the courtyard is the scene of Peter's denial. A similar irony is manifest in the shift from the jubilation of the many (11:8, *polloi*) blessing Jesus and following (11:9, *akoloutheō*) him into Jerusalem to the tumult of the crowd demanding his crucifixion there a few days later (15:8, 11, 15, *ochlos*). Perhaps the hearers/readers of Mark's Gospel experienced the ironic tension of simultaneous desires to follow the crucified one and difficulties in denying themselves and taking up their own crosses.

Coming and Going

Jesus' activity of calling to himself both disciples and crowds and the activity of both disciples and crowds in following Jesus suggest certain parallels between the two groups. Other activities, however, distinguish them. Repeat-

---

14. Mark 8:34 presents something of a problem for Best (*Following Jesus*, 31–32), since he posits a definite distinction between the crowd ("the unevangelised mass") and the disciples ("the church") and 8:34 links the two groups.

edly the crowd is said to come to Jesus, the disciples are said to go with him. The crowd comes to Jesus seeking the healing (1:32, *pas* [all]; 2:2, *polloi* [many]; 3:8, *plēthos polu* [great multitude]) that he offers. Jesus also offers the gathered crowd teaching (*ochlos* [crowd]: 2:13; 3:32; 4:1 twice; 10:1; *polloi*: 2:2); and, even though the pursuing crowd hinders the freedom of Jesus and his disciples to eat (3:20, *ochlos*; 6:31, *polloi*), Jesus offers the crowd food (6:39, 41, 42, *pas*; 8:1, *ochlos*). Wherever Jesus goes the crowd comes to him (*ochlos*: 5:21; 9:15; 9:25; *eis ek tou ochlou* [one of the crowd]: 9:17; *polloi* [many, masculine]: 6:33; *pollai* [many, feminine]: 15:41), or, when he is temporarily unreachable, to his disciples (9:14, *ochlos*). Even near the end, at Gethsemane, a crowd (14:43, *ochlos*)—this time with Judas and from the chief priests, scribes, and elders—comes to Jesus. Unlike the earlier crowds who sought manifestations of Jesus' power in teaching, healing, and miraculous feeding, this final crowd seeks the restraint of Jesus' power in his arrest.

While the crowd continually comes to Jesus, the disciples continually go with him. Jesus withdraws with some of his disciples (the four—Peter and Andrew and James and John: 1:29; 13:3; the three—Peter, James, and John: 5:37; 9:2; 14:33) or with his disciples as a group (*mathētai*: 2:15; 3:7; 4:34; 4:35–36 [they]; 6:31–32 [they]; 7:17; 8:10; 8:13ff. [they]; 8:27 twice; 9:28; 10:10; 10:32a [they]; 10:46; 14:32; *dōdeka*: 4:10; 10:32b; 11:11; 14:17). Once, rather early in the narrative, Jesus asks his disciples to have a boat ready for him in case he needs to withdraw with them from the crowd (3:9, *mathētai*, *ochlos*). Another time, rather late in the narrative, Jesus withdraws (from Jericho toward Jerusalem) with his disciples and a great crowd together (10:46, *mathētai*, *ochlou ikanou* [large crowd]). At the close of the narrative Jesus is reported to be "going before" his disciples to Galilee (16:7, *mathētai*, *Petros* [Peter]).

Often Jesus' withdrawal with his disciples is the setting for special instruction of them, instruction not offered the crowd (*dōdeka*: 4:10; *mathētai*: 4:34; 7:17; 9:28; 10:10).[15] More often Jesus' withdrawal with his disciples is part of the overall pattern of their accompanying Jesus wherever he goes (*mathētai*: 2:15; 3:7; 3:9; 4:35–36 [they]; 6:31–32 [they]; 8:10; 8:13ff. [they]; 8:27 twice; 10:32a [they]; 10:46; 14:32; 16:7; *dōdeka*: 10:32b; 11:11; 14:17).[16] Twice Jesus is alone with the four— Peter (Simon) and Andrew and James and John: once in Simon's house, where Jesus heals Simon's mother-in-law (1:29), and once on the Mount of Olives, where, at the initiative of the four, Jesus speaks of the end of time (13:3). Thrice Jesus takes the three—Peter, James, and John—aside with him: at the raising of Jairus's daughter (5:37), at the transfiguration (9:2), and at Gethsemane (14:33), giving these three episodes a special prominence in Jesus' story.

Like the disciples, the crowd is called by Jesus, and, like the disciples, the crowd follows Jesus. But although they continually come to Jesus, the crowd, unlike the disciples, is not—with one significant exception (10:46, the close of the "way" section)—said to go with Jesus. While Jesus frequently withdraws *with* the disciples, he frequently withdraws *from* the crowd (3:9, *ochlos*, potential withdrawal; 4:36, *ochlos*; 6:31–33, attempted withdrawal from the many [6:31, 33, *polloi*]; 6:45, *ochlos*; 7:17, *ochlos*; 7:33, *ochlos*). The disciples are distinguished from the crowd as those *with* whom Jesus frequently withdraws; yet on occasion Jesus withdraws *from* the disciples as well as *from* the crowd. Of course, when Jesus withdraws with a small group of his disciples he withdraws from the majority (5:37; 9:2; 13:3; 14:33); but Jesus also withdraws from all his disciples, either from all twelve at once (6:45–47, them [6:45, *mathētai*]) or first

---

15. These references are categorized by Best under "They are recipients of private instruction from Jesus" ("Role of the Disciples," 385–86.)

16. Some of these references are categorized by Best as "They journey with Jesus" (ibid.).

from the nine (14:33) and then from the three (14:35, 39, 41). At 1:35 Jesus withdraws by himself, and, since the twelve are not appointed until 3:13–19, Jesus cannot be said to have withdrawn specifically from the disciples; yet he is pursued by "Simon and those who were with him" (1:36). When Jesus withdraws from the crowd it is usually to be with his disciples (3:9; 4:36; 6:31–33; 7:17); 7:33 is exceptional—Jesus withdraws from the crowd with the deaf-mute in order to heal him. But when Jesus withdraws by himself—from the crowd and his disciples (6:45–47), or from the three (14:35, 39, 41), or from unspecified people (1:35)—it is always for prayer.

To recapitulate: the disciples are called, and the crowd is called; the disciples follow, and the crowd follows; the crowd comes to Jesus, but the disciples go with him; yet sometimes Jesus is all alone. The multiple references to the crowd's coming appear to be the narrative manifestations of the Markan Jesus' understanding of why he "came out" (1:38); the multiple references to the disciples' going appear to be the narrative manifestations of his appointment of the twelve "to be with him" (3:14). Jesus comes out to preach and to cast out demons (1:38–39); Jesus appoints twelve apostles or disciples not only "to be with him" but also "to be sent out to preach and have authority to cast out demons" (3:14–15). Jesus journeys to Jerusalem with the disciples and the crowd (10:32, crowd?; 10:46), and, after his death and resurrection there, it is reported to the women who seem to emerge from the crowd and to act like disciples (15:40–41, *akoloutheō* [follow], *diakoneō* [serve], *pollai* [many, feminine]) that he is going before them to Galilee.

Teaching, Healing, Feeding

The people of the crowd are the chief beneficiaries, the disciples, the chief assistants, of Jesus' ministry of teaching and healing. Yet in order to assist in teaching (6:30, *apostoloi*), the disciples must first receive Jesus' teaching; thus the Markan Jesus teaches both the disciples and the crowd, as many passages throughout the narrative illustrate. Here those passages that employ *didaskō*, teach, or *didachē*, teaching, specifically will serve as examples.[17] As has often been noted, the Markan narrator frequently refers to Jesus as teaching without giving—or even suggesting—the content of his teaching; this is especially the case in those scenes in which Jesus teaches the crowd (*ochlos*: 2:13; 4:1–2; 6:34;[18] 10:1; cf. 11:18; *pas*: 1:21–28 [1:27, *pas*]; *polloi*: 6:2; *tas kōmas kuklō* [the surrounding villages]: 6:6). The content of Jesus' teaching in the temple is specified—or at least exemplified; just how much of this teaching the crowd hears, however, is uncertain: 11:17? probably not, since 11:18 (*ochlos*) appears to be a general reference; 12:35–37? probably so, since 12:37 (*ochlos*) appears to conclude 12:35–37; 12:38–40? impossible to judge. Whether the crowd is intended as part of the audience at the flashback at 14:49 is also impossible to judge, and furthermore, 14:49 is a generalized reference to teaching. As noted above, when Jesus withdraws with his disciples it is often for private, more detailed teaching on a topic he has just covered more generally and more openly. When Jesus is explicitly said to be teaching (*didaskō*) the disciples, however, the content of his teaching is his coming passion and resurrection (8:31, they; 9:31, *mathētai*); this the crowd is not taught. Thus, the Markan Jesus teaches the disciples more about what the crowd is taught and more than the crowd is taught.[19]

---

17. See R. T. France, "Mark and the Teaching of Jesus," in *Gospel Perspectives: Studies of History and Tradition in the Four Gospels*, ed. R. T. France and David Wenham (Sheffield: JSOT Press, 1980), I: 101–36, esp. 105–6.

18. Best regards *ochlos* at 6:34 as "a symbol for the instruction of Mark's church" and, thus, as an exception to Mark's "normal" use of the crowd to denote "the unevangelised mass" (*Following Jesus*, 210–11).

19. See ibid., 235–36.

Closely related to specific references to Jesus teaching (*didaskō* or *didachē*) the disciples or the crowd are references to Jesus commanding the disciples or the crowd to "hear," or statements reporting that they "heard" Jesus. The parable of the sower is framed by Jesus' exhortations to the very large crowd (4:1a, *ochlos pleistos*), the whole crowd (4:1b, *pas ho ochlos*): "Hear" (4:3, *Akouete*); "Whoever has ears to hear, let that one hear" (4:9, author's translation of *Hos echei ōta akouein akouetō*). The interpretation of the parable of the sower is concluded by Jesus' exhortation to "those who were about him with the twelve" (4:10—a complex phrase apparently indicating more than the disciples and less than the whole crowd[20]): "If any one has ears to hear, let that one hear" (4:23, author's translation of *ei tis echei ōta akouein akouetō*). The "parable" (7:17) concerning defilement is introduced by Jesus' exhortation to the crowd (7:14, *ochlos*): "Hear me, all of you, and understand" (7:14, *Akousate mou pantes kai sunete*). The paired feeding stories, as enacted parables, are concluded by Jesus' exclamation to the disciples (8:10, *mathētai*): ". . . having ears do you not hear? . . . Do you not yet understand?" (8:18, 21, . . . *ōta echontes ouk akouete*; . . . *Oupō suniete*;). Finally, the voice from the cloud speaks on behalf of Jesus at his transfiguration before Peter, James, and John: "hear him" (9:7, *akouete autou*). Thus both the disciples and the crowd are directly exhorted by Jesus to hear.

And both groups do hear—to a certain extent. Jesus questions the disciples' hearing—and understanding (8:18, 21; cf. 4:13)—and the hearing and understanding of "those outside" (4:10, the crowd?[21] part of the crowd?), who "may indeed *hear*

---

20. Thus both Best and F. C. Synge oversimplify—in opposite directions. According to Best, "the twelve together with those about Jesus (4:10) are identical with the disciples (4:34)." ("Twelve," 32; see n. 9 above). According to Synge, "the crowds were the 'arounders'" (53), "the publicans and sinners, Gentiles" ("A Plea for the Outsiders: Commentary on Mark 4:10–12," *JTSA* 30 [1980]: 58).

21. So Best, *Following Jesus*, 235.

but [do] not understand" (4:12).[22] The narrator comments
(4:33) that "with many such parables he [Jesus] spoke the word
to them [the crowd? see 4:1–2, 10, 34], as they were able to
hear it" and that the disciples *heard* (11:14, *mathētai*) Jesus
curse the fig tree on his way into Jerusalem and into the temple. In addition, the many who *heard* Jesus in the synagogue
(6:2, *polloi*) were astonished, and the great crowd who *heard*
Jesus in the temple (12:37, *polus ochlos*) "heard him gladly." But
the latter phrase, *ēkouen autou hēdeōs*, is an ominous one: when
Herod *heard* John, Herod "was much perplexed; and yet he
heard him gladly" (6:20, *hēdeōs autou ēkouen*), but such gladness
did not save John. Neither does the gladness of the crowd at
hearing Jesus save him, although it does make the chief priests,
scribes, and elders more circumspect in plotting his arrest
(11:18; 12:12; 14:2). Yet Jesus was arrested and brought before
the chief priests, scribes, and elders; there "many (*polloi*) bore
false witness against him" (14:56), saying, "We *heard* him say,
'I will destroy this temple that is made with hands, and in three
days I will build another, not made with hands'" (14:58). This
the Markan Jesus has not said; false speakers report a false
hearing. Neither the disciples nor the crowd finds it easy to
hear Jesus truly.

The response of the crowd or of individuals from the crowd
to hearing about Jesus is more encouraging. In Capernaum,

---

22. One could hardly find a view more distant from the view presented here than David J. Hawkin's interpretation, based on 4:10–12,
that "the disciples are made to be figures representative of the church,
and the crowds are made to be figures representative of Israel" ("The
Incomprehension of the Disciples in the Marcan Redaction," *JBL* 91
[1972]: 497). Synge also regards the "outsiders" at 4:10–12 as "the
orthodox" or "Israel," but he contrasts this group not with the disciples but with "the crowd": "The almost unanimity of commentators
in equating the 'outsiders' with the crowds makes it necessary to reit-
erate that the 'outsiders' are those who disapproved of the crowds
that encircled Jesus, that the crowds were the 'arounders,' and that
the 'outsiders' were the orthodox" (53; see n. 20 above).

"many (*polloi*) gathered together" (2:2) when they *heard* that Jesus was at home (2:1); from all of Palestine and beyond, "a great multitude, *hearing* all that he did, came to him" (3:8) at the sea; at Gennesaret, they "ran about the whole neighborhood and began to bring sick people on their pallets to any place where they *heard* he was" (6:55). From amid the crowd the woman with the hemorrhage came to Jesus with faith after having *heard* reports about him (5:27); the Syrophoenician woman *heard* of Jesus and came with courage to him who "could not be hid" (7:24–25); Bartimaeus *heard* that Jesus was passing by and cried out, "Jesus, Son of David" (10:47), despite being rebuked by many (10:48, *polloi*). Hearing about Jesus, and especially about his healing power, the crowd gathers to him. To the gathered crowd and to the disciples Jesus says, "Hear—and understand." Both the crowd and the disciples hear; both have difficulty understanding.

Given the opportunity for hearing and the difficulty in understanding that the disciples and the crowd share, it is not surprising that they also share a response of amazement, astonishment, and even fear in relation to Jesus.[23] The crowd is amazed, astonished at Jesus' teaching—

1:22   they (1:27, *pas*), *ekplēssesthai* (astounded)
1:27   *pas, thambeisthai* (amazed)
6:2   *polloi, ekplēssesthai*
11:18   *ochlos, ekplēssesthai*

---

23. Arguments can be made, of course, for analyzing reactions of fear separately from amazement and astonishment, and I have made such an analysis of the material presented here. For my present purpose, however, the results of the twofold and the combined analyses did not differ significantly. (In my discussion I have listed the specific word/s for fear, astonishment, etc., employed in each relevant passage.) Best, seeking to distinguish tradition from redaction, does separate amazement and fear on the part of the disciples ("Role of the Disciples," 387–88).

at Jesus' healing—
  2:12   *pas, existasthai* (astonished)
  5:15   they (5:14, *eis tēn polin kai eis tous agrous* [in the city
          and in the country]), *phobeisthai* (afraid)
  5:20   *pas, thaumazein* (filled with wonder)
  5:33   woman from crowd (*ochlos*: 5:24, 27, 30, 31),
          phobeisthai
  7:37   they (7:33, *ochlos*), *ekplēssesthai*

at Jesus himself—
  9:15   *pas ho ochlos* (the whole crowd), *ekthambeisthai*
          (awe-struck).

The disciples are amazed, astonished at Jesus' teaching—
  10:24   *mathētai, thambeisthai* (amazed)
  10:26   they (10:24, *mathētai*), *ekplēssesthai* (astounded)

at Jesus' power over the sea—
  4:41   they (4:34, *mathētai*), *phobeisthai* (afraid)
  6:50   they (6:45, *mathētai*; 6:50, *pas*), *tarassesthai* (terrified)
  6:51   they (6:45, *mathētai*), *existasthai* (astonished)

at Jesus' transfiguration—
  9:6   they (the three; see 9:2), *ekphobos* (frightened)

at Jesus' prediction of his passion and resurrection—
  9:32   they (9:31, *mathētai*), *phobeisthai*.

Mark 10:32 is an especially important verse within the narrative pattern of amazement and fear of the disciples and the
crowd. "And they [Jesus and the disciples; see 10:23, 24] were
on the road, going up to Jerusalem, and Jesus was walking
ahead of them [the disciples]; and they [the disciples] were
amazed (*thambeisthai*), and those who followed [from the
crowd?] were afraid (*phobeisthai*)."[24] For both the disciples and
the crowd Jesus' power is amazing; and, in light of that power,

---

24. See n. 10 above.

Jesus' suffering is amazing. Yet the reverse is also true. Jesus' suffering, his death, is amazing; and, in light of that death, his resurrection, his ongoing power, is amazing. It is no wonder that the three women who emerge from the crowd and act like disciples[25] (15:40–41, *akoloutheō* [follow], *diakoneō* [serve], *pollai* [many, feminine]) are amazed (16:5, *ekthambeisthai*), astonished (16:8, *ekstasis* [ecstatic]), and afraid (16:8, *phobeisthai*) at the empty tomb.[26] Amazement, astonishment, and even fear are not unknown by—and not inappropriate for—the followers of Jesus, whether these followers are disciples or the crowd. Not all who are amazed follow (12:17, *ekthaumazein*), but all who follow are amazed.

Whereas the disciples and the crowd share amazement and astonishment at Jesus' actions, the disciples' amazement is never noted (with the possible exception of the inclusion of the three at 5:42) and the crowd's amazement most frequently noted in response to Jesus' healing activity. It is, after all, the crowd and not the disciples who are healed by Jesus. Jesus does heal one member of one disciple's family, Simon's mother-in-law (1:29–31); but otherwise Jesus' healing is offered to the crowd and to members of the crowd (1:32, *pas*; 1:34, *polloi*; 2:2–12, the paralytic [2:2, *polloi*; 2:4, *ochlos*; 2:12, *pas*]; 3:10, *polloi*; 5:1–20, the Gerasene demoniac [5:20, *pas*]; 5:24–34, the woman with a hemorrhage [5:24, 27, 30, 31, *ochlos*]; 7:32–37, the deaf-mute [7:33, *ochlos*]; 9:14–29, the epileptic boy [9:14, 15, 17, 25, *ochlos*; 9:26b, *polloi*]; 10:46–52, blind Bartimaeus [10:48, *polloi*]).

Jesus teaches, Jesus heals; the disciples and the crowd relate to Jesus somewhat differently in regard to these two actions,

25. Best ("Role of the Disciples," 386) lists "xvi.8 (the women)" under the category of *the disciples* "are afraid at what he says or does or at what may happen to them" (Table 2. From the redaction).

26. Cf. David Catchpole, "The Fearful Silence of the Women at the Tomb: A Study in Markan Theology," *JTSA* 18 (1977): 8–9.

although both groups are amazed and astonished at Jesus. Jesus also feeds, and this activity also distinguishes the disciples and the crowd while uniting them as those for whom Jesus expresses concern. Jesus feeds the crowd bread in the desert (6:39, 41, 42, *pas*; 8:2, 6a, 6b, *ochlos*) and asks the disciples to help him with the distribution (6:41, *mathētai*; 8:6, *mathētai*). Jesus feeds the disciples bread and wine in the upper room (14:22–25, they [14:23, *pas*]). The feedings of the five thousand and the four thousand seem "miraculous," the feeding of the twelve seems ordinary; but both are to be understood in relation to the kingdom of God (see especially 14:25), and neither is immediately understood by the participants (see especially 8:14–21). Since all three accounts—the feeding of the five thousand, the four thousand, the twelve—are marked by eucharistic language, those who participate and those who need to understand include not only the disciples and the crowd but also the hearers/readers of the Markan narrative.

Assisting and Questioning

Jesus feeds both the disciples and the crowds, asking assistance of the disciples (6:41; 8:6). Jesus teaches both the disciples and the crowd, asking assistance of the disciples (3:14; 6:12, 30). Jesus heals the crowd, asking assistance of the disciples (3:15; 6:7, 13). Throughout the narrative the Markan Jesus enlists the assistance of his disciples, sometimes for a rather specific task involving arrangements for his ministry and movement throughout Palestine—

3:9	*mathētai*
6:37	you (6:35, *mathētai*)
6:41	*mathētai*
6:45	*mathētai*
8:6	*mathētai*
11:1	*duo tōn mathētōn autou* (two of his disciples)
14:13, 16	*duo tōn mathētōn autou*

14:32   *mathētai*
14:33–42   the three, especially Peter (see 14:33, 37)

sometimes in more general terms that are often read as paradimatic for later "disciples" of Jesus—particularly:

1:16–20   the four (esp. 17; see 1:16, 19)
3:13–19   *dōdeka*, [*apostoloi*], the twelve by name
6:7   *dōdeka*

but also:

6:41   *mathētai*
8:6   *mathētai*
14:32   *mathētai*
14:33–42   the three.

Despite the recent emphasis on discipleship failure in Mark, the disciples frequently succeed in giving the assistance Jesus requests. Peter's statement that "we have . . . followed you" (10:28) fulfills Jesus' earlier command to "Follow me" (1:17). The apostles successfully preach and exorcise demons (6:12–13, 30), as Jesus appointed them to do (3:14–15). Jesus' disciples procure the boat (3:9), the colt (11:7), and the room (14:16) he requests. They are unable to multiply bread in the wilderness (6:37), but they do help Jesus distribute it (6:41; 8:6). They do not manage to go before Jesus to Bethsaida (6:45), but they do arrive there later with Jesus (8:22). They do wait with Jesus while he prays at Gethsemane (14:32), although Peter, James, and John cannot stay awake (14:33–42); yet, as the Markan Jesus notes, "the spirit indeed is willing, but the flesh is weak" (14:38).[27]

---

27. It is not entirely clear whether the three women at the empty tomb, who are not quite disciples but are asked to speak to them, give the aid enlisted by the young man, who is not quite Jesus but speaks for him. It would appear that the narrator assumes that the hearer/reader assumes that the women did tell the disciples, because later someone surely told the narrator who now tells the hearer/reader! In addition,

Where the disciples get into real difficulty is in volunteering assistance that Jesus has not specifically requested. They are willing in their intentions, but their judgments are weak. The disciples seem to mean well in volunteering assistance to Jesus and his ministry, but their exuberance must often be redirected by Jesus. It was not necessary for "Simon and those who were with him" (1:36) to pursue Jesus, for Jesus had not intended to withdraw for long (1:38). It was unnecessary for Peter to offer to build three booths for the transfigured Jesus, Moses, and Elijah (9:5), for Jesus would soon be on his way to Jerusalem. Yet Peter was eager to assist Jesus' ministry, to honor Jesus. It was inappropriate for John and the other disciples to forbid the unknown exorcist (9:38). It was inappropriate for the disciples to rebuke those bringing children to Jesus (10:13). But in each case the disciples intended to assist Jesus' ministry; they were surprised to learn their actions displeased Jesus.

The ten who were indignant at James and John probably thought to please Jesus in contrast to those two (10:41), but Jesus seems to have directed his correcting response to all twelve (10:42–45).[28] Peter's exclamation upon seeing the fig tree withered (11:21) seems to be offered as homage to Jesus, but Peter's surprise suggests as well his lack of faith in contrast

---

the phrase "they said nothing to any one" (*oudeni ouden eipan*) may mean "they said nothing to any one else," or "they said nothing to any one in general." At 1:44 Jesus charged the healed leper to "say nothing to any one (*mēdeni mēden eipēs*); but go, show yourself to the priest, and offer for your cleansing what Moses commanded, for a proof to the people." Surely in showing himself to the priest the former leper would say something to the priest; the priest, however, would not be just any one, but the very one the leper was instructed to inform. At the close of Mark, the disciples and Peter are not just "any one," but the very ones the women are instructed to tell. And in this case too, as at 1:45, the word does seem to have gotten out.

28. So also Best, "Role of the Disciples," 380, and *Following Jesus*, 129.

to the faith Jesus calls for (11:22–24). The exclamation of one of the disciples upon coming out of the temple (13:1) is immediately reversed by Jesus (13:2), but certainly the disciple expected assent to his rhetorical remark. In each of these episodes, the disciples intend to do or say that which will please Jesus, but they misjudge Jesus' reaction. They do not yet realize what following Jesus entails.

At 9:18 we learn that the disciples have been asked to exorcise an unclean spirit, that they have been willing to do so, and that—although they have been successful in exorcisms previously (6:13)—this time they have failed.[29] It is not, however, their willingness that has failed, and they are eager to learn why they have been unsuccessful (9:28). At 14:12 the disciples volunteer to make preparations for the celebration of the Passover with Jesus. In this case their voluntary assistance is directed by Jesus' specific commands (14:13–15), and their assistance is accepted and successful (14:16). Many of these references are categorized by Best under "They act as a foil to Jesus, giving him the opportunity to teach and act."[30] Each episode does contribute to a fuller understanding of the demands of discipleship.

At 14:29 and 14:31, Peter emphatically—and all the disciples as well—insist, against Jesus' warnings, that they will follow Jesus always. They volunteer their unfailing loyalty. Peter

---

29. Friedrich Gustav Lang argues that the failure is to be attributed not to the disciples' lack of faith but to the father's lack of faith ("Sola Gratia im Markusevangelium: Die Soteriologie des Markus nach 9, 14–29 und 10, 17–31," *Rechtfertigung*, ed. J. Friedrich, W. Pöhlmann, P. Stuhlmacher [Tübingen: J. C. B. Mohr (Paul Siebeck), 1976], 321–37). More fruitfully, I think, Sharyn Dowd has suggested to me that the "story is ambiguous as to *whose* is the failure. At 9:18 the father blames the disciples. At 9:28 the disciples blame themselves. At 9:23 Jesus seems to blame the father." Perhaps the ambiguity is not to be resolved; perhaps the failure is not the father's alone or the disciples' alone but, as the Markan Jesus says in 9:19, the failure of this "faithless generation."

30. Best, "Role of the Disciples," 385–86.

even makes an attempt to follow (14:54). But Jesus' judgment is right; their judgments are wrong—as they always are when not under the explicit direction of Jesus. When the disciples *respond* to Jesus' request for assistance, they are often successful; when they *volunteer* assistance on their own, they are usually off course. Apparently, to follow Jesus, the disciples must follow Jesus' lead.

The crowd seems to err in the opposite direction: following Jesus too closely; not offering that which is not asked for, but asking continually for that which is offered. The crowd seeks out Jesus' healing power (1:37, *pas*—the crowd in addition to "Simon and those who were with him"?; 2:4, *ochlos*; 3:9, *ochlos*), sometimes obstructing by its very size those who seek healing (2:4, *ochlos*), sometimes obstructing them by direct rebuke (10:48, *polloi*). And sometimes the ever-present crowd denies Jesus and his disciples the opportunity to eat (3:20, *ochlos*; 6:31, *polloi*), or even threatens Jesus' safety (3:9, *ochlos*). In short, the crowd crowds Jesus. For all its gathering to Jesus, however, the crowd does not always trust Jesus' healing power; "most of them" (9:26, *tous pollous*) thought the epileptic boy had died when Jesus commanded the unclean spirit to come out of him.[31]

Yet the crowd overeager in its desire for healing from Jesus, like the disciples overeager in their desire to assist and please Jesus, does not in fact impede the ministry of Jesus. Rather, the interaction between Jesus and the crowd, like that between Jesus and the disciples, helps illustrate the true nature of the ministry of Jesus and the discipleship of his followers. The crowd too is a foil for Jesus.[32]

Still, the disciples serve as the most significant foil for Jesus. And this is nowhere more clear than in the constant stream of

---

31. In the future, Jesus warns, some of the crowd may be misled by others, perhaps also of the crowd, for many (*polloi*) will come in Jesus' name and lead many (*polloi*) astray (13:6).

32. Contra Best, "Role of the Disciples," 392.

questions Jesus asks his disciples and his disciples ask him. Generally accompanied by his disciples, Jesus naturally asks them questions throughout his ministry of teaching (4:21; 4:30; 9:12; 13:2), healing (5:30; 9:16, disciples?), and feeding (6:38; 8:5). But, more importantly, Jesus questions the disciples concerning their understanding of the parables (4:13; 7:18), of the feedings (8:17–21), of the demands of discipleship (8:36–37; 9:33; 9:50; 10:36, 38; 14:37, 41), of himself (8:27, 29). He questions their faith (4:40; 9:19). Jesus questions the crowd (or individuals amid the crowd) as well as the disciples, as he teaches (3:33; 4:13, those about him with the twelve; 4:30, crowd?; 8:36–37; 12:35, 37) and heals (5:30; 5:39; 9:16, 19, 21; 10:51). But Jesus' questions of the crowd are less frequent and—with the exception of 3:33—less profound at the metaphorical level than his questions of the disciples.

The contrast is even greater in regard to the questions the disciples and the crowd ask Jesus. Strictly speaking, no direct questions from the crowd to Jesus are reported by the Markan narrator; twice, however, the crowd questions itself concerning Jesus, and in his presence (1:27, *pas*; 6:2, *polloi*). On the other hand, both indirect (4:10, those about him with the twelve; 7:17; 10:10) and direct questions from the disciples to Jesus are narrated, and twice the narrator notes that the disciples had questions they did not raise (9:10; 9:32). The disciples ask Jesus about parables (4:10; 7:17), teaching (9:11; 10:10), healing (9:28), feedings (6:37; 8:4), salvation (10:26), the signs of the end (13:4). They cannot bring themselves to ask about Jesus' death and resurrection (9:10; 9:32).[33] Almost always their questions betray their lack of faith and/or understanding (4:10; 4:38; 4:41, among themselves; 5:31; 6:37; 7:17; 8:4; 9:11; 9:28; 10:10; 10:26; 13:4; 14:4, disciples?; the exceptions are 14:12 and 14:19). But at least

---

33. As Best notes of 9:32, "[T]heir failure to understand is only partial: they understand enough to be afraid to ask to understand more" (*Following Jesus*, 73).

the disciples remain willing to question Jesus, and to be questioned by Jesus, and to question themselves (9:28; 14:19).

In some important ways the disciples and the crowd are distinguished from one another by their relation to Jesus. The crowd comes to Jesus and he heals them. But Jesus gives more time to his disciples: he frequently withdraws with them. And Jesus asks more in return from his disciples: he enlists their assistance (and they also volunteer their assistance); he questions them (and they also question him). Yet in other important ways the disciples and the crowd are parallel in their relation to Jesus: Jesus calls both to himself; both follow Jesus; Jesus teaches both and commands both to hear; both are amazed and astonished at Jesus; Jesus feeds both. And in two final ways the disciples and the crowd are also parallel: both find themselves, because of their relation to Jesus, in opposition to Jewish leaders; yet both, in the end, abandon Jesus to the opposition of Jewish leaders.

Abandoning

In the first half of the Markan narrative the disciples of Jesus find themselves in opposition to Jewish leaders, particularly the Pharisees (2:15–17, scribes of the Pharisees; 2:18, Pharisees and disciples of the Pharisees; 2:23–27, Pharisees; 7:1–8, Pharisees and scribes; 8:15, Pharisees and Herodians; 9:14, scribes).[34] On the surface the disputes have to do with eating and bread (2:15–17, eating with sinners; 2:18, not fasting; 2:23–27, plucking grain; 7:1–8, eating unwashed; 8:15, the leaven of the Pharisees and Herodians), but the more fundamental issues are purity and authority. In the second half of the

---

34. Thomas L. Budesheim points out, especially in regard to 9:14, that the Markan Gospel presents a parallel between the disciples and their teacher in that both debate with the scribes ("Jesus and the Disciples in Conflict with Judaism," *ZNW* 62 [1971]: 190–209, esp. 206–9).

Markan narrative the crowd that follows Jesus finds itself in opposition to Jewish leaders, particularly the chief priests and the scribes (11:18, chief priests and scribes; 11:32, chief priests, scribes, and elders; 12:12, chief priests, scribes, and elders; 14:2, chief priests and scribes). At this stage in the story the chief priests and scribes (and elders) hesitate to move against Jesus because they fear the crowd that supports him. After one of Jesus' disciples betrays him to the chief priests (14:10), however, they are able to stir up the crowd against Jesus (15:11).

Thus, both the disciples and the crowd, who were in opposition to Jewish leaders because they followed Jesus, abandon Jesus, who must then face the opposition of Jewish leaders alone. Judas betrays Jesus (14:10, Judas Iscariot, *heis tōn dōdeka* [one of the twelve]; 14:43, Judas, *heis tōn dōdeka*), as the narrator had noted (3:19, Judas Iscariot) and Jesus had implied (14:20, *heis tōn dōdeka*) he would. All the disciples forsake Jesus (14:50, *pas* [all]), as Jesus had warned (14:27, *pas*) and the disciples had denied (14:31, *pas*) they would. Peter denies Jesus (14:66–72), as Jesus had predicted (14:30) and Peter had denied (14:29, 31) he would. At Gethsemane Jesus faces a newly formed group: "Judas . . . one of the twelve, and with him a crowd with swords and clubs, from the chief priests and the scribes and the elders" (14:43). Presumably the many (14:56, *polloi*) who bear false witness against Jesus before the assembled chief priests and scribes and elders (14:53) emerge from this crowd. By the time Jesus is delivered to Pilate, the chief priests have the crowd well under their control (15:8, 11, 15). The crowd is co-opted; the disciples have fled. His followers have failed him; Jesus is alone.

Conclusion

Both the disciples and the crowd follow Jesus. Both the disciples and the crowd are fallible. Yet the Gospel of Mark is not an allegory in which a group of characters in the story may be equated with a group of persons beyond the narrative. The disciples are equivalent to neither Mark's supposed opponents nor Mark's imagined hearers/readers.[35] The Gospel of Mark is, however, metaphoric and imagistic, and the disciples and the crowd—especially taken together—do evoke a composite image of the followers, the fallible followers, of Jesus. Were only the disciples depicted as followers, the demands of discipleship would be clear, but discipleship might appear restrictive. Were only the crowd depicted as followers, the outreach entailed in following Jesus would be clear, but followership might appear permissive. With both disciples and the crowd depicted as followers, as fallible followers, the Markan narrative message is plain: discipleship is both open-ended and demanding; followership is neither exclusive nor easy.

In addition to the complementarity of the disciples and the crowd in this composite portrait of followers, there exists a kind of complementarity of the part and the whole within each group. The disciples, as the inner group specifically chosen and commissioned by Jesus, have a higher positive connotation as a group than does the crowd. But the individual disciples, and groups of two, three, or four disciples set apart from the twelve, generally have a negative connotation (see the Appendix to Chapter 3 for references). On the other hand, when individuals are singled out of the crowd, their connotative value is highly positive as illustrated in the following passages:

---

35. Likewise Best's identification of the crowd as "the unevangelised mass" or "the uncommitted" (*Following Jesus*, 29, 101, 136, 154), the disciples as "the church" or "Christians" (29, 113, 136), and the twelve as "missionaries" (184, 195, 204–5) is overschematized. But with Best (*Following Jesus*, 46 n. 12) I reject E. Lohmeyer's identification of the crowd with the laity and the disciples with ecclesiastical officials.

2:2–12	four men and the paralytic (2:2, *polloi*; 2:4, *ochlos*; 2:12, *pas*)
2:13–14	Levi—from the crowd? (2:13, *ochlos*; 2:15b, *polloi*)
5:1–20	Gerasene demoniac (5:20, *pas*)
5:24–34	woman with hemorrhage (5:24, 27, 30, 31, *ochlos*)
7:32–37	deaf-mute (7:33, *ochlos*)
9:14–29	father of epileptic boy (9:17, *heis ek tou ochlou* [one from the crowd]; 9:14, 15, 25, *ochlos*; 9:26b, *polloi*)
10:46–52	Bartimaeus (10:48, *polloi*)
12:41–44	poor widow (12:41, *ochlos*; 12:43, 44a, *pas*)
15:40–41	three women—from the crowd? (15:41, *pollai*)

Perhaps this arrangement counters stereotyping; perhaps it challenges the assumptions of the hearers/readers. One expects disciples to be exemplary; their fallibility is surprising. One expects little of the crowd; their followership is surprising.

It hardly needs to be said that there are crucial differences between the disciples and the crowd—in terms of both narrative roles and theological significance. The concern here has been to illustrate the narrative and theological points of contact between the two groups. That both the disciples and the crowd are portrayed in positive and negative ways in relation to Jesus is indicated by the various—and parallel—kinds of activities that characterize each group's relationship with Jesus. That the disciples and the crowd are more complementary than competing groups in the Markan narrative, contributing to a composite portrait of followers of Jesus, is suggested by the distinctive—but compatible—kinds of activities that characterize each group's relationship with Jesus. The Markan extension of both the invitation and the demand of followership from the disciples to the crowd sets up its further extension—to the hearers/readers. The pattern of movement from the disciples to the crowd to the hearers/readers is suggested especially by: (1) Jesus' statements of the "whoever" type, addressed—within the story—to the disciples and/or the crowd, but reaching

beyond; and (2) Jesus' statements about "many" and "all,"
addressed—within the story—to the disciples, employing
terms usually designating the crowd, and pointing outward to
the hearer/reader.[36]

Jesus addresses "whoever" type statements to his followers—
most frequently the disciples but also the crowd (8:34): whoever
has ears to hear (4:23; cf. 4:9), whoever would come after me
(8:34), whoever would save his or her life (8:35), whoever would
be first (9:35), whoever gives you a cup of water (9:41), whoever
causes a little one to sin (9:42), whoever does not receive the
kingdom of God like a child (10:15), whoever leaves house or
family or lands (10:29), whoever does not doubt in his or her
heart (11:23). Surely the twelve and members of the crowd are
among the "whoever," but so may be the hearers/readers. Here
we can look at but one example. Jesus' saying at 10:29–30,
"there is no one who has left (*aphēken*) . . . who will not receive
. . . ," echoes Peter's immediately prior statement, "we have left
(*aphēkamen*) everything . . ." (10:28). Thus by their actions the
disciples are linked with the "whoever" of 10:29–30; the disciples, as the hearer/reader realizes, are among those who have
left families, houses, lands. But the disciples alone do not necessarily comprise the "whoever" at 10:29–30, for not only does
the "receiving" remain in the narrative future, but also the way

---

36. On Mark's implied readers, see Robert M. Fowler, *Loaves and
Fishes: The Function of the Feeding Stories in the Gospel of Mark*, SBLDS
54 (Chico, Calif.: Scholars Press, 1981), 149–79; and Fowler, "Who
Is 'the Reader' of Mark's Gospel?" *SBLSP* 22 (1983): 31–53. On
Mark's hearers/readers, see Werner H. Kelber, *The Oral and the Writ-
ten Gospel* (Philadelphia: Fortress, 1983). Both Fowler's reading and
Kelber's reading of the disciples in Mark are different from mine,
similar to each other's, and related to Weeden's. See also H.-J.
Klauck, "Die erzählerische Rolle der Jünger im Markusevangelium,"
NovT 24 (1982): 1–26; K. Stock, *Boten aus dem Mit-Ihm-Sein: Das Ver-
hältnis zwischen Jesus und Zwölf nach Markus*, AnBib 70 (Rome: Pon-
tificio Istituto Biblico, 1975).

is left open for others to be included among those who leave lands and regain lands for Jesus' sake "and for the gospel" (10:29)—others including, if not especially, whoever hears or reads Mark's "gospel of Jesus Christ, the Son of God" (1:1).

Other statements addressed by the Markan Jesus to the disciples are centered on the words many (*polloi*) and all (*pas*), familiar Markan designations for the crowd. Jesus informs his disciples that he gives his life, pours out his blood, for the many (10:45, *polloi*; 14:24, *polloi*). And, concerning followership, Jesus instructs his disciples that "many that are first will be last, and the last first" (10:31 *polloi*) and that "If any one would be first, he must be last of all and servant of all" (9:35, *pas*, *pas*) or "slave of all" (10:44, *pas*). The Markan Jesus addresses the disciples, but the words he employs—many and all—are open-ended. The disciples are surely among the many for whom Jesus gives his life; the crowd is also among the many; but the many embraces as well the hearers/readers of the Markan narrative. Whoever—disciples, crowds, hearers/readers—would be first of all, must be servant of all. What the Markan Jesus says to the four disciples he says to all (13:37, *pas*). What the Markan narrative says about discipleship it says to all. Both separately and together, the disciples and the crowd serve to open the story of Jesus and the narrative of Mark outward to the larger group—whoever has ears to hear or eyes to read the Gospel of Mark.

4

Text and Contexts

Interpreting the Disciples In Mark

It is a cliché, of course, to say that one must read the text in context, not use the text for a pretext.[1] The cliché may indeed be true, but its view of truth is oversimplified, for a text has not one but many contexts. Different interpreters, focusing on one or another of these contexts, may come to conclusions that are mutually complementary or competitive. A more systematic understanding of the relations between a text and its contexts and between contextual foci and interpretive conclusions would aid us in evaluating interpretations and thus in interpreting texts. The present essay will propose a typology of contextual foci of interpreters and apply it to a significant work of New Testament scholarship: Werner Kelber's *The Oral and the Written Gospel*.[2] Kelber's study is concerned (among

---

1. It seems appropriate to note that the original (external historical) *context* of this paper was a session of the Structuralism and Exegesis Section of the SBL in 1985.

2. Werner H. Kelber, *The Oral and the Written Gospel: The Hermeneutics of Speaking and Writing in the Synoptic Tradition, Mark, Paul, and Q* (Philadelphia: Fortress, 1983). The precursor to this book was Kelber's article, "Mark and Oral Tradition," *Semeia* 16 (1979): 7–55.

other things) with interpreting the story of Jesus and the disciples as it unfolds in the Markan narrative, and that concern will serve as a "test case" for asking questions about the relation of text and contexts in the interpretive task.[3]

A Typology of Contextual Foci of Interpreters

One must refer to the contexts of a text, not its singular context. As Dominick LaCapra persuasively argues: "For complex texts, one has a set of interacting contexts whose relations to one another are variable and problematic and whose relation to the text being investigated raises difficult issues in interpretation."[4] It would perhaps be an impossible task to enumerate all the contexts of a text, but a simplified typology of contextual foci may be of use in registering the different interests, approaches, and assumptions of interpreters of texts and their contexts.

The proposed typology of contextual foci of interpreters is based on the intersection or crossing of two familiar distinctions: internal/external and literary/historical. Murray Krieger's

---

3. In the original context of this paper (see note 1), I also discussed as a "test case" Vernon K. Robbins, *Jesus the Teacher: A Socio-Rhetorical Interpretation of Mark* (Philadelphia: Fortress, 1984). The interpretation of the disciples in Mark serves as a test case for the application of redaction criticism for C. Clifton Black (*The Disciples according to Mark: Markan Redaction in Current Debate*, JSNTSup 27 [Sheffield: Sheffield Academic Press, 1989]), who focuses on the work of Robert P. Meye, Ernest Best, and Theodore J. Weeden, Sr., but discusses an extensive bibliography. Black's final appraisal is judicious but not surprising: Researchers' presuppositions predict their outcomes better than their stated methodologies do; redaction criticism has tended toward "methodological imperialism" and has sought to answer questions that are, by definition, unverifiable; a more synthetic interpretation—including historical, tradition, literary, authorial-theological (i.e., modified redaction), and reader-response criticism—is needed. See my review in *Int* 45 (1991): 82, 84.

4. Dominick LaCapra, *Rethinking Intellectual History: Texts, Contexts, Language* (Ithaca, N.Y.: Cornell University Press, 1983), 35.

images of the text as mirror and the text as window[5] suggest metaphorically what is meant here by the "internal" and the "external" contexts of a text. When an interpreter focuses on the text's "internal" context (text as mirror) he or she looks to "the text itself"—its words and sentences, its characters and settings, its plot and action, its rhetoric and imagery—for the text's meaning and significance. When an interpreter focuses on the "external" context of a text (text as window) she or he looks through the text to its situation in some larger world—whether cultural, political, religious, or literary.[6] "Literary" and "historical" have often been characterized as two distinctive (if not opposing) approaches to texts. To focus on the "literary" context of a text is to concentrate more on how the text is read than on why it was written, more on function—perhaps in relation to the conventions of a genre—than on intention. To focus on the "historical" context of a text is to investigate its place in societal/cultural processes of continuity and change. The quotation marks enclosing the four main terms of the typology are intended to indicate the problematic nature of the terms and the impossibility of their pure manifestation except as abstractions.

Crossing the "internal"/"external" distinction with the "literary"/"historical" distinction results in four contextual foci of interpreters of texts (see diagram): A, the interrelations of the

5. Murray Krieger, *A Window to Criticism: Shakespeare's Sonnets and Modern Poetics* (Princeton, N.J.: Princeton University Press, 1964). See also Norman R. Petersen, *Literary Criticism for New Testament Critics*, GBS (Philadelphia: Fortress, 1978), 19.

6. With Krieger (*Window to Criticism*, 28) and with Kelber ("Narrative as Interpretation and Interpretation of Narrative: Hermeneutical Reflections on the Gospels," *Semeia* 39 [1987]: 107–33, esp. 121–27), I agree that both views of the text—as mirror and as window—are not only legitimate but necessary to the interpretive task in its fullest sense. The difficulty lies in relating the two views in a way that does justice to both. See also Werner H. Kelber, "Apostolic Tradition and the Form of the Gospel," in *Discipleship in the New Testament*, ed. Fernando F. Segovia (Philadelphia: Fortress, 1985), 24–46, esp. 32–34; and note 55 below.

Contextual Foci (of Interpreters)

	"internal" context	"external" context
"literary" context	**A** the interrelations of the elements of the text	**B** the interrelations of the text with other texts
"historical" context	**C** the immediate societal/cultural situation of the text (esp. its origin or preservation)	**D** the broader societal/cultural situation of the text

Arrows reflect relationships in Werner H. Kelber, *The Oral and the Written Gospel.*

elements of the text; B, the interrelations of the text with other texts; C, the immediate societal/cultural situation of the text (especially its origin and/or preservation); D, the broader societal/cultural situation of the text. It is here assumed (although it will not be discussed) that "the text" is an abstraction employed to refer to the communication process involving an author (real and implied), a text (variously transmitted), and an audience (real and implied).[7] The audience of particular concern here is

---

7. Thus I am in agreement with Paul B. Armstrong that "A text is not an independent object which remains the same regardless of how it is construed. The literary work is not autonomous but 'heteronomous,'" that is, "paradoxically both dependent and independent, capable of taking on different shapes according to opposing hypotheses about how to configure it, but always transcending any particular interpreter's beliefs about it" (*Conflicting Readings: Variety and Validity in Interpretation* [Chapel Hill: University of North Carolina Press, 1990], 11, x).

the community of scholarly interpreters. The parentheses around "of Interpreters" in the title of the diagram indicates that the role of the interpreter (reader, literary critic, historian), although integrally involved with a text's multiple contexts, is not the focus of this typology. Yet it is important to note here that these are contextual foci *of interpreters*. The interpreter is omnipresent in interpretation. Thus we will need to return, in the concluding section, to a brief explicit consideration of the role of the interpreter in relation to text and contexts.[8] The immediate task is to apply this typology to the work of a real interpreter.

The title of Kelber's 1983 book, *The Oral and the Written Gospel*, suggests its underlying concern: the dynamic interaction of orality and textuality manifested in New Testament texts—especially Paul's letters and Mark's Gospel. This interaction is, for Kelber, a central element—and perhaps the central element—of the broader societal/cultural situation of the New Testament—a D focus. To indicate that Kelber is concerned with the "external"/"historical" context is not to identify linguistics with history, but only to point out that Kelber focuses on the interactions and shifts between linguistic media as they occur in time, in history. Although Kelber does, of course, concern himself with the interrelations of the elements of the text (A) of Mark—especially its characters—this does

---

8. One might, of course, *focus* on the role of the interpreter, as reader-response critics do, or on the movement from the reader/interpreter's preunderstanding to explaining the text (perhaps from an A focus) to understanding (with a second focus on the role of the interpreter). On this latter option see Lynn M. Poland, *Literary Criticism and Biblical Hermeneutics: A Critique of Formalist Approaches*, AAR Academy Series 48 (Chico, Calif.: Scholars Press, 1985), especially the final discussion of Ricoeur. See also Armstrong, *Conflicting Readings*, who presents a theory of "limited pluralism," in which conflicting readings of interpreters may be evaluated and appreciated without absolute claims to "truth" or "correctness."

not appear to be his focal concern, and this observation seems
even more true of *The Oral and the Written Gospel* than of his
two earlier books, *The Kingdom in Mark*[9] and *Mark's Story of
Jesus*.[10] Kelber's focal concern—in all three books in distinctive
ways—is the immediate societal/cultural situation of the
Markan text, especially its origin (C). The concluding chapters of *Kingdom* and *Mark's Story* very explicitly deal with the
historical situation of the genesis of Mark's Gospel. The concluding chapter of *Oral and Written* shares this concern as well,
but in terms of contextual foci it adds an interesting new twist:
a focus on the genre of Mark, which entails examining the
interrelation of the Markan text with other texts (B). For Kelber, Mark's genre—parable—is the only one appropriate for
the occasion of its genesis. Thus Kelber ignores none of the
contextual foci of the typology; but concerns for A and D seem
to serve C, that is, the "internal"/"literary" context and the
"external"/"historical" context seem primarily useful in clarifying the "internal"/"historical" context. B also serves C, that
is, the "external"/"literary" context serves to clarify the "internal"/"historical" context; but one gets the feeling at the close
of *Oral and Written* that genre (B) is becoming as intriguing to
Kelber (and as focal) as genesis (C). This feeling is confirmed
in Kelber's 1985 article, "Apostolic Tradition and the Form of
the Gospel," which presents Mark's Gospel as "an anti-genre
to the genre of a sayings tradition," the parabolic reversal of
"the revelation dialogue that has been embedded in 4:1–33"
and is exemplified by the Gospel of Thomas.[11]

Although Kelber manifests awareness of multiple contexts,
no interpreter can focus on everything at once. The arrows on

---

9. Werner H. Kelber, *The Kingdom in Mark: A New Place and a New
Time* (Philadelphia: Fortress, 1974).

10. Werner H. Kelber, *Mark's Story of Jesus* (Philadelphia:
Fortress, 1979).

11. Kelber, "Apostolic Tradition," 42.

the diagram suggest the ways in which these four contextual foci are interrelated for Kelber. The arrow moving from D to C indicates that the broader societal/cultural situation of the text forms the background for the immediate societal/cultural situation of the text (especially its origin), which is in the foreground for Kelber. The two-directional arrow between A and C represents the interaction between Kelber's interpretation of the text and his presentation of its immediate context, seen most clearly in his understanding of the polemical nature of both. The arrow from C to B suggests the movement of Kelber's concern from his primary focus (genesis) to his secondary—but increasingly important—focus (genre). Basically Kelber studies the relation of text (A) and history (D) in Mark and comes to an understanding of, firstly, Mark's genesis (C) and, secondly, Mark's genre (B).

This typology of contextual foci is intended to be descriptive not evaluative, although, clearly, judgments about what is the central thrust in a work are required in order to apply the typology. Now, having presented this (admittedly schematic) view of how various textual contexts are related, I do wish to pose some questions about all contextual readings. Again Kelber's contextual reading of the text of Mark will serve as an example.

Questions about Contextual Readings

I introduce my questions by reference to Dominick LaCapra's critique of the book by Allan Janik and Stephen Toulmin, *Wittgenstein's Vienna*. This book is "an exemplar of a contextualist approach to interpreting the meaning of an important text"—Wittgenstein's *Tractatus Logico-Philosophicus*.[12] But LaCapra raises questions about Janik and Toulmin's book based on his reading of Wittgenstein's book. LaCapra

---

12. LaCapra, *Rethinking*, 86.

describes the goal of the former in this way: "The explicit intention of Janik and Toulmin is to relate the *Tractatus* (first published in 1921) to a precise context: fin-de-siècle Vienna. This context was characterized by a widespread cultural concern with the crisis of language and the problem of ethics. Their argument is that the ignorance of this context has led to significant distortion in the way the *Tractatus* has been read."[13] But LaCapra's judgment is as follows:

> In Janik and Toulmin's account, the idea that the *Tractatus* is essentially "ethical" rather than "logical" in meaning depends upon an extremely reductive interpretation of the text which, not surprisingly, coincides with an extremely reductive interpretation of the context. This dual reduction serves the interest of a fully unified interpretation. . . . In Janik and Toulmin, the context serves ultimately to saturate the text with meaning. The paradoxes and silences of the text are not questioned precisely because they are filled in or smoothed over by generous helpings of context, and the paradoxes of the context itself are transcended through a methodology that ties everything together.[14]

> In a circular fashion, the notion of context as a synchronic whole, situated in time and place, further serves to bring about a coincidence between the author's intentions and the meaning of the text.[15]

LaCapra complains that what Janik and Toulmin either seek or assume—the context—does not exist. No text has just one context; contexts are always plural, and they present the same problems and challenges as texts: they demand interpretation in themselves and in relation to other "more or less pertinent contexts."[16] LaCapra realizes that "it would of course be

---

13. Ibid.
14. Ibid., 87–88.
15. Ibid., 91.
16. Ibid., 95–96.

humanly impossible to treat adequately all these contexts," but he insists that "the awareness of the 'intertextual' horizon of any contextual reading serves both as the (recurrently displaced) ideal limit for research and as a check against unsubstantiated claims for the primordiality of any given context."[17] Thus LaCapra's point is "not to fault Janik and Toulmin for not being exhaustive" but "to question the concept of exhaustiveness, including the form it takes in Janik and Toulmin: that of contextual saturation of the meaning of a text."[18]

One way to test the relative importance of any one context is "to examine critically the extent to which it informs a reading of the text,"[19] a task that LaCapra carries out in relation to *Wittgenstein's Vienna* and Wittgenstein's *Tractatus*.[20] While LaCapra admits that "'contextualism' in the sense practiced by Janik and Toulmin . . . may seem liberating in contrast with a narrowly literary or 'history-of-ideas' point of view,"[21] he fears that it has limits of its own. The text should not "be identified with the self-enclosed, unique aesthetic object"[22] nor overidentified with the context. "The relationship between text and context," LaCapra concludes, "would then become a question of 'intertextual' reading, which cannot be addressed on the basis of reductionist oversimplifications that convert the context into a fully unified or dominant structure saturating the text with a certain meaning. Meaning is indeed context-bound, but context is not itself bound in any simple or unproblematic way."[23]

Certainly Kelber does not believe that the simple, unproblematic context of Mark is to be sought, much less found. In fact, *The Oral and the Written Gospel* serves to awaken New

---

17. Ibid., 99.
18. Ibid.
19. Ibid.
20. Ibid., 100–114.
21. Ibid., 114–15.
22. Ibid., 116.
23. Ibid., 117.

Testament scholars to certain of Mark's multiple contexts that have been neglected. And certainly Kelber's work "informs a reading of the text" of Mark to a considerable extent. Yet it is instructive, as an example, to ask (1) whether Kelber's book tends toward the "contextual saturation of the meaning" of the Markan text and (2) what are the limits of the extent to which his work "informs a reading of the text." My questions are, thus, less pointed than LaCapra's questions; but, like his, they are raised in order to highlight general methodological assumptions and strategies as much as to critique specific interpretations.

Kelber is concerned to show how Mark stands out in its broader context: it confronts orality with textuality; it confronts tradition with parable. Of course Mark has both continuities and discontinuities with its historical/cultural context, as Kelber is aware. But the continuities seem underexplained (not quite *not* explained) by Kelber. It is a matter of the interpreter's *telos*, his or her end, in the sense of both *goal* and *conclusion*. If one reaches one's goal, conclusions seem in order. If one is interested especially in the relation of a text to a particular context, and one works out a reasonable interpretation of the text and a plausible reconstruction of the context, and the two fit together nicely, one may be tempted not to ask further questions of the text or the context (especially from the point of view of yet another context) that might upset that delicate balance. It seems very unlikely that Kelber had a fully worked out view of a Markan ("historical" or "external") context before working out a Markan exegesis. More probably, exegesis influenced understanding of the context, as well as vice versa, throughout the process of interpretation. It is the neatness of the final fit between the text and the focal context that gives pause and raises the question of the contextual saturation of the meaning of the text.

In relation to Kelber's *Oral and Written* the problem is especially complex, for we may need to ask not only about the possible contextual saturation of the meaning of the text but also about the possible textual saturation of the meaning of the context! Does an understanding of the context of Mark as polemical (textuality versus orality) lead to an understanding of the story of the Markan disciples as polemical? Or does the reading of the Markan story of the disciples as polemical influence the reading of the Markan context as polemical? Each of Kelber's three books asserts a polemical reading of the story of the disciples and a polemical reading of the Markan context—although the foundation for the polemic is different in each case. The disciples are portrayed negatively in Mark because they represent those who, in Mark's historical context, held the "wrong" eschatology (*Kingdom*), belonged to the "wrong" church (*Mark's Story*), employed the "wrong" linguistic medium (*Oral and Written*), and/or embraced the "wrong" genre ("Apostolic Tradition and the Form of the Gospel"). In order to resolve this chicken-or-egg problem of Kelber's work, one would probably have to trace it back to the relation of text and context in Weeden's work on the disciples in Mark[24] and from there back to Georgi's work on text and context in regard to the opponents of Paul in 2 Corinthians.[25]

A more important question would seem to be whether the mutual saturation (or especially "neat" fit) between text and

---

24. Theodore J. Weeden, "The Heresy That Necessitated Mark's Gospel," *ZNW* 59 (1968): 145–58; and Weeden, *Mark—Traditions in Conflict* (Philadelphia: Fortress, 1971).

25. Sharyn Echols Dowd (*Prayer, Power, and the Problem of Suffering: Mark 11:22–25 in the Context of Markan Theology*, SBLDS 105 [Atlanta: SBL, 1988], 6–24), traces the influence of Dieter Georgi's *Die Gegner des Paulus im 2. Korintherbrief*, WMANT 11 (Neukirchen-Vluyn, 1964) on Weeden's dissertation (reflected in his publications cited above), and then to Norman Perrin and his students. Kelber was a doctoral student of Perrin at Chicago and dedicated his first book (his revised dissertation) to him. See Kelber, "Apostolic Tradition," 26–28, 42, on Perrin and Weeden.

focal context leads Kelber to misread some of his own cues. Kelber presents a rather thorough analysis of "Mark's Oral Legacy,"[26] that is, the "oral forms and conventions" that "have gained admittance into the written document" even though "the pre-gospel transmission does not in itself account for the extant gospel."[27] On this basis it would seem more accurate to describe Mark as shaping and interpreting oral tradition, rather than opposing and rejecting it.[28] Furthermore, if (1) oral tradition is not completely rejected by Mark (as Kelber's discussion of its "oral legacy" would seem to suggest), and (2) the disciples in Mark represent oral tradition (as Kelber asserts explicitly), then (3) it would seem more consistent to argue that the disciples are *not* completely rejected but, rather, interpreted—in ways that preclude their simple idolization. As oral tradition is curtailed and contained but not eliminated, Kelber might well argue, so the disciples are critiqued and chastened but not discredited. But his understanding of the Markan context as polemical blocks such a reading. The argument can be made from a different angle as well. If, as Boomershine[29] persuasively argues, the Gospel of Mark was intended to be told and heard, not read individually and silently, was Mark really as opposed to orality as Kelber suggests? It would appear, rather, that the author was presenting his own interpretation—written, to be sure, but written to be spoken—but his own interpretation of oral tradition for his own situation.[30]

---

26. Kelber, *Oral and Written*, chap. 2.

27. Ibid., 44.

28. See also Theodore J. Weeden, Sr., "Metaphysical Implications of Kelber's Approach to Orality and Textuality," in *SBLSP* 16 (1979) 2: 153–66, esp. 158–60.

29. Thomas E. Boomershine, "Mark, the Storyteller: A Rhetorical-Critical Investigation of Mark's Passion and Resurrection Narrative" (Ph.D. diss., Union Theological Seminary, New York, 1974).

30. See also Weeden, "Metaphysical Implications," 162–63.

And, if this is true, an interpretation of the disciples as representatives of the opposed oral tradition loses crucial support.[31]

It is clear that Kelber does not present orality/textuality as "the context" of the Markan Gospel. Kelber comments, for example, that the "early and radical" shift from orality to textuality that Mark represents is "not fully accounted for without the stimulus of environmental factors," especially the destruction of the temple in 70 C.E.[32] But the shift from orality to textuality that Kelber takes as an extremely important element of the Markan context he then depicts as essential and central to an understanding of the disciples. At one point Kelber presents the argument compactly:

> the relationship between Jesus and his disciples is constructed on the oral principle of *imitatio magistri*, or in Platonic terms on *mimesis*, which has as its chief concern the preservation of tradition.
>
> In Mark's gospel the twelve personify the principal, oral representatives of Jesus. They function in a mimetic process whose function is to assure continuity of tradition. . . . [However,] [*b*]*oth the model of a mimetic relationship and the drama of failing discipleship are drawn with equal care by Mark.* This leads us to suggest that the dysfunctional role of the disciples narrates the breakdown of the mimetic process and casts a vote of censure against the guarantors of tradition. Oral representatives and oral mechanism have come under criticism.[33]

Kelber's argument that his observations about orality and textuality are central to the search for the "original form" of the

---

31. Kelber's attempt to resolve this problem by distinguishing between primary orality (Mark's oral legacy) and secondary orality (the reading aloud of Mark's Gospel) is not convincing, even though the distinction itself is of interest (*Oral and Written*, 217–18).

32. Ibid., 210.

33. Ibid., 197; Kelber's emphasis.

sayings of Jesus is more convincing than his argument that they are central to Mark's story of Jesus and the disciples.[34] (The contextual view of Mark from which I make this statement will be made explicit below.)

Yet it seems only fair to remind ourselves that, in his insistence that the distinction between the oral and the written be taken seriously, Kelber was, in 1983, almost a voice crying in the wilderness. This does not free his work from the danger of the contextual saturation of the meaning of the text, but it does raise the possibility of a certain degree of understandable over-compensation. The contextual saturation of the meaning of the text may be a built-in danger when one seeks to interpret a text and yet focuses not on the text itself (contextual focus A) but on the "internal"/"historical" context, especially the genesis of the text (C). *The Oral and the Written Gospel* is not immune to this danger, although Kelber is not unaware of it. The difficulty of the interpretive task makes the struggle all the more important. A theory of the text's genesis is no substitute for an interpretation of its significance. To explain the text's emergence in history is not to explain the text.

I have borrowed LaCapra's metaphor of "saturation" to speak of this danger. Concretizing this image may clarify its significance for the interpretive situation. When a sponge is saturated with water it does not really do a very good job of wiping off the kitchen table; it leaves a watery trail, and it cannot absorb any cleanser, should some be needed for a more thorough job. (Of course, a dry sponge, one that is totally unsaturated, is equally unsuited for this task.) Analogously, when a text like Mark's Gospel is saturated with meaning from

---

34. One might also ask: Can there be a contextual saturation of the understanding of the *form* of the text as well as of its *meaning*? This question could be applied to Kelber's discussion of the Gospel's form as parable. See Elizabeth Struthers Malbon, "Mark: Myth and Parable," *BTB* 16 (1986): 8–17.

one or another of its contexts, it does not function at its best either; it does not tell its story fully. If the questions a text raises tend to be quite completely answered by information from one of the text's "external" contexts, for example, then information from the text's "internal" relations may simply not be absorbed. Sometimes an interpreted text, like a sopping sponge, needs to be squeezed out.

A metaphor more often employed in discussing this issue is the hermeneutical "circle." Scholars of ancient literature and ancient history are accustomed to the problem of the circularity of analyzing the text for information about the context, then reconstructing the context on the basis of that analysis, and finally reinterpreting the text in terms of that reconstructed context. Kelber breaks out of this potentially vicious circle in an important way: he brings to his analysis of Mark significant information about the first-century context that could not be gleaned from Mark alone by the twentieth-century reader. But the hermeneutical circle spins in another way when Kelber relies heavily on this new contextual information either to answer or not to raise basic questions about the text itself, the interrelations of its elements, its characters, plot, and so on. Then the relations between orality and textuality in a reconstructed context become *the key* to interpreting the relations between Jesus and the disciples in Mark. The questions the characters and plot of Mark present to the reader tend to be answered on the basis of the reconstructed context of its genesis, to the (relative) neglect of the context of the text's own interrelations. One way to break open the interpretive circle again is to move to another context. Such a move is my goal in the following section.

Questions about the Disciples in Mark

My questions about the disciples are raised from a different contextual focus from Kelber's—from a focus on the interrelations of the elements of the text (A). And it may be that this different focus can suggest a reading of the story of the disciples in Mark that supplements, complements, and in some cases corrects the reading of Kelber.

My first question is in essence a restatement of my contextual focus: Do we not need, at some point, to read the text with primary reference to its own "internal" relations, as a check on readings of the text in close relation to "external" history or "external" literature (with their contingent dangers of contextual saturation of the meaning of the text)? Of course, reading the text with *no* reference to history or other texts is impossible; and, of course, focusing on the internal relations of the text has its own dangers. Yet there is still something to be said for preliminary investigations of the text and of history in relative isolation, so that the two may thereafter inform each other rather than risk forming or deforming each other initially. In terms of the Markan story of the disciples, my first question might be rephrased: Does not a reading of Mark with primary reference to its own "internal" relations suggest (for example) that two of the narrator's critical decisions must be interpreted together—the decision to end chapter 16 with questions about the disciples' future actions unanswered and the decision to include in chapter 13 Jesus' description of the disciples' future actions? And does not this reading serve as a check on readings (often made in close connection with a reconstructed historical context) of the Markan disciples as "failures"?

Readings of the disciples in Mark as "failures" (such as Kelber's) frequently include several interpretations of elements of chapters 13 and 16 not supported by a reading that focuses on the internal relations of the text. For example, the assumption that the disciples remain in Jerusalem is not shared by the Markan Jesus, whose message is not, "Tell the disciples and Peter to go to Galilee so they will see me," but rather, "Go, tell the disciples and Peter that I am going before them to the same place they are going—home, to Galilee; there they will see me as I told them earlier." Nor is the assumption that the disciples never hear of or respond to Jesus' resurrection supported by the narrator's choice to end the chronological narration with the women's fear and silence. Jesus' descriptions of the disciples' future responses, narrated proleptically in chapter 13, are given not as commandments that the disciples may or may not succeed in keeping, but as predictions: "You *will* be beaten . . . and you *will* stand before governors and kings for my sake," not "you *should* stand . . ." Were these projections judged to be inaccurate, it would not be the disciples who were discredited, but Jesus (contra Kelber[35]). And this is clearly not the case in Mark.

Based on a contextual focus on the interrelations of the elements of the text, one might say that the Markan Gospel has a double ending: the passion of the community (chapter 13) paralleling the passion of Jesus (chapters 14–16).[36] Or one might say, with Frank Kermode,[37] that Mark 13 is intercalated between 1–12 and 14–16 and, with most Markan interpreters, that intercalation serves an interpretive function. This arrangement of chapters 13 and 16 allows the narrator to suggest something very important about Jesus the teacher. The climactic teaching of Jesus is his teaching about suffering and death, about taking up one's cross for the sake of the other. But Jesus' lessons on this subject are not over until he dies, because talking about dying is not at all the same thing as dying. The

---

35. Kelber, *Oral and Written*, 128; "Apostolic Tradition," 35–36, 39–40.

36. See Elizabeth Struthers Malbon, *Narrative Space and Mythic Meaning in Mark*, New Voices in Biblical Studies (San Francisco: Harper & Row, 1986; reprint, The Biblical Seminar 13; Sheffield: Sheffield Academic Press, 1991), chap. 5.

37. Frank Kermode, *The Genesis of Secrecy: On the Interpretation of Narrative* (Cambridge, Mass.: Harvard University Press, 1979), 127–28.

disciples' learning cannot be complete until Jesus' teaching is complete. Reporting suffering and possibly death for the disciples (the completion of their learning) proleptically in chapter 13 rather than chronologically in chapter 16 has the crucial function of ending the Gospel story dramatically with Jesus' death and resurrection. Thus the Markan hearers/readers are left to stand *with* the characters in the story (especially the women) at the empty tomb—face-to-face, as his followers were, with the challenge and the promise of Jesus' death.

My second question about the disciples that challenges the extent to which Kelber's book informs a reading of the text is this: In terms of the internal relations of the text, are not the disciples more closely related to the other Markan characters and to the readers than Kelber suggests? In Kelber's interpretation the reader is completely at odds with the disciples. More convincing is Robert Tannehill's view[38] that the reader is intended to identify with the disciples (with their strengths first but later with their weaknesses), not just in chapter 16 but throughout the narrative, and Joanna Dewey's refinement of this view:[39] the implied reader identifies both with the disciples and with Jesus; the implied reader's situation is that of the disciples, but his or her values are those of Jesus.

Furthermore, the relation between the disciples as characters within the narrative and the hearers/readers as respondents beyond the narrative is prepared for in the Markan Gospel by the relations between the disciples and other characters within the narrative. There is a movement outward from the disciples to the crowd; the crowd (*ochlos*) serves to complement the disciples in a composite portrait of the followers of Jesus. Jesus calls to himself both the disciples and the crowd,

---

38. Robert Tannehill, "The Disciples in Mark: The Function of a Narrative Role," *JR* 57 (1977): 386–405.

39. Joanna Dewey, "Point of View and the Disciples in Mark," in *SBLSP* 21 (1982): 97–106.

and both the disciples and the crowd follow Jesus. Jesus teaches and feeds both the disciples and the crowd—and also heals the crowd—and both the disciples and the crowd are amazed or astonished at Jesus. Again and again the crowd comes to Jesus; time after time the disciples go with Jesus. Jesus spends more time with the disciples and asks more assistance from them—in teaching, feeding, and other tasks. Yet the crowd crowds Jesus, and the disciples misunderstand discipleship. Although both the disciples and the crowd find themselves in opposition to Jewish leaders because they follow Jesus, in the end both abandon Jesus, who must then face the opposition of Jewish leaders alone. Both the disciples and the crowd are fallible followers. The encompassing movement from the disciples to the crowd within the narrative continues in the direction of the implied readers, as may be seen in the "whoever" statements of Jesus to his followers (most frequently the disciples but also the crowd): for example, whoever would come after me must deny self and take up his or her cross and follow me (8:34).[40]

The relation of the disciples to other characters or character groups in Mark also has a direct bearing on the hearer/reader's relation to the disciples. According to Kelber, the disciples of Jesus are actually portrayed in Mark (by stages) as opponents of Jesus, along with the Jewish leaders and others; this is because they represent the opponents of the author of the Markan Gospel. My view is that the disciples are depicted first of all as "round" characters, in contrast to the demons and the Jewish leaders—who are "flat" characters on the negative side,[41] and in contrast to the so-called "little

---

40. See Elizabeth Struthers Malbon, "Fallible Followers: Women and Men in the Gospel of Mark," *Semeia* 28 (1983): 29–48, esp. 31–32; and Malbon, "Disciples/Crowds/Whoever: Markan Characters and Readers," *NovT* 28 (1986): 104–30 [here chapters 2 and 3].

41. See Elizabeth Struthers Malbon, "The Jewish Leaders in the Gospel of Mark: A Literary Study of Marcan Characterization," *JBL* 108 (1989): 259–81, esp. 275–81 [here chapter 5].

people"[42]—who are "flat" characters on the positive side (the classic discussion of "flat" and "round" characters is that of Forster[43]). Whereas the hearer/reader might hiss the opponents and cheer the "little people," he or she would find more to identify with in the characterization of the disciples. If there is a connotative coloring to Mark's Gospel, the disciples represent neither white nor black but gray. The shading of the Gospel of Mark—and especially of its portrait of the disciples—is thus more subtle than that to which a polemical reading is sensitive. And the challenge of being a follower of Jesus is thus more intricately drawn. The Markan Gospel discredits not the disciples, but the view of discipleship as either exclusive or easy.

In Kelber's 1985 article "Apostolic Tradition and the Form of the Gospel," based on a 1982 paper at a conference on the theme of discipleship in the New Testament, this polemic between the disciples and the readers still stands. Kelber writes, "Nowhere in the canon does a text generate in readers as much alienation from the disciples as in this Gospel [of Mark];"[44] "*the full narrative impact* of the disciples' story is a negative one;"[45] "Mark enforces discipleship that is discontinuous with the Twelve and also with women."[46] Whereas Kelber seems to suggest that his view of the disciples challenges

---

42. David Rhoads and Donald Michie, *Mark as Story: An Introduction to the Narrative of a Gospel* (Philadelphia: Fortress, 1982), 129–35. The second edition of *Mark as Story* (Minneapolis: Fortress, 1999), with Joanna Dewey added as second author, refers to the "People," not "The Little People," and the discussion of the minor characters is significantly revised.

43. E. M. Forster, *Aspects of the Novel* (New York: Harcourt, Brace & Co., 1927; reprint, 1954).

44. Kelber, "Apostolic Tradition," 24.

45. Ibid. (emphasis original).

46. Ibid., 36.

as too conservative (or traditional) the views of other interpreters,[47] Kelber's own understanding of Mark's narrative seems to me not radical enough. (Polemical is not the same thing as radical.) Kelber hears the Markan Gospel as an attack on the disciples as the claimed authority of an esoteric group;[48] I sense in it the pulling of the rug out from under any and all such groups, including the audience.[49] Neither the disciples nor the hearers/readers can rest on their insider status; in this the two groups are alike, not different. Kelber's negative reading of the disciples and positive reading of the audience risks encouraging the readers' shared sense of superiority. I think Mark pulls the rug out from under us too.

However, in the conclusion to Kelber's 1988 article "Narrative and Disclosure: Mechanisms of Concealing, Revealing, and Reveiling," there is a shift in the presupposed disciples/readers polemic. While the disciples are still viewed negatively (as chosen insiders who have made themselves outsiders), the readers' natural advantage over the disciples is questioned.

> In view of parabolic mystery at the peak of the narrative, the role reversal of the disciples from insiders to outsiders should have a chilling effect on us, the new insiders. In thinking that we are inside the narrative, we are perpetually reminded of what happens to insiders. It will not let us stay inside for long, if at all[.] And if we think we are inside, it is a sure sign that we are already outside.[50]

---

47. E.g., Petersen, Tannehill, and Boomershine; Kelber, "Apostolic Tradition," 34–37.

48. Kelber, "Apostolic Tradition," 41–42.

49. Similarly, earlier Kelber heard in Mark a rejection of Jerusalem as the site of the parousia in favor of Galilee (Kelber, *Kingdom*), whereas I heard a rejection of the notion that the place of the parousia could be predicted (Malbon, *Narrative Space*).

50. Werner H. Kelber, "Narrative and Disclosure: Mechanisms of Concealing, Revealing, and Reveiling," *Semeia* 43 (1988): 1–20; quotation from 17.

In such a situation, I would add, how can we be so sure that the disciples are irrevocably outsiders? Or that being inside and being outside are polemically opposed rather than connected in process and in mystery? In the conclusion to Kelber's 1991 address to the Bible in Ancient and Modern Media Group of the Society of Biblical Literature, it is the absoluteness of the polemic between the oral and the written that is questioned. What is demanded, Kelber admits, is

> a new sensitivity toward the interworkings of Scripture [the written] and Logos [the oral] whereby each comes into its own by interaction with the other.
>
> What this suggests is that Scripture versus Logos, this great divide thesis, which pits oral tradition vis-à-vis the gospel text, cannot in the end supply the answer to the questions concerning tradition and gospel. . . . To grasp the overlaps and interfaces, we have to understand the hermeneutics of speech and writing, even if they rarely existed in a pure state. And yet, the longer one works with the strong thesis, the more we are aware of its character as a mastertrope. We need to force the dichotomy in order to erase it.[51]

Would this new sensitivity to the interrelations between the oral and written as media enable a less polemical interpretation of the interrelations of the disciples within and the readers of Mark's Gospel?

My questions about the disciples in Mark, directed here primarily to the conclusions concerning the disciples drawn by Kelber in his three books, serve to complicate his analysis. Can the disciples really serve as vehicles for polemic if Markan patterns of characterization show them not as black or white but

---

51. Werner H. Kelber, "Scripture and Logos: The Hermeneutics of Communication" (paper presented to the Bible in Ancient and Modern Media Group at the annual meeting of the SBL, Kansas City, Mo., 1991), 14.

gray? Can the Markan Gospel really be said to lack disciple-ship fulfillment if chapter 13 is not forgotten in interpreting chapter 16?

Of course one could ask whether my reading of the disci-ples in Mark, barely sketched out here, tends toward the con-textual saturation of the meaning of the text. It would be a fair question, since the danger is inherent in the interpretive situ-ation. It is, perhaps, somewhat more difficult to apply the metaphor of "contextual saturation" to an approach that focuses on the internal relations of the elements of the text since such an approach is sometimes accused of ignoring con-texts altogether.[52] But, given that the internal relations of the elements of the text also comprise a context (A), what would characterize "contextual saturation" from this standpoint? Anachronism in interpretive strategies would seem to be the chief problem—reading the text in ways common enough in twentieth-century literary criticism but contraindicated or undocumented in the ancient world. Eccentricity on the part of the interpreter could also be a means of contextual satura-tion of the meaning of the text from this standpoint—reading in one's own views more than reading out the text's views. But eccentricity and eisegesis are not the prerogatives only of those focusing on the internal relations of the text. I believe I could defend my reading of the disciples in Mark against the charges of anachronism and eccentricity, although the present

---

52. See the critique of "formalism" (which would appear to include interpretations focused on the interrelations of the elements of the text) presented by Lynn M. Poland. Poland argues that for-malism in New Testament interpretation gains some of its strengths and some of its weaknesses from its borrowings from New Critical theory. For example: "Since New Critical theory is itself unclear about how a literary text is related to contexts of meaning outside of it, biblical scholars appropriating these critical assumptions may repeat these ambiguities in their own work" (*Literary Criticism and Biblical Hermeneutics*, 160).

study is not the place to attempt this.[53] But I would certainly not see my own approach—or anyone's—as inherently protected from either the danger of contextual saturation of the meaning of the text or the opposite threat of contextual isolationism (ignoring too many relevant contexts).

I would argue, however, that a certain "pride of place" or "veto power"—to suggest metaphors for the initial and final roles—is appropriate to an interpretation with a contextual focus on the interrelations of the elements of the text, especially when one's goal is to interpret the text. When one's goal is to depict the history of Christian origins or the scope of ancient literary genres, the internal relations of individual texts, while still important, might well move into the background—although not too far into the background.[54] But

---

53. In any such defense, the three criteria of validity presented by Armstrong would be of importance: (1) inclusiveness ("If understanding is a matter of fitting together parts into a whole, then that belief about their relations will be superior which can encompass the most elements in the configuration it projects" [*Conflicting Readings*, 13]); (2) intersubjectivity ("Inasmuch as interpretation requires us to project beliefs, our reading becomes more credible if others assent to it or at least regard it as reasonable" [14]); (3) efficacy (that is, "the evaluation of a hypothesis or a presupposition on pragmatic grounds to see whether or not it has the power to lead to new discoveries and continued comprehension" [15]). Armstrong makes it clear that "these tests are capable of ruling out some interpretations as demonstrably illegitimate, although they cannot conclusively identify a single correct reading and must consequently allow genuine, irreconcilable hermeneutic conflict" (83).

54. Questions about the internal relations of the elements of texts must not move too far into the background because assumptions are always being made about them. As Armstrong notes, "An appeal to origins cannot settle disputes about interpretation because in both arenas suppositions about part-whole relations are at stake. . . . A historical source seems self-evident to the critic only because it corroborates his or her sense of the whole that is the type of the story" (*Conflicting Readings*, 105). See also LaCapra's discussion of social history and intellectual history in the final essay of his book *Rethinking Intellectual History*: "The difference between social and intellectual

when one claims to say what the text says, one must be willing to be guided not only by fruitful suggestions from multiple contexts but especially by the "internal"/"literary" context, the interrelations of the elements of the text.[55]

It is because of the multiple dimensions of texts and contexts and the human limits of their interpreters that a more systematic understanding of the relations between a text and its contexts and between contextual foci and interpretive conclusions is essential to the ongoing process of evaluating interpretations and, more basically, interpreting texts. "In an ideal world," writes LaCapra, "each historian [or interpreter] would be responsible for the treatment of all problems from the most comprehensive of all possible perspectives. In the real world, certain choices must be made. Only when these choices are self-conscious and thought out can genuine cooperation among historians [or interpreters] with different emphases be undertaken in a noninvidious spirit."[56]

Text, Contexts, and Interpreters

A contextual reading in itself provides no guarantee of the adequacy of a textual interpretation. *The* context does not

---

history is primarily one concerning the direction of interest. Social history uses texts to reconstruct a context or a past social reality. . . . Intellectual historians should, I think, try to provide good, close readings" (343–44).

55. In his 1985 article "Apostolic Tradition," Kelber would seem to agree: "That a gospel lives by its own internal logic is a principle of special relevance for discipleship, which is one of the most circumspectly plotted features in Mark. It may not be amiss, therefore, to withhold credence from any theory on Markan discipleship that has not seriously attempted to decode the full narrative pattern" (33). But, of course, one does not attempt "to decode the full narrative pattern" without presuppositions. See note 57 below. And yet, in the same article Kelber concludes: "[T]he answer to Markan discipleship will in the last analysis come from the history of the tradition" (41).

56. LaCapra, *Rethinking*, 67.

exist, and the text's multiple contexts seem to raise as many interpretive questions as they answer. Yet, to understand the text we must have contextual readings, and multiple contextual readings, and, in most cases, multiple contextual *readers*. Thus, in considering the relation of text and contexts, we have concerned ourselves with the interrelations of the contextual foci *of interpreters*. The critical question is how to interrelate the multiple readings of a single text that result from multiple interpreters focusing on multiple contexts.[57] *The* answer, like *the* context, does not exist. But we may try out a couple of images that give direction.[58]

The first image is advocacy, and it comes from the legal field. Perhaps we interpreters are like attorneys defending our clients (our contextual foci or contextual readings), always dedicated to our own clients' best interests. One obvious advantage of this metaphor is that it makes room for areas of expertise; if one wanted to argue an interpretive case concerning orality and textuality, one would surely retain Kelber as a consultant! Another useful application of the metaphor is this: just as attorneys have limited free choice of their clients (specialty, location, financial needs or desires dictate accepting some clients; others may be assigned by the court system), so

---

57. Of course, the multiple and differing presuppositions of interpreters is an equally critical and even more fundamental question. As Armstrong writes: "Conflicting readings can occur because interpreters with opposing presuppositions about language, literature, and life can generate irreconcilable hypotheses about the meaning of a text. The role of belief in understanding makes disagreement inevitable in interpretation" (*Conflicting Readings*, ix). Differing presuppositions have much to do with the critical question of *why* interpreters choose the contextual foci they do from among the text's multiple contexts.

58. These images are presented in a slightly different form in the conclusion to Elizabeth Struthers Malbon, "The Poor Widow in Mark and Her Poor Rich Readers," *CBQ* 53 (1991): 589–604 [here chapter 6].

many interpreters select their contextual foci neither at random nor with perfect freedom and fully conscious deliberation (I doubt that the feeling of being "drawn" by one's approach—or one's text—is rare). In addition, the image of advocacy suggests the strength of the bond between an interpreter and his or her contextual focus. But the legal analogy breaks down in the end. Scholarly debates, although sometimes heated, are not basically adversarial situations. To suggest that one contextual focus or one contextual reading could be adjudicated "innocent" and another "guilty" assumes not only an acknowledged judge and jury of interpretation but also *a* standard that all are sworn to uphold: *the* (right, best, whatever) context. In fact, it may make more sense to conceive of the text as the client of all its interpreters, in which case our common advocacy defuses our adversarial relations. Thus the advocacy image is inadequate.

A second image that might provide direction as we struggle to interrelate multiple contexts and multiple interpretations of the text is neither as concrete nor as striking as the first, but it may prove more useful. It is the image of complication. To complicate, not to clarify, is the task of the historian or historian of religions, according to Jonathan Z. Smith.

> The philosopher has the possibility of exclaiming with Archimedes: "Give me a place to stand on and I will move the world." . . . There is, for such a thinker, at least the possibility of a real beginning, even of achieving *the* Beginning, a standpoint from which all things flow, a standpoint from which he has clear vision. The historian or the historian of religions has no such possibility. There are no places on which he might stand apart from the messiness of the given world. There is for him no real beginning, but only the plunge which he takes at some arbitrary point to avoid the unhappy alternatives of infinite regress or silence. His standpoint is not discovered; rather it is erected with no

claim beyond that of sheer survival. The historian's
point of view cannot sustain clear vision.
        The historian's task is to complicate, not to clarify.[59]

As a historian of the New Testament period, as well as an
interpreter of New Testament texts, Kelber has certainly "complicated"—in this positive, if hyperbolic, sense—our picture of
Mark's Gospel. No longer can we assume an unbroken linear
connection between oral tradition and the written text; Kelber's foundational work has complicated our understanding of
media and media shifts. But it seems that in the very act of *complicating* the overall picture in Smith's positive sense, Kelber
does sometimes *clarify* Markan interpretation in Smith's negative sense. The aspect of the historical *context* that "complicates" existing understandings (because it compensates for a
lack of serious attention in previous scholarship) becomes the
key to "clarifying" the *text*. For Kelber, the oral/written media
shift "complicates" early Christian history but "clarifies" the
Markan text.[60] This relation between "complicating" history
and "clarifying" text points to the central issue raised above: the
contextual saturation of the meaning of the text.

The concept of "contextual saturation," borrowed from
LaCapra, together with the typology of contextual foci developed here, helps me to identify where and why I have certain
difficulties with the reading of Jesus and the disciples in Mark
presented by Kelber. First, I tend to be focally aware of aspects
of the text of which he is subsidiarily aware (and vice versa, of

---

59. Jonathan Z. Smith, *Map Is Not Territory: Studies in the History
of Religions* (Leiden: Brill, 1978), 129.

60. According to LaCapra (*Rethinking*, 340): "The general problem facing the 'human sciences' is to arrive at a differential understanding of the relation between documentary and other than merely
documentary components of various texts and types of text." Certainly that is a problem here.

course). Second, I judge that sometimes his focal awareness of certain of the text's contexts overinforms ("saturates") his understanding of the text, that "information" from one context is used either to answer or to deflect important questions that are more sharply raised in another context. Accordingly, as an interpreter with a contextual focus more on text and less on history than Kelber, I feel responsible, first, to be attentive to the more complicated view of Markan history he enables me to share and, second, to share alternative views of the Markan text that may serve to "complicate" his own. Kelber and others will, in turn, evaluate whether my "complication" fulfills the positive role Smith has in mind. All "complications" are not equally helpful, just as all interpretations are not equally compelling.

Still, *the* interpretation does not exist. "Complication" continues to renew the perhaps inevitable search for "clarity."[61] As James Kincaid puts it: "Readers proceed with the assumption that there must be a single dominant structuring principle and that it is absurd to imagine more than one such dominant principle."[62] But texts themselves resist such "clarity" (or "coherence," as he calls it): "most texts, at least, are, in fact, demonstrably incoherent, presenting us not only with multiple organizing patterns but with organizing patterns that are competing, logically inconsistent"—with "a structure of mutually competing coherences."[63] As he argues against the text's single determinant meaning, Kincaid is not arguing for the text's indeterminacy.[64] These seem to him, and to me as well, false alternatives. We are not free to assume that the text can mean anything just because it can mean many things. The argument is, rather, that texts "complicate" readings of themselves. Thus

---

61. See Frank Kermode, *The Sense of an Ending: Studies in the Theory of Fiction* (New York: Oxford University Press, 1967).

62. James R. Kincaid, "Coherent Readers, Incoherent Texts," *Critical Inquiry* 3 (1977): 781–802; quotation from 783.

63. Ibid., 783.

64. Ibid., 789–90.

interpreters of the text take up their task from the text itself: to "complicate" interpretation. Both of these images, advocacy and "complication," are consistent with Paul Armstrong's suggestion for how to deal with *Conflicting Readings*:

> Interpreters must be forceful in applying their beliefs and assumptions to the text even as they remember that their convictions about textual configurations are only hypotheses and are therefore provisional and open to change and refutation. As hypotheses, guesses about meaning must be held with conviction even as they must also be viewed tentatively and warily. The paradox that hermeneutic power requires limitation to be effective is a reflection of the doubleness of belief as an epistemological structure. A belief is a guess about what we do not know, and it must consequently be both embraced with faith and questioned with skeptical detachment.[65]

Such faithful yet detached interpreters, interpreters who seek to be advocates of the text in its multiple contexts and yet to "complicate" and thus enliven interpretation, might well be described by the words Smith applies to historians: their "manner of speech is often halting and provisional"; they approach their "data" with "tentativeness"; in their work they detect "clues, symptoms, exemplars"; they provide us with "hints that remain too fragile to bear the burden of being solutions."[66] Or, in the words of LaCapra: "The point here is to do everything in one's power not to avoid argument but to make argument as informed, vital, and undogmatically open to counterargument as possible,"[67] although "the process of gaining perspective on our own interpretations does not exclude the attempt to arrive at an interpretation we are willing to defend."[68]

---

65. Armstrong, *Conflicting Readings*, 139.
66. Smith, *Map Is Not Territory*, 129–30.
67. LaCapra, *Rethinking*, 38.
68. Ibid., 45.

LaCapra's words (argument, counterargument, defend) return us to the image of advocacy, which, despite its final limitations, is not without useful application. It would appear unlikely that an interpreter could become an advocate for many different contexts. For this reason we must all, as interpreters of texts, seek to meet two requirements: (1) to understand as many approaches and appreciate as many contexts as possible, and (2) to read, listen to, and argue with other interpreters—especially those who are also working at the first requirement. We must argue our positions with conviction—but in order to "complicate." We must share our interpretations with faith—and also with skepticism.

5

The Jewish Leaders in the
Gospel of Mark

A Literary Study of Markan Characterization

As any reader or hearer of stories knows, characters—whether human or nonhuman, animate or inanimate—are essential to stories. Thus characterization is an essential element of any critical theory of narrative,[1] and as any reader of Markan scholarship knows, certain aspects of characterization have received particular attention in Markan studies of the last decade or so.[2] The Markan disciples of Jesus have been the chief characters

---

1. In Seymour Chatman's exposition of narrative structure, for example, "characters" are one of the four elements of story. The narrative text is comprised of story (the what) and discourse (the how). Story consists of existents (characters and setting) and events (actions and happenings) (Chatman, *Story and Discourse: Narrative Structure in Fiction and Film* [Ithaca, N.Y.: Cornell University Press, 1978]). "Character" is also one of the four elements of narrative isolated by Wesley Kort; the other three elements are atmosphere (or setting), plot, and tone (*Narrative Elements and Religious Meanings* [Philadelphia: Fortress, 1975]).

2. For a very brief review, see David Rhoads, "Narrative Criticism and the Gospel of Mark," *JAAR* 50 (1982), esp. 417–19. Perhaps the most suggestive study of the characters in Mark is the brief overview of David Rhoads, Joanna Dewey, and Donald Michie in *Mark as Story: An Introduction to the Narrative of a Gospel*, 2d ed. (Minneapolis: Fortress, 1999), chaps. 5 and 6. In addition, their notes provide a helpful beginning bibliography.

investigated, and the key study in this area has been Theodore
Weeden's *Mark—Traditions in Conflict*.[3] Weeden's work is key
not only because he centers his interpretation of Mark on the
characterization of the disciples but because he justifies his
interpretation on the basis of the importance of characterization in first-century literary interpretation and creation. I find
Weeden's observations concerning characterization—but not
his interpretation of the disciples—to be an appropriate starting point for subsequent attempts, including the present one,
to understand and interpret patterns of characterization in
the Gospel of Mark. The present study has a second starting
point in the work of Michael Cook concerning a second
group of Markan characters: the Jewish leaders.[4] From these
starting points I will move to literary observations about the
Jewish leaders as they are characterized in Mark's narrative,
and from those observations to three suggestions about the
broader narrative contexts in which these and other characters are embedded.

Two Starting Points:
Characterization; Jewish Leaders

When Weeden refers to characterization or character portrayal, he has in mind not "character study in the modern sense
but rather presentation of characters as a medium through
which an ancient author dramatizes the theses of his compo-

---

3. Theodore J. Weeden, Sr., *Mark—Traditions in Conflict*
(Philadelphia: Fortress, 1971). See also the very different positions
taken by two students of Norman Perrin, Werner H. Kelber (with
parallels to Weeden) and John R. Donahue, S.J., in two small but significant books: Kelber, *Mark's Story of Jesus* (Philadelphia: Fortress,
1979); and Donahue, *The Theology and Setting of Discipleship in the
Gospel of Mark* (Milwaukee: Marquette University Press, 1983).

4. Michael J. Cook, *Mark's Treatment of the Jewish Leaders* (Leiden:
Brill, 1978).

sition."[5] On the basis of H. I. Marrou's *History of Education in Antiquity*,[6] Weeden summarizes the focus of Greek and Roman education from the first century B.C.E. through the second century C.E. as the "pedantic study of the great literary works of the past," particularly the epic poems and the tragedies. Interest in characters was a "particularly pronounced" part of such study.[7] The heroes and villains of the ancient works served as models for human virtues and vices.[8] Furthermore, Weeden argues, these cardinal tenets for literary interpretation guided literary creativity as well—as is especially the case with the Hellenistic historians, by whom the heroes are idealized and the villains denigrated so that history may have its proper interpretation. Finally, Weeden concludes: "the nature of the Gospel genre" suggests "that the first reader would have approached the Gospel guided by the same hermeneutical principles that he used when he read the tragedians or the historians." The Markan Gospel "approximates the style of the Greek drama and the popular lives of the times." Thus the Markan reader "would have perceived that character portrayal and the events in which the major characters are involved are the points of focus from which one understands the message of the Gospel."[9]

---

5. Weeden, *Mark*, 14 n. 18.

6. H. I. Marrou, *A History of Education in Antiquity*, trans. George Lamb (New York: Sheed & Ward, 1956), esp. 160–70, 277–81.

7. Weeden, *Mark*, 12, 13.

8. Perhaps this first-century approach is not so distant from the treatment of character in the modern novel as the centuries might suggest. Kort, at least, asserts: "Character in narrative is an image of human possibilities, either for good and creativity or for evil and destruction, and the rise of modern narrative is very much tied to the effort to explore or to render paradigms of those possibilities" (*Narrative Elements*, 40). See below under the subheading "Exceptional Jewish Leaders."

9. Weeden, *Mark*, 17.

Further study of the appropriate literary background against which Mark's first-century work is to be read has been done and remains to be done,[10] but Weeden's insistence on the importance of characterization seems legitimate. Weeden's interpretation of the disciples as characters in Mark, however, is another matter. Weeden's approach is redaction *historical*; his ultimate concern is to explain—historically—the genesis of Mark's Gospel. Following Johannes Schreiber and Joseph Tyson in seeing Mark's "portrayal of the disciples . . . as a literary device in the service of polemic,"[11] Weeden differs from them in identifying the target of the polemic: advocates of Jesus as a *theios anēr*, a "divine man."[12] For Weeden the overall portrayal of the disciples is negative (moving from unperceptiveness to misconception to rejection) because of Mark's polemical purpose, and Mark's purpose is polemical because Mark's historical situation is polarized.[13] As I have argued elsewhere, I find Mark's Gospel

---

10. See, e.g., Charles H. Talbert, *What Is a Gospel: The Genre of the Canonical Gospels* (Philadelphia: Fortress, 1977); and Vernon K. Robbins, *Jesus the Teacher: A Socio-Rhetorical Interpretation of Mark* (Philadelphia: Fortress, l984).

11. Weeden, *Mark*, 25. Weeden adds that both Schreiber and Tyson understand this as "a polemic against a conservative Jewish Christian group in Palestine which placed no positive meaning in Jesus' death, held to the long-established Jewish practices, and rejected the necessity of the gentile mission" (25). Johannes Schreiber, "Die Christologie des Markusevangeliums," *ZTK* 58 (1961): 175–83; Schreiber, *Theologie des Vertrauens* (Hamburg: Furche-Verlag H. Rennebach, 1967), 101 n, 112ff., 127–29, 165ff.; Joseph Tyson, "The Blindness of the Disciples in Mark," *JBL* 80 (1961): 261–68.

12. Schreiber identifies the opposition group as Peter, James, and John, whereas Tyson suggests the family of Jesus. Kelber, agreeing with the polemical interpretation of Mark, identifies a fourth alternative opposition group: the Jerusalem church (*The Kingdom in Mark: A New Place and a New Time* [Philadelphia: Fortress, 1974]; Kelber, *Mark's Story of Jesus*).

13. A perceptive and convincing argument concerning the influences on and of Weeden's polemical view of Mark was presented by

more pastoral and its portrayal of the disciples—as fallible followers—more complex and more subtle.[14] Another problematic aspect of Weeden's characterization of the disciples as Jesus' opponents is that it masks the obvious fact that the Jewish leaders function as Jesus' opponents in Mark.[15] My methodology is, in contrast to Weeden's, a literary one, and at this point I wish to apply it to an examination of this other group of characters in Mark: the Jewish leaders.

Mark's portrayal of the Jewish leaders is the focus of Michael J. Cook's work, *Mark's Treatment of the Jewish Leaders*, which sets a second starting point for my present work. Cook's methodology is more source historical than redaction historical, but he shares with Weeden a central concern for explaining—historically—the genesis of Mark's Gospel.[16] New Testament scholars do not, of course, accept the antagonism between the Markan Jesus and the Jewish leaders as descriptive of "the historical Jesus," but rather as reflective of the subsequent struggles of the

Sharyn Dowd at the March 1985 meeting of the Southeastern Region of the SBL in Atlanta, in a paper entitled "The Influence of Georgi's *Die Gegner* on Markan Scholarship in the United States" and incorporated into her Emory University doctoral dissertation, *Prayer, Power, and the Problems of Suffering: Mark 11:22–25 in the Context of Markan Theology*, SBLDS 105 (Atlanta: Scholars Press, 1988).

14. Elizabeth Struthers Malbon, "Fallible Followers: Women and Men in the Gospel of Mark," *Semeia* 28 (1983): 29–48 [here chapter 2]; Malbon, "Disciples/Crowds/Whoever: Markan Characters and Readers," *NovT* 28 (1986): 104–30 [here chapter 3]. See also Robert Tannehill, "The Disciples in Mark: The Function of a Narrative Role," *JR* 57 (1977): 386–405; and Joanna Dewey, "Point of View and the Disciples in Mark," *SBLSP* 21 (1982): 97–106.

15. Of course, there may be more than one class of opponents, as will be made clear at the close of this chapter.

16. In terms of my typology of contextual foci, Cook focuses on the external literary context and Weeden focuses on the external historical context, whereas I focus on the internal literary context ("Text and History: Interpreting the Disciples in Mark," paper presented at the annual meeting of the SBL, Anaheim, Calif., November 1985) [here, revised, chapter 4].

early Christian church and the Judaism from which it had just recently separated[17]—or was in the very process of separating.[18] This position, however, simply projects the "historical" questions from the time of Jesus to the time of the early church; it does not make them any easier to answer. What is the relationship of Mark's Pharisees, scribes, and others to actual Jewish groups in the first century? And what—even within Mark's Gospel—is the relationship of the various groups to one another?

In answer to the first question, Cook has argued that

> the Evangelists *themselves* were unclear as to who all these Jewish leadership groups had actually been in Jesus' time; they did not adequately define and describe them or adequately distinguish among them because they *could* not. Moreover, some of the group titles ("chief priests," "Herodians," "elders") are merely general constructs, i.e., literary devices serving the convenience of the Synoptists themselves and lifted from their sources; they are not reflective of leadership groups actually functioning in Jesus' time or later.[19]

---

17. See, e.g., Michael J. Cook, "Jesus and the Pharisees: The Problem as It Stands Today," *JES* 15 (1978): 441–60; and Arland J. Hultgren, *Jesus and His Adversaries: The Form and Function of the Conflict Stories in the Synoptic Tradition* (Minneapolis: Augsburg, 1979).

18. See the dissertation of Moston Robert Mulholland, Jr., "The Markan Opponents of Jesus" (Ph.D. diss., Harvard University, 1977), the central thesis of which is clearly stated in the abstract: "This study of the general element of persecution, set within the more specific context of the synagogue, and illustrated by the very specific issues of controversy by the opponents of Jesus, gives support to the hypothesis that the Markan editorial use of the opponents reflects a *Sitz-im-Leben* in which the followers of Jesus have experienced opposition from the Jewish community, are being disciplined at the hands of that Jewish community, and now find themselves on the verge of being thrust out of that Jewish community as the Jews begin to involve secular/political authorities in their opposition to the followers of Jesus" (6).

19. Cook, *Jewish Leaders*, 1. For a different view, see below, under the subheading "Jewish Leaders Distinguished."

Cook's greater interest—and my own as well—is with the second question, the intra-Markan relationship of the various groups. His thesis is that Mark's portrayal of Jewish leadership groups reflects the redactional combination of three written sources: "1) an early Passion source, furnishing him with chief priests, scribes and elders, based in Jerusalem; 2) a source focusing on scribes only, setting them in Jerusalem; and 3) a source focusing on Pharisees and Herodians, possibly set in a Galilean context."[20] It is thus Mark's editorializing that gives us, in the words of Cook, the "radical segregation of the Jewish leadership groups into two separate camps of conspirators—chief priests + scribes + elders, on the one hand, and Pharisees + Herodians, on the other."[21]

I find Cook's theory of sources unconvincing for several reasons, among them being a fundamental suspicion of hypothetical sources created by twentieth-century interpreters from first-century texts.[22] But the greatest danger of Cook's thesis seems to me to be that, in accepting a source hypothesis as explaining the existence of differences between the Jewish groups in Mark, one might fail to go on to consider the narrative effect of these differences for the Markan Gospel as a whole. One might substitute a theory of genesis for an interpretation of significance. (A similar danger is present in Weeden's explanation of the Markan portrayal of the disciples as

---

20. Ibid., 4–5.

21. Ibid., 4.

22. For arguments that work against Cook's assumption of an early passion source, see Werner H. Kelber, ed., *The Passion in Mark: Studies on Mark 14–16* (Philadelphia: Fortress, 1976); and Donald Juel, *Messiah and Temple: The Trial of Jesus in the Gospel of Mark*, SBLDS 31 (Missoula, Mont.: Scholars Press, 1977). For arguments that work against Cook's reconstruction of two pre-Markan controversy collections, see Joanna Dewey, *Markan Public Debate: Literary Technique, Concentric Structure, and Theology in Mark 2:1–3:6*, SBLDS 48 (Chico, Calif.: Scholars Press, 1980).

generated by an attack on a rival Christian group.[23]) There is nothing wrong, of course, with wanting to explain the genesis of a narrative text, but one must not thereby explain away the significance of the narrative. It is my present goal to take a careful look at the actions and the groupings of the members of the Jewish religious establishment characterized in the Markan narrative in order to interpret their significance in and to the Gospel as a whole. With Weeden I am drawn to focus on characterization; with Cook I am drawn to examine the Jewish leaders. Because of this double starting point and my literary approach, my conclusions will involve setting the Jewish leaders in their larger narrative contexts in Mark.

Literary Observations:
The Jewish Leaders as Characters

While the disciples sometimes appear as friends, sometimes as enemies, a second major character group or cluster of groups—the Jewish leaders, or the Jewish religious establishment—may clearly be labeled enemies of the Markan Jesus. In Mark's Gospel, members of the Jewish religious establishment include scribes; Pharisees; Herodians; chief priests, scribes, and elders; the high priest; Sadducees; and two named individuals, Jairus, a ruler of a synagogue, and Joseph of Arimathea, a member of the council (*bouleutēs*).[24]

---

23. Because of his view of the Gospel as polemic and the disciples as representatives of Mark's enemies, Weeden cannot integrate into his interpretation the elements of positive characterization of the disciples—which he does recognize (see, e.g., *Mark*, 23); thus he dismisses or ignores them.

24. All biblical quotations presented in English are from the RSV. All textual analysis relies on *The Greek New Testament*, ed. Kurt Aland et al., 3d ed. (New York: United Bible Societies, 1975).

Scribes and Pharisees

In the first ten chapters of Mark, the opposition of the Jewish religious establishment to Jesus is seen primarily in the actions of scribes and Pharisees as characters and in generalized statements about scribes and Pharisees.[25] Conflict with scribes and with Pharisees is concentrated chiefly in the controversy stories of chapters 2–3 and in the discussion of the tradition of the elders in chapter 7. Both scribes and Pharisees are linked in the Markan narrative with other groups of characters.

Scribes are involved in conflict with Jesus in the following controversies: healing and forgiving the paralytic (2:6), eating with tax collectors and sinners (2:16), the question of possession by Beelzebul (3:22), eating with hands defiled (7:1, 5). Scribes are in conflict with the disciples of Jesus at 9:14: "And when they [Jesus and Peter, James, and John—from the Mount of Transfiguration] came to the [other] disciples, they saw a great crowd about them, and scribes arguing with them." But on one occasion, one of the scribes and Jesus are not in conflict but in agreement (12:28, 32): in a discussion of which commandment is first of all, the scribe says to Jesus, "You are right, Teacher" (12:32), and Jesus says to the scribe, "You are not far from the kingdom of God" (12:34). Clearly this is an exceptional scribe.

The general Markan view of scribes is underlined in four statements about their customary behavior. The first such statement—and the first Markan reference to any member of the Jewish religious establishment—is the narrator's comment

---

25. In an unpublished paper Anthony J. Saldarini emphasizes that the Pharisees are "competing for influence on the people with Jesus and/or the early Palestinian Christian community" ("The Pharisees, Scribes and Sadducees in Mark," 8). A revised (and shortened) version of this paper appears as "The Social Class of the Pharisees in Mark," in *The Social World of Formative Christianity and Judaism: Essays in Tribute to Howard Clark Kee*, ed. Jacob Neusner et al. (Philadelphia: Fortress, 1988), 69–77.

on Jesus' first activity in the synagogue: "And they were astonished at his teaching, for he taught them as one who had
authority, and not as the scribes" (1:22). Two additional statements concern not *how* but *what* the scribes teach; both are
presented as questions, and both question the scribe's teaching and/or understanding (9:11, concerning the coming of
Elijah; 12:35, concerning Christ as the son of David). Jesus
answers both his own question (12:35) and the disciples'
(9:11); and, whereas he seems to disagree with the scribal
teaching about the Christ as David's son, he seems to agree
with the scribal teaching that Elijah must come first, although
the implication is that the scribes (and others) have failed to
realize that Elijah has come first in John the Baptist. A final
generalized statement about the scribes appears as a warning
from Jesus at the close of his teaching in the temple: "Beware
of the scribes, who like to go about in long robes, and to have
salutations in the market places and the best seats in the synagogues and the places of honor at feasts, who devour widows'
houses and for a pretense make long prayers. They will receive
the greater condemnation" (12:38–40). Thus the scribes in
general—according to the Markan narrator and the Markan
Jesus—teach without authority and without understanding
and act with pride and without compassion.[26]

The scribes active as characters in Mark are related to other
members of the Jewish religious establishment. Because
scribes on two occasions are specified as having come down
from Jerusalem (3:22; 7:1), they are linked with the scribes of
the chief priests/scribes/elders of Jerusalem (chapters 11–15).
Scribes are also linked with Pharisees; together they *see* and

---

26. Cf. Saldarini, "The Pharisees, Scribes and Sadducees in
Mark," 10: "The scribes are the point of reference for Jewish religious teaching and Mark implies that they are the ordinary teachers
with whom people are familiar. Jesus, who also teaches, is contrasted
with them, especially because of the way he teaches, rather than the
content of his teaching."

ask: about his "eat[ing] with tax collectors and sinners" (2:16), and about his disciples' eating "with hands defiled, that is, unwashed," and thus not "according to the tradition of the elders" (7:1–2, 5). Mention of the tradition of the elders (7:5) may also link the scribes and (especially) the Pharisees (7:3) with the elders of the Jerusalem chief priests/scribes/elders.

The Pharisees, who are linked with several other groups in opposition to Jesus, are, at their first Markan reference, linked with the scribes (2:16). Although the significance of the phrase "scribes of the Pharisees" at 2:16 (rather than the more usual "scribes and the Pharisees") is not clear, the more difficult text is generally accepted.[27] In either case there is a link between scribes and Pharisees. The controversy at 2:16 concerns eating with tax collectors and sinners. Other controversies involving the Pharisees are these: the fact that Jesus' disciples do not fast, as John's disciples and the disciples of the Pharisees do (2:18), plucking grain on the Sabbath (2:24), healing on the Sabbath (3:6), eating with hands defiled (7:1, 3, 5), seeking a sign from heaven (8:11), the question of divorce (10:2), and paying taxes to Caesar (12:13). Two of these references—the two in which Pharisees and Herodians join together against Jesus—are more general in their import (3:6; 12:13). While 3:6 follows immediately the controversy about healing on the Sabbath, this statement that the Pharisees and Herodians held counsel on how to destroy Jesus also serves as the conclusion to the entire series of controversy stories in 2:1–3:6.[28] While 12:13 precedes immediately the controversy about paying taxes to Caesar, the issue of taxes seems secondary to the motive of entrapment:

---

27. Bruce M. Metzger, *A Textual Commentary on the Greek New Testament* (New York: United Bible Societies, 1971), 78: "The more unusual expression *hoi grammateis tōn Pharisaiōn* is to be preferred, since the tendency of scribes would have been to insert *kai* after *hoi grammateis* under the influence of the common expression 'the scribes and the Pharisees.'"

28. See Dewey, *Markan Public Debate*, esp. 46–47.

"And they sent to him some of the Pharisees and some of the Herodians, to entrap him in his talk."

On the one hand, 3:6 and 12:13 may be said to be generalized because they depict the underlying antipathies of the Pharisees as Markan characters. On the other hand, 7:3 and 8:15 depict the behavior and attitudes of the Pharisees in general (not in particular actions as characters)—as that behavior is interpreted by the Markan Jesus and the Markan narrator. In an address to his disciples, the Markan Jesus cautions: "Take heed, beware of the leaven of the Pharisees and the leaven of Herod" (8:15). In an aside to his hearers/readers in 7:3, the Markan narrator explains: "(For the Pharisees, and all the Jews,[29] do not eat unless they wash their hands, observing the tradition of the elders; . . .)." Clearly, what the Pharisees do, their typical action, remains a problem for the Markan narrator as it is for the Markan Jesus.

The Pharisees involved in particular conflicts with Jesus are related to several other groups also antagonistic to him. The Pharisees' link to the scribes (2:16; 7:1, 5) connects them to the Jerusalem group of chief priests/scribes/elders—especially since, as noted above, the scribes are said to have come down from Jerusalem (7:1). The fasting of the Pharisees (2:18a) and their disciples (2:18b) parallels the fasting of the disciples of John. The Pharisees and the Herodians (who are mentioned only in connection with the Pharisees in Mark) join together to plot Jesus' destruction (3:6), "to entrap him in his talk" (12:13). Thus the Markan Pharisees seem, at least in their antagonism to Jesus, to have common interests with several other groups. Certainly the concerns of the Pharisees and the

---

29. The only other Markan use of the term "Jews" is in the title given—whatever the tone—to Jesus by Pilate: "King of the Jews" (15:2, 9, 12, 18, 26). Contrast the title given sarcastically—and ironically—by the chief priests and the scribes: "the Christ, the King of Israel" (15:32). (The only other reference to Israel is Jesus' recitation of the *Shema Israel* at 12:29.)

scribes overlap, although the Markan Pharisees are perhaps more concerned with the observance of the Sabbath and the food laws (e.g., 2:16; 2:18; 2:24; 3:6; 7:1) and the Markan scribes perhaps more involved in teaching in general (e.g., 1:22; 2:6; 9:11; 12:28, 32; 12:35).

What bothers both the scribes and the Pharisees about the Markan Jesus is that he challenges the tradition—the tradition of the elders (7:5). What bothers the elders—and the chief priests and the scribes and the whole council—is that the Markan Jesus appears to be attracting a large following in this challenge. Thus the challenge of the Markan Jesus is not merely theoretical; it has practical consequences. The scribes and the Pharisees raise religious objections, based on their interpretation of Scripture and tradition. The chief priests, scribes, and elders raise also what must be called political objections, based on their struggle with Jesus for authority and influence over the people.[30]

Chief Priests, Scribes, Elders, and Others

In the Markan passion narrative (beginning with the entry into Jerusalem in 11:1) the core group of the Jewish religious establishment in opposition to Jesus is comprised of the chief

---

30. It was not, unfortunately, until the conclusion of this work on the Jewish leaders in Mark that I read Mulholland's dissertation on "The Markan Opponents of Jesus." His work "examines the role of the opponents of Jesus (Scribes, Pharisees, Herodians) who appear as the only opponents in Mark 1:1–8:26, and appear intermingled with the Passion Narrative opponents (Chief Priests, Elders, Scribes) in 8:27–13:37" (abstract, p.1). Mulholland's approach is redaction critical and his focus is historical—the Markan *Sitz im Leben*; but he has noticed a broader literary pattern in Mark that merits further attention. I present his summarizing chart (from p. 1 of his abstract) in full (next page):

priests, scribes, and elders.[31] This group is mentioned five
times, including one passion prediction: 8:31; 11:27; 14:43;
14:53b; 15:1. The order of listing the three subcategories is
not invariable: once the elders precede the chief priests and
scribes (8:31); twice the elders follow the chief priests but precede the scribes (14:53b; 15:1); and twice the elders follow the

---

(*cont.*)

Scribes	2:1–12 Jesus' nature and activity (healing)	3:22–30 Jesus' nature and activity (exorcism)	9:11, 14 Jesus' nature and activity (exorcism)
Scribes and Pharisees	2:13–17 Ritual cleanliness in eating	7:1–23 Ritual cleanliness in eating	(lacking in the third appearance of the opponent cycle)
Pharisees	2:18–28 Fasting and lawful activity	8:11–12 Seek a sign	10:1–12 Lawful activity
Pharisees and Herodians	3:1–6 Plot to destroy Jesus	8:15 Jesus warns followers	12:13–17 Seek to entrap Jesus

As Mulholland observes: "While the order of appearance and issues
of controversy are not in total harmony, the high degree of correlation between them suggests a Markan utilization of these opponents"
(abstract, 1).

31. The historical context is described by Saldarini ("The Pharisees, Scribes and Sadducees in Mark," 14–15): "The relationships
and interests of the Jewish leadership groups are reasonably clear.
The chief priests go to Pilate because they are clearly the dominant
group, especially in dealing with the Romans and the larger political
and social issues of the Jewish community. They object to Jesus' large
following among the people and their resultant loss of control over
the community as a whole and they also fear disorder from the activities of an unauthorized teacher. Their concerns are mainly political
and in these interests they are joined by the elders, probably the traditional leaders of the community who were senior members of

chief priests and the scribes (11:27; 14:43). Once the tripartite group is expanded by an additional reference to the whole council (*holon to synedrion*,15:1). Four times, including one passion prediction, reference is made to a two-part subgroup: the chief priests and the scribes (10:33; 11:18; 14:1; 15:31). The chief priests are mentioned without reference to the other two groups on five occasions, including one reference in combination with the whole council (*holon to synedrion*, 14:55[32]): 14:10; 14:55; 15:3; 15:10; 15:11. The high priest is mentioned alone on four occasions: 14:53a; 14:60; 14:61; 14:63.[33]

The actions of the two-part subgroup (chief priests and scribes) do not differ significantly from the actions of the tripartite group (chief priests, scribes, and elders). The chief priests and scribes—to whom the Markan Jesus predicted he would be handed over (10:33)—seek to destroy him out of fear because of the astonishment of the crowd at his teaching (11:18), seek to arrest him by stealth and kill him (14:1), and mock him as he hangs on the cross (15:31). The chief priests, scribes, and elders—by whom the Markan Jesus predicted he would be rejected (8:31)—question him about his authority

---

prominent families, and by the scribes, who were, as we have already seen, recognized teachers in the community. The scribes who are associated with the chief priests had some governing authority over the community, according to Mark. This view of the scribes, chief priests and elders is consistent with what we know of ancient society."

32. A third Markan reference to *synedrion*, in addition to 14:55 and 15:1, appears at 13:9 in Jesus' warning to Peter, James, John, and Andrew—and through them to "all" (13:37): "But take heed to yourselves; for they will deliver you up to councils (*synedria*). . . ." As Jesus is delivered up to the council, so his followers will be delivered up to councils.

33. The Markan Jesus refers to the "high priest" Abiathar and "the priests" in telling the story of how David ate the bread of the Presence (2:26) and instructs a healed leper to "go, show yourself to the priest, and offer for your cleansing what Moses commanded, for a proof to the people" (1:44). But in neither case are the priests involved as characters in the Markan story.

(11:27), send a crowd with swords and clubs to arrest him
(14:43), assemble to examine him (14:53b), and hold a consultation and bind him over to Pilate (15:1). Because the chief
priests are members of the tripartite core group *and* members
of the two-part subgroup *and* active on their own in the passion narrative, the hearer/reader of the Markan narrative
comes to regard them as the leaders of the opposition to Jesus
in Jerusalem. Their leadership in the actions resulting in Jesus'
death is perhaps initiated by the betrayal of Judas Iscariot
(14:10). Once Jesus is in custody, the chief priests—and the
whole council—seek testimony against him to put him to
death; but they do not initially succeed (14:55). It is the high
priest's questioning that leads to the charge of blasphemy
(14:60–64) and Jesus' condemnation by "all" (14:64). The
chief priests are most active and most successful as adversaries
of Jesus before Pilate: they accuse Jesus of many things (15:3)
and stir up the crowd to have Pilate release Barabbas instead
of Jesus (15:11). Pilate recognizes both the leadership and the
motive of the chief priests: "For he perceived that it was out of
envy that the chief priests had delivered him up" (15:10). In
some contexts, the high priest might be considered the leader
of the leaders (the chief priests), but this is not really the case
in the Markan passion narrative. It is the high priest who offi-
cially questions Jesus (14:60, 61) and renders the symbolic
judgment against him (14:63, tearing his own garments).[34] But
the high priest performs these actions "in the midst" (14:60)
of the chief priests and the whole council (14:55) or the chief
priests, scribes, and elders (14:53b) after "they" (14:53a, refer-
ring back to 14:43?) have led Jesus to him.

One final group that is a part of the Jewish religious establishment receives a brief mention in the Markan narrative: the
Sadducees (12:18). The Sadducees serve to fill out the picture

---

34. The conflict between the high priest and Jesus is extended to
the servants of the high priest and the followers of Jesus. While Jesus
is being arrested with no personal resistance, an unnamed follower of

of Jewish groups that are, one by one, gotten the best of by the Markan Jesus as he completes his teaching in the temple. The long scene (11:27–12:44) is wonderfully effective. Jesus (with his disciples) comes into Jerusalem again and into the temple, and the various groups of the Jewish religious establishment *come to him* there. First the chief priests, scribes, and elders try to trick him (into what they would regard as blasphemy?) with a question about his authority, but he tricks them instead with a question they dare not answer about John's authority (11:27–33). Then Jesus tells the parable of the wicked tenants, which the chief priests, scribes, and elders perceive is told "against them" (12:1–12). When the tripartite group is unable to arrest Jesus because of their fear of the crowd, they send to him "some of the Pharisees and some of the Herodians, to entrap him in his talk" (12:13). Not surprisingly, those who would be trappers are trapped. The foes' question about taxes to Caesar is meant to get Jesus into trouble with the Roman authorities, but Jesus' clever answer results in challenging not the authority of the Romans but the devotion of the Jewish questioners (12:13–17). The Pharisees and Herodians are amazed (12:17). The Sadducees are the third group to approach Jesus in the temple, and they also strike out. Their trick question has to do with the resurrection (which they deny), and Jesus' answer preludes his own resurrection—which is, in an important sense, the final answer of the Markan narrator to the questioning Jewish religious establishment. Jesus says: "He is not God of the dead, but of the living; you are quite wrong" (12:27). Not only Sadducees, but also Pharisees and

---

Jesus strikes the slave of the high priest and cuts off his ear (14:47). While Jesus is being questioned by the high priest, Peter—who "had followed him at a distance, right into the courtyard of the high priest" (14:54)—is questioned by one of the maids of the high priest and denies his association with Jesus. The two episodes, however, serve primarily to illustrate the contrast between Jesus and his followers rather than the opposition between Jesus and his enemies in the Jewish religious establishment.

Herodians and chief priests, scribes, and elders are quite
wrong, according to the Markan narrative.

But the Markan Jesus still stands in the temple, and one of the
scribes (not a group of them) approaches him with a question:
"Which commandment is the first of all?" (12:28). It does not
appear to be a trick question, and Jesus does not turn it against
the scribe. Rather, the questioner and the questioned commend
each other (12:28–34). "And after that no one dared to ask him
any question" (12:34). But Jesus himself asks a question, concerning not one exceptional scribe but the scribes in general:
"How can the scribes say that the Christ is the son of David?"
(12:35). Jesus answers his own question, and the great crowd
hears him gladly (12:36–37). Presumably the Markan Jesus has
been "walking in the temple" all this time while the various characters walk by to question him. Now Jesus sits—and sitting is the
usual position of rabbis when teaching.[35] He sits down opposite
the treasury, and the one who comes by is not a member of the
religious establishment but the lowest of the low—a woman, a
widow, and poor. But she, Jesus points out to his disciples, gives
her whole life (*holon ton bion autēs*, 12:41–44). With that comment, the Markan Jesus leaves the temple (13:1)—the focus of
the Jewish religious establishment—never to return.

Three Suggestions:
Narrative Contexts of the Jewish Leaders

From these literary observations about the Jewish leaders as
characters I wish to draw three inferences concerning Mark's
portrayal of the Jewish leaders: the first concerning their unity
as a group opposed to the Markan Jesus, the second concerning
their distinctions as reflective of a particular Markan literary

---

35. Herbert G. May and Bruce M. Metzger, eds., *The New Oxford
Annotated Bible* (New York: Oxford University Press, 1962, 1973),
1175, n. on Matt. 5:1.

pattern, the third concerning their exceptional members as a key to a basic aspect of Markan characterization. Each of these three aspects of Mark's portrait reminds us that we must interpret the Jewish leaders in their broader narrative contexts—contexts (plural) because Mark's narrative is multilayered.

Jewish Leaders Unified: Opponents of Jesus

First, the Pharisees, Herodians, chief priests, scribes, elders, and Sadducees are united as characters by their active opposition to the Markan Jesus. This active opposition begins with questioning Jesus, progresses to plotting against him and accusing him, and culminates in condemning him to death. This kind of opposition is unique among the Markan characters. Even in Weeden's extreme reading, the disciples move from unperceptiveness to misconception to rejection—which is clearly distinguishable from questioning and attacking and condemning. Thus, one conclusion to be drawn from my literary observations concerning Mark's portrayal of the Jewish leaders is that all the characters must be seen in relation to all the other characters in order to understand their functioning in Mark's story.[36] If one is to call the disciples "opponents" of

---

36. "Contrast" is one of the techniques of characterization discussed by Adele Berlin in her very helpful book, *Poetics and Interpretation of Biblical Narrative* (Sheffield: Almond Press, 1983)—along with "description," "inner life," and "speech and actions" (33–42). As Berlin points out, contrast can be with another character, with an earlier action of the same character, or with the expected norm (40). All three types of contrast can be seen in Markan characterization; but in the case of the Jewish leaders, contrast with other characters is the most important. In fact, we perceive the significance of the (minimal) descriptions, the (minimal) revelations of inner life, and the speech and actions of the Jewish leaders by reading them *in contrast with* those of other Markan characters. Cf. Baruch Hochman, *Character in Literature* (Ithaca, N.Y.: Cornell University Press, 1985), 51: "In the end, we tend to think of character—of people, to begin with—in terms of conflict, which may be moral, social, or psychological in nature."

the Markan Jesus—an extremely misleading label for them, from my point of view—one must clearly distinguish their type and level of "opposition" from the opposition of the Jewish leaders.

A brief look at chapter 7 may serve to suggest the importance of following Mark's own clues for interpreting any particular characters around Jesus in relation to other characters around Jesus. The coming together, at 7:1, of the Pharisees "with some of the scribes, who had come down from Jerusalem," links the chief opponents of Jesus in Galilee (the Pharisees) and representatives (symbolic if not literal) of his chief opponents in Jerusalem (the chief priests, scribes, and elders).[37] This narrative suggestion of the greater conflict yet to come is a fitting introduction to the Markan Jesus' most extended and explicit teaching against the tradition of the elders. In terms of the Jewish establishment characters and their relations to the Markan Jesus, the dispute in 7:1–13 is a bridge between the controversy stories of 2:1–3:6 and the passion of Jesus in chapters 11–16. In addition, those who struggle against Jesus—here Galilean Pharisees and Jerusalem scribes—are set in narrative contrast with those who struggle to understand and follow Jesus—both here and throughout Mark, the crowd and especially the disciples. In terms of the disciples and the crowd as potential followers of Jesus, 7:14–23 is an echo of 4:1–34, the parable chapter. In chapter 7, as in chapter 4, both the crowd and the disciples hear Jesus' parable and the disciples hear Jesus' explanation of the parable as well.

The three character groups of 7:1–23 illustrate three types of relations with Jesus. The Pharisees and scribes question the behavior of Jesus' disciples on the basis of the tradition of the elders. Rather than offer a direct and immediate defense of his

---

37. I see this linking as an effective narrative technique. Cook argues that it reflects Mark's redaction of written sources (*Jewish Leaders*, 58–67).

disciples, Jesus first attacks the attackers. He questions the tradition of the elders on the basis of the Scriptures—on which the tradition of the elders itself is ultimately based.[38] And, as even the scribes and Pharisees must recognize, the authorities Jesus cites (Isaiah, Moses) outrank the authorities they themselves cite (the elders). At stake is the "commandment of God" versus "the tradition of men" (7:8), the "word of God" versus "your tradition which you hand on" (7:13).[39] No rebuttal of Jesus' argument is offered by the Markan Pharisees and scribes. Whereas the Pharisees and some of the scribes had "gathered together" to Jesus (7:1), Jesus *calls* the crowd to him (7:14). Furthermore, this calling is specified as a calling *again*, and the obedience of the crowd in gathering to Jesus is assumed by the Markan narrative. Thus the arrangement seems a familiar one. Jesus begins, "Hear" (*akousate*, 7:14; cf. *akouete*, 4:3); the crowd apparently listens, but their response to the parable is not indicated. Rather, the disciples, who have obviously heard the parable along with the crowd, ask Jesus "about the parable" (7:17), and Jesus questions their lack of understanding (7:18; cf. 4:13 and 8:21). This dialogue opens the third section of 7:1–23—Jesus' explanation of the parable to the disciples (in the house). After the explanation, the disciples raise no further questions. Thus, although Jesus *initiates* the conversation only with the crowd, Jesus has the last word with each of the three groups of characters. Against those who argue from authority (Pharisees and scribes), Jesus argues from a higher authority. To those who will listen (the crowd), Jesus speaks. With those who ask questions (the disciples), Jesus enters into a dialogue to enable understanding.

---

38. In Mark 7 and Matthew 15, *paradosis* refers to "Jewish tradition outside the Law" (F. Büchsel, "*didōmi . . . paradosis*," *TDNT* 2: 172).

39. The opposition between the things of God and the things of humanity is, of course, an important Markan theme; see, e.g., 8:33; 11:30; 12:14.

The three direct intrusions of the narrator in 7:1–23—one in each section—rest on the assumption that the hearers/readers need explanations of "things Pharisaical" or even "things Jewish": washing hands and utensils (7:3–4), Corban (7:11), clean and unclean foods (7:19). These intrusions, therefore, manifest the distance assumed by the narrator to exist between the hearers/readers and the Pharisees/Jews; but, expressed from the other side, the intrusions themselves serve to distance the hearers/readers from the Pharisees/Jews. The Pharisees—"and all the Jews" (7:3)—are "them"; the narrator and the hearers/readers are "us." The crowd (whose hearing is actual, but whose response remains potential) and the disciples (whose engagement is actual, but whose full understanding remains potential) are, thereby, not unlike the hearers/readers (whose attention is assumed by the narrative, but whose response remains beyond it). The crowd and the disciples, like the narrator and the hearers/readers, are "us" as opposed to "them."

Jewish Leaders Distinguished: Narrative Escalation

The distinctions among the groups of Jewish leaders and their respective spheres of interest, activity, and influence in Mark's Gospel parallel key distinctions between spatial settings in Mark. In the first half of Mark's story, Jesus' chief opponents among the Jewish leaders are scribes and Pharisees; in the final half his primary opposition comes from the chief priests, scribes, and elders. In terms of spatial settings, the two halves of the Markan narrative depict a general movement from Galilee to Jerusalem and from synagogue to temple. A quick look at these spatial shifts will suggest how they form an appropriate background for the shift in emphasis between groups of Jewish leaders opposed to Jesus.

As I have argued elsewhere, given the cultural connotations that seem to underlie the narrative, the Markan presentation of Galilee and Jerusalem is surprising in two ways: Galilee—not Jerusalem—is the sphere of culminating action (1:14; 14:28; 16:7), and Galilee—not Jerusalem—bears the positive connotations within the pair of spatial terms. In these two ways, the traditional (Jewish) valuation of Galilee and Jerusalem is reversed in the Markan narrative.[40]

A second spatial shift in Mark is from synagogue to temple.[41] For the traditional Jew this movement (like that from Galilee to Jerusalem) represents an increase in holiness, but for the Markan Jesus it brings an escalation of conflict. Jesus teaches and heals in synagogues (in Galilee—see 1:39), but such activities lead, in terms of the people's response, first to amazement at Jesus (1:22, 27) and later to rejection of him (6:2–6) and, in terms of the response of the Jewish leaders, first to suspicions of Jesus (3:2) and then to plotting his death (3:6). Never after the first six chapters of Mark is Jesus reported to be in a synagogue. In chapters 11–12 Jesus teaches in the temple (in Jerusalem), and, one by one, the various groups of the Jewish religious establishment appear before him and are reduced to silence by his words. The Markan account of Jesus' teaching in the temple is framed by the intercalated episodes of the cursing of the fig tree and the casting out of the temple's sellers and buyers in chapter 11 and the dramatic departure of Jesus and his disciples from the temple to the Mount of Olives in chapter 13. The Markan Jesus and the Markan narrator reject Jerusalem, the temple, and the chief priests, scribes, and elders.

---

40. For a discussion of the views of E. Lohmeyer, R. H. Lightfoot, W. Marxsen, and W. Kelber, and an alternative view, see my "Galilee and Jerusalem: History and Literature in Marcan Interpretation," *CBQ* 44 (1982): 242–55; reprinted in *The Interpretation of Mark*, ed. William R. Telford (London: T. & T. Clark, 1995), 253–68. See also my *Narrative Space and Mythic Meaning in Mark*, New Voices in Biblical Studies (San Francisco: Harper & Row, 1986; reprint, The Biblical Seminar 13; Sheffield Academic Press, 1991).

41. See my *Narrative Space*, esp. chap. 4.

Thus the conflict Jesus experiences with the scribes and with the Pharisees (chapters 2–10) escalates with the chief priests, scribes, and elders (chapters 11–15). There is trouble in Galilee and in Jerusalem, trouble in the synagogue and in the temple, and trouble among scribes and Pharisees and among chief priests, scribes, and elders; but the trouble gets worse. For Jesus, a rough life leads to a terrible death. Whereas the scribes and the Pharisees may protest Jesus' teaching and his "impurity," the chief priests, scribes, and elders can judge and condemn him. The second half of the story is a narrative escalation of the first half, as both its patterns of spatial settings and its patterns of characterization show.[42]

Michael Cook, of course, would attribute a twofold Markan grouping—Pharisees and Herodians, on the one hand, and chief priests, scribes, and elders, on the other—to Mark's redactional combination of his sources. Even if I found Cook's source hypothesis convincing (which I do not), I would still want to be attentive to the narrative effect of the Gospel of Mark as a whole—as hearers and readers have been responding to it for nearly two thousand years.[43] I do not mean to remove Mark's Gospel (as a literary work) from its historical context, but neither do I accept hypotheses concerning its historical genesis as precluding interpretations of its literary (and theological) significance. Rather, I affirm that historical and literary approaches put constraints upon each other. A literary

---

42. On escalation in the Markan "opponent cycle" see also Mulholland, especially 173–74, 207–8.

43. I certainly do not mean to imply that hearers and readers of Mark have understood or interpreted Mark's Gospel in the same way for nearly two thousand years! My point is, rather, that the literary approach to Mark as an integral whole is, at the most basic level, not really new; it is the usual way most readers approach stories. To be sure, for many Christian readers or hearers, Mark's canonical status has interfered with an integrated reading, especially by the breaking up of the Gospel into portions for the lectionary.

approach to Mark undercuts the "necessity" to explain all distinctions and shifts in the narrative by reference to different
sources.[44] But a literary approach to Mark—as a first-century
work[45]—is bounded by our understanding of its probable historical context.

In the present study, for example, the recent work of
Anthony Saldarini on the Jewish leaders in Palestine in the
first century of the Common Era has been of special importance. Saldarini argues that "Mark's literary presentation, the
historical facts and social patterns may both confirm and aug-
ment one another."[46] By applying, especially to the Pharisees,
a "sociological analysis of groups by class and status, with
stress on their function and power in society,"[47] Saldarini
reaches the following conclusion:

> In Mark's Gospel, as in Josephus's history of the first
> century, the Pharisees are a religious-interest group
> with political goals, but they are not a dominant
> group. Mark's Pharisees are not based in Jerusalem,

---

44. Cf. the similar position, even more strongly argued, of Adele
Berlin in the fifth chapter of *Poetics and Interpretation of Biblical Narrative*, "Poetic Interpretation and Historical-Critical Methods."

45. It is possible, of course, to take a literary approach to biblical
texts without concern for their historical contexts; and, especially
because of their canonical status in a living religion, this is frequently
done—with greater or lesser degrees of self-awareness and sophistication. For an example with a great degree of self-awareness and
sophistication, see Dan Otto Via, Jr., *The Parables: Their Literary and
Existential Dimension* (Philadelphia: Fortress, 1967).

46. Saldarini, "The Pharisees, Scribes and Sadducees in Mark," 2.
Saldarini assumes that, "Since most commentators date Mark near
the war with Rome (66–70), it is unlikely that Mark is reflecting the
changes in Jewish leadership in the decades following the war and it
is likely that he is reflecting something of the mid first-century situation, either through his own knowledge or the data in his traditions"
(1).

47. Ibid., 2.

contrary to Josephus, but the dominant social pattern remains. The Pharisees exercise influence on the people and compete with Jesus for control . . . they enter into political alliances with the Herodians and are associated with the scribes, who do have some political control. . . .

Even if Mark does not know much about the historical Pharisees or scribes, as Michael Cook argues, he does reproduce the dominant social pattern of ancient society and place the Pharisees at the edges of the governing class. They are a political-interest group which is out of power. Consequently, they are not seen as active in Jerusalem, and their sphere of action is in the towns of Galilee. Though we cannot be certain that Mark and his sources give us a completely accurate picture of the Pharisees as a strong community force in Galilee in the early and middle first century, their general role in Jewish society is intrinsically probable.[48]

My analysis suggests that Mark's narrative builds on this historical reality and elaborates it—by literary techniques, for theological purposes. Whereas Cook concentrated on taking apart the Markan narrative on the basis of its references to Jewish leadership groups in order to see if sources that could explain why the different groups appear as they do and when they do in the narrative could reasonably be constructed, I have been seeking an understanding of the characterization of the Jewish leadership groups that makes sense of the Markan Gospel in its historical context but as a literary and theological whole.

---

48. Saldarini, "The Social Class of the Pharisees in Mark," 74–75. See also Saldarini, "The Social Class of the Pharisees in Josephus," in *Pharisees, Scribes, and Sadducees in Palestinian Society: A Sociological Approach* (Wilmington, Del.: Glazier, 1988).

Exceptional Jewish Leaders: Response to Jesus as Key

It is as part of that whole, the Gospel of Mark as a literary and theological whole, that the encounter between Jesus and "one of the scribes"—the exceptional scribe who is "not far from the kingdom of God" (12:34)—is of special interest. Although the scribes are members of the Jewish religious establishment portrayed as enemies of Jesus, the group characterization (although sometimes not far from caricature) does allow this individual exception. Scribes are free *not* to be enemies of Jesus. Of this exceptional scribe, Saldarini observes: he "heard Jesus disputing with the Sadducees, was impressed with his answer and so asked him a friendly question of his own in order to enter into discussion with him. . . . [T]he scribe is impressed with Jesus' teaching ability and authority and questions him as a disciple would question a master or a teacher his colleague."[49] Thus, the exceptional scribe is more like a follower than a foe, and these two categories are seen to be open-ended.[50]

Two other exceptional members of the Jewish religious establishment receive slightly more development in the Markan narrative: Joseph of Arimathea and Jairus. Perhaps the Markan

---

49. Saldarini, "The Pharisees, Scribes and Sadducees in Mark," 11.

50. Mulholland interprets this encounter differently, arguing that Jesus' reply (12:34a) and the following pericope are to be understood as "belonging together in Mark's arrangement of his materials" ("Markan Opponents," 117). "When Jesus informs the scribe that he is not far from the Kingdom of God (v. 34a), there is a lack implied, a lack which prevents the Scribe from entering the Kingdom of God. The following pericope provides an explication of that which is implied—the Scribes (and, by inference, the synagogue) are mistaken in their understanding of the Messiah (12:35–37). Thus, the Scribe's added remark in v. 35b may reflect the debate between Christians and the Jewish community over the person of Jesus and, especially, the relationship between Jesus and God. . . . This seemingly irenic encounter between Jesus and the Scribe is, in reality, a mask which clothes the central issue of the controversy—the Jewish community is so close to the followers of Jesus, yet so far" (118).

narrator intends the hearers/readers to remember the exceptional scribe "not far from the kingdom of God" when Joseph of Arimathea is introduced as one "who was also himself looking for the kingdom of God" (15:43). Joseph is "a respected member of the council" (15:43), and although the word used for council here is *bouleutēs*, not *synedrion* as at 14:55 and 15:1, it still serves as an official designation. Thus one is surprised to learn that Joseph "took courage and went to Pilate, and asked for the body of Jesus" (15:43), and, being granted the body, wrapped it in a linen shroud he had bought and laid it in a tomb (15:44–46). This is the service John's disciples performed for him (6:29), but it is performed for Jesus by one who might well be expected to be his enemy. Similarly, although Jesus was often in conflict in synagogues (3:1–6; 6:2–6), "one of the rulers of the synagogue [*archisynagōgos*, 5:22, cf. 36], Jairus by name" (5:22), apparently followed Jesus' command—"Do not fear, only believe" (5:36)—even though his daughter had been reported dead not long after Jairus made his request for her healing. This is the only resuscitation narrated in the Markan Gospel, and it is set in the house of a ruler of the synagogue (5:35, 38).

Thus, it would seem, although members of the Jewish religious establishment are generally characterized as foes of the Markan Jesus, they may not be automatically so categorized. The Markan Gospel does indeed schematize the Jewish religious leaders as foes of Jesus, but it refuses to absolutize that schema. Being a foe of the Markan Jesus is a matter of how one chooses to relate to him, not a matter of one's social or religious status and role. And the same is true of being a friend of Jesus.

Furthermore, the Jewish religious establishment (although subdivided) is but one major category of foes of the Markan Jesus. Other categories are the Roman political establishment (Herod, Pilate, soldiers) and nonhuman foes (unclean spirits, demons, Satan). And Jesus also has several categories of friends—or, since "friends" is not quite the right term, several categories of those on the same "side" as Jesus (which is, in a reversal of the text of 8:33, not the side "of men" but "the side of God"). Those on the side of Jesus include both nonhuman "characters" (God, the Holy Spirit) and human characters (e.g., suppliants and exemplars—although these two overlap). The disciples, of course, are basically on the side of Jesus, having "left everything and followed" him, as Peter reminds Jesus (10:28). But, because of their difficulties in following Jesus ("you are not on the side of God, but of men," Jesus had earlier [8:33] rebuked Peter), I think a case can be made for treating the disciples (and, in certain aspects, the crowd and the women at the cross and tomb as well[51]) in a separate (and third) major category: followers.

In terms of "content," the disciples have commonalities with both extreme groups: they share the faith and commitment of other human characters on the side of Jesus, and yet they share the misunderstanding and fear of those opposed to Jesus. But in terms of "form," it is the two extreme groups that have commonalities as distinct from the disciples or followers. For, whereas those on the side of Jesus and those opposed to him are "flat" in their characterization—to use the terminology of E. M. Forster—Jesus' followers, and especially his disciples, are "round."[52] Their responses exhibit multiple aspects

---

51. See Malbon, "Fallible Followers" and "Disciples/Crowds/Whoever" [here chapters 2 and 3].

52. E. M. Forster, *Aspects of the Novel* (New York: Harcourt, Brace & Co., 1927; reprint, 1954), 103–18. Forster's distinction between "flat" and "round" characters has been widely adopted—and adapted. I have not found useful the discussion of it by Grahame C. Jones ("'Flat' and 'Round' Characters, the Example of Stendahl," *Australian Journal of French Studies* 20 [1983]: 115–29) in relation to the novels of Stendahl. More applicable to biblical (and/or ancient) literature is Berlin's reformulation of Forster's "flat" and "round" characters into three types (thought of as points on a continuum): "1) the agent, about whom nothing is known except what is necessary for the plot; the agent is a function of the plot or part of the setting; 2) the type, who has a limited and stereotyped range of traits, and who represents the

of their relation to Jesus: both faith and doubt, both trust and fear, both obedience and denial.

We know that characterization by "types" was conventional in ancient literature, including history writing as well as epic, drama, and other forms.[53] The *Characters* of Theophrastus (thirty sketches of extreme examples of vices, apparently written around 319 B.C.E) were a fixed point in that ancient tradition.[54]

---

class of people with these traits; 3) the character, who has a broader range of traits (not all belonging to the same class of people), and about whom we know more than is necessary for the plot" (*Poetics*, 32; also cited here in chapter 6, n. 45). It is not yet clear to me whether this threefold categorization is more helpful in interpreting Mark's Gospel than Forster's twofold distinction. Hochman proposes a "taxonomy" or "a sequence of eight categories [and their opposites] that describe aspects of characters in literature": stylization/naturalism, coherence/incoherence, wholeness/fragmentariness, literalness/symbolism, complexity/simplicity, transparency/opacity, dynamism/staticism, closure/openness (Hochman, *Character*, 88–89). My preliminary work suggests that Hochman's categories will be useful in establishing profiles of *all* the characters and character groups in Mark for the purpose of comparing them with each other.

53. See Weeden, *Mark*, 12–19; and Fred W. Burnett, "Characterization in Matthew: Reader Construction of the Disciple Peter" (paper presented to the annual meeting of the SBL, Anaheim, Calif., November 1985), esp. 38–58; and the literature cited by both Weeden and Burnett. An intriguing suggestion offered by William Charles Korfmacher bears following up in relation to Markan characterization: "[I]n comedy, tragedy, and epic at least the fixed type characters of rhetorical theory were subjected to modifications in accord with the *genre* in which they chanced to appear" ("Three Phases of Classical Type Characterization," *Classical Weekly* 27 [1934]: 86).

54. For a discussion of Theophrastus and classical rhetoric, see Benjamin Boyce, *The Theophrastan Character in England to 1642* (London: Frank Cass, 1967), 11–36; Warren Andersen, *Theophrastus: The Character Sketches—Translated, with Notes and Introductory Essays* (Kent, Ohio: Kent State University, 1979), xi–xx; and J. W. Smeed, *The Theophrastan 'Character': The History of a Literary Genre* (Oxford: Clarendon, 1985), 1–11.

An ancient editor of the sketches, it would appear,[55] added a letter of dedication (or proem), attributing these words of explanation to Theophrastus:

> I have often marvelled, when I have given the matter my attention, and it may be I shall never cease to marvel, why it has come about that, albeit the whole of Greece lies in the same clime and all Greeks have a like upbringing, we have not the same constitution of character. I therefore, Polycles, having observed human nature a long time (for I have lived ninety years and nine and moreover had converse with all sorts of dispositions and compared them with great diligence), have thought it incumbent upon me to write in a book the manners of each several kind of men both good and bad. And you shall have set down sort by sort the behavior proper to them and the fashion of their life; for I am persuaded, Polycles, that our sons will prove the better men if there be left them such memorials as will, if they imitate them, make them choose the friendship and converse of the better sort, in the hope they may be as good as they. But now to my tale; and be it yours to follow with understanding and see if I speak true.[56]

No Theophrastan sketches of good characters have come down to us, but such a goal—to describe the two extremes—would have been appropriate for Theophrastus, a student of Aristotle, who perceived virtue as a golden mean between two extremes.[57]

---

55. R. C. Jeeb, *The Characters of Theophrastus: An English Translation with Introduction and Notes*, ed. J. E. Sandys (New York: Arno, 1979), 18.

56. J. M. Edmonds, ed. and trans., *The Characters of Theophrastus*, LCL (Cambridge, Mass.: Harvard University Press; London: Heinemann, 1961), 37–38.

57. See Boyce, *Theophrastan Character*, 5, 11–16; Jeeb, *Characters*, 13–16; Andersen, *Theophrastus*, xi–xiii; Smeed, *Theophrastan 'Character*,' 3–7. It may be that contemporary readers of Mark's Gospel are

I am certainly not suggesting that Mark's Gospel depicts followership as the golden mean between the unqualified faith of the hemorrhaging woman and the fearful plotting of the Pharisees, chief priests, scribes, and elders! But followership *is* characterized in Mark as involving the lively struggle between faith and doubt, trust and fear, obedience and denial. The author of Mark wishes to show who Jesus is and who Jesus' followers are. To do this he schematizes the characters of his story; he paints extreme cases of enemies and exemplars as the background against which the trials and joys of followers may stand out more boldly.[58] If Mark's Gospel is in any sense a

---

not, in fact, in a completely different realm from first-century hearers/readers of Mark in regard to perceiving "typical" characters. Baruch Hochman argues that "both in literature and life . . . we reduce characters, as we reduce plots (or sequences of events), to what we take to be their essential meaning or their animating principle" (*Character*, 41). He elaborates: "Yet our perception of people is typological, in life as well as in literature, just as all of our perceptions are essentially typological and categorical. We tend to perceive anyone (as we perceive any*thing*) in terms of some system or classification and only then come to conceive of him or her, if the signs point that way, in terms of his or her uniqueness or individuality" (46). And, Hochman concludes: "Just as we recognize the typefying nature of perception, so we should also insist on the potentially schematic nature of character, in life as well as in literature . . ." (47). See also n. 8 above.

58. Those (simply) on Jesus' side and those (simply) opposed to him are background characters; Jesus' followers are—to use the terminology of W. J. Harvey—*ficelles*, that is, characters who, while more delineated than the background characters, exist primarily to serve some function or functions (*Character and the Novel* [Ithaca, N.Y.: Cornell University Press, 1965], 52–73). These functions, Harvey suggests, might include acting as a foil for the protagonist (in the case of Mark's Gospel, Jesus); by misunderstanding and a partial view, focusing the protagonist's dilemma more clearly; and, especially when the experience of the protagonist is "exceptional," serving as "the springboard from which we launch ourselves into the turbid depths of the central figure" (63). Furthermore, the *ficelle* (Jesus' disciples/followers as a group in Mark) can, because of his or her "generalized and representative value," "in various ways extend the story of the protagonist" and serve as "the reader's delegate in the story" (67).

polemic, it is a polemic not against the Jews as a group[59] or an opposition Christian group supposedly represented by the disciples,[60] but against a simplistic view of discipleship (or followership) that sees unfailing support or unfailing enmity as the only options, rather than as the background against which the complex relations of Jesus and his followers must be worked out.

Mark's Gospel seems to be typical of ancient literature in its characterization by types—"good" types to emulate and "bad" types to eschew. Additional research will be needed to determine whether or not Mark's Gospel is typical in two ways in which it increases the complexity and subtlety of characterization by types. First, in addition to the contrast of "good" and "bad" types, Mark's Gospel presents a contrast between "flat" and "round" character groups; the "flat" are either good *or* bad, the "round" are both good *and* bad. And, second, Mark offers the contrast of a typical character group and exceptional characters, who function not to "round" out the "flat" group but to prevent the type from becoming a stereotype. It is the exceptional characters that indicate most clearly that the functional character groups in Mark are delineated on the basis of typical responses to Jesus, not on the basis of stereotypical characteristics associated with given statuses and roles.[61] Thus

---

59. The author of Mark seems to have taken care to portray Jesus' opponents as the Jewish *leaders*, not all the Jewish people—especially in contrast to the authors of Matthew and John. The struggle is presented as that between a nontraditional *Jewish* leader and his *Jewish* followers (Jesus and his disciples) and the traditional Jewish leaders. For a discussion of the Markan *Sitz im Leben* relevant to this issue, see Mulholland, "Markan Opponents."

60. Weeden, *Mark*; Kelber, *Kingdom*; Kelber, *Mark's Story*; Kelber, *The Oral and the Written Gospel: The Hermeneutics of Speaking and Writing in the Synoptic Tradition, Mark, Paul, and Q* (Philadelphia: Fortress, 1983).

61. Difficulties remain in integrating these two pairs of terms: "flat" and "round" and typical and exceptional. As I complete my examination of all the characters in Mark, I hope to clarify this terminology.

Mark challenges both the absolutism of "good" and "bad" (no one is a perfect disciple) and the absolutism of types determined by status and role (no one is ruled out as a disciple). By suggesting that even presumed foes can be followers, Mark opens up the category of disciples; by indicating that even known followers can sometimes fail, Mark deepens the meaning of discipleship.

Thus, in their narrative contexts, the Jewish leaders in Mark's Gospel are characterized as "flat" and "bad"; they are simply Jesus' opponents—but not quite without exception.[62]

---

62. Cf. Jack Dean Kingsbury on the characterization of the Jewish leaders in Matthew: "Given the fact that the Jewish leaders in Matthew's story constitute a flat character whose root trait is that they are 'evil,' one should not find it surprising that the implied author's characterization of them should prove to be uniformly, and even monotonously, negative" ("The Developing Conflict between Jesus and the Jewish Leaders in Matthew's Gospel: A Literary-Critical Study," *CBQ* 49 [1987]: 60; see also Sjef Van Tilborg, *The Jewish Leaders in Matthew* [Leiden: Brill, 1972], esp. 166–72). In Matthew, Jairus is described as simply a ruler (*archōn*, 9:18, 23), not a ruler of a synagogue; the leader who discusses with Jesus the great commandment is a Pharisaic lawyer (*nomikos*, 22:35, although not universally attested), not a scribe, and he neither commends nor is commended by Jesus; and Joseph of Arimathea is identified not as "a respected member of the council" but as "a rich man . . . , who also was a disciple of Jesus" (27:57). Thus two of the three Markan "exceptional" Jewish leaders are not identified in Matthew as Jewish leaders at all, and the one who is so identified is not portrayed as exceptional! This contrast makes Mark's portrayal all the more striking. Luke's treatment of these three characters is more similar to Mark's. In Luke, Jairus is identified as "a ruler of the synagogue" (8:41); the questioner is a "lawyer" (10:25), who is told simply that he has "answered right" (10:28, but cf. 10:29); and Joseph of Arimathea is described as "a member of the council, a good and righteous man, who had not consented to their purpose and deed, and he was looking for the kingdom of God" (23:50–51). But Robert C. Tannehill has argued that in Luke-Acts, the story of Israel—not just the story of the Jewish leaders—is a tragic story because in it the initial expectation of salvation for Jews and Gentiles is not fulfilled ("Israel in Luke-Acts: A Tragic Story," *JBL* 104 [1985]: 69–85).

And the exceptions suggest that being a foe of Jesus is not simply a matter of one's social or religious status and role, but a matter of how one responds to Jesus. Of course, responding *appropriately* to Jesus, being a follower, is not a simple matter either. The complexity of Markan patterns of characterization reflects the complexity of Markan religious and theological affirmations. In this, the Gospel of Mark is a literary and theological whole.[63]

---

63. I am pleased to express my gratitude to: (1) the Center for Programs in the Humanities at Virginia Polytechnic Institute and State University for a 1986 Humanities Summer Stipend in support of the work reflected here; (2) the Virginia Tech Educational Foundation for a travel grant enabling me to present a version of this paper at the fourth international meeting of the SBL, Jerusalem, August 1986; (3) Anthony J. Saldarini of Boston College for offering encouraging and helpful comments on an earlier draft and for sharing drafts of his work in progress on the Pharisees in first-century Palestine; and (4) Charles H. Talbert of Wake Forest University for suggesting that I take a look at Theophrastus's *Characters*.

6

The Poor Widow in Mark
and Her Poor Rich Readers

> And sitting opposite the treasury, he was observing how the crowd cast money into the treasury. And many of the rich cast in much. And one poor widow, coming, cast in two *lepta*, which is [in value] a *quadrans*. And calling his disciples, he said to them, "Amen, I say to you, the poor widow herself cast in more than all of those casting into the treasury. For all (of them) cast in from their surplus, but she from her need cast in all of whatever she had, her whole life."[1]
>
> Mark 12:41–44

Reviewing and adding to the varying interpretations of this small story in Mark's Gospel offer a way of raising an important methodological issue in the larger story of New Testament or, more broadly, biblical interpretation. Here examination of the interpretations presented in three representative commentaries—historical critical (Swete), form critical (Taylor), redaction critical (Nineham)—and one intriguing article (by

\

---

1. Author's (fairly literal) translation. The translation of *bios* as "life" rather than as "means of living," both of which are legitimate translations, is based on the narrative contexts of the passage, as will become clear below.

Addison Wright) preludes my reading of the story of the poor widow in six Markan narrative contexts. These multiple interpretations provide a basis for reflection on the methodological issue of dealing with differences in interpretation. There are a wealth of readings of the poor widow's story, yet one must sometimes wonder whether our embarrassment of riches as readers is not akin to poverty: both can be paralyzing.

Three Commentaries

The Markan commentary of Henry Barclay Swete was first published in London in 1898.[2] Swete is especially interested, in his comments here and elsewhere, to clarify matters of the Greek text and the ancient historical background. The "treasury" referred to in this passage, he tells us, would have been the colonnade in the temple's Court of the Women, under which thirteen chests of trumpetlike shape, and thus known as *Shopharoth* (trumpets), were placed.[3] The two coins involved were Greek *lepta*, which, "as Mc. explains for the benefit of his Roman readers," were each worth half a Roman *quadrans*, and which, as Swete explains for the presumed benefit of his English readers, were the eighth part of an *as* or the one one-hundred-twenty-eighth part of a denarius or the seventh part of a *chalkous*.[4]

But Swete also expands the details of the minimal Markan story in colorful ways. "Passover was at hand," he notes, "and wealthy worshippers were numerous and liberal."[5] "The Lord's attention is attracted by the rattling of the [widow's] coin[s] down the throats of the Shopharoth. He looks up . . . from the

---

2. Henry Barclay Swete, *Commentary on Mark* (Grand Rapids: Kregel, 1977; reprint of 3d ed., 1913).

3. Ibid., 292.

4. Ibid., 293.

5. Ibid.

floor of the Court [of the Women] on which his eyes had been resting, and fixes them on the spectacle. . . ."[6] Delightful as these imagined sights and sounds may be, more striking are Swete's observations of verbal and narrative contrasts. "The widow stands out on the canvas, solitary and alone," he notes, "in strong contrast to the *polloi plousioi* [the many rich], and is detected by the Lord's eye in the midst of the surrounding *ochlos* [crowd]."[7] "The rich cast in . . . *polla* [much], the widow *panta* [all]."[8]

For Swete the point of the story is the lesson "the Lord" would teach the disciples about giving. "The lesson is taught, as usual," he notes, "by an example—in the concrete, not in the abstract."[9] The difficulty and yet importance of the lesson are indicated by "the use of the solemn formula *amēn . . . legō humin* [Amen, I say to you]."[10]

The magisterial Markan commentary of Vincent Taylor, published in England in 1952, fifty-four years after Swete's, also seeks to explain the intricacies of the Greek text and (to a lesser extent) to fill in details about the historical background. Taylor's focus, however, is on both the *Sitz im Leben Jesu*, the situation in life of Jesus, and the *Sitz im Leben* of the early church reflected in the oral tradition behind the Markan text.[11] According to Taylor, the "narrative is a Pronouncement-story," that is, the "story is told, not for its own sake, but because it leads to a significant saying of Jesus about almsgiving."[12] Taylor also reports other form critical opinions: Bultmann "classifies it as a Biographical Apothegm"; Redlich as

---

6. Ibid., 292.

7. Ibid., 293.

8. Ibid., 294.

9. Ibid.

10. Ibid.

11. Vincent Taylor, *The Gospel according to St. Mark* (Grand Rapids: Baker, 1981; reprint of 2d ed., 1966).

12. Ibid., 496.

"an Apothegm-story"; Dibelius "prefers to regard it as a narrative constructed by Mark on the basis of a saying of Jesus,
and especially a parable."[13] "The position of the narrative,"
Taylor observes, "is due to topical reasons. The reference to
widows in xii.40 and its connexion with the Temple account
for its place in the Marcan outline."[14]

In terms of historical backgrounds, Taylor's references to
trumpet-shaped chests and the *lepta* and *quadrans* are much
briefer than Swete's, but Taylor discusses in addition the historical literary parallels to the story in other religious traditions: Jewish, Indian, and Buddhist. Particularly he cites
(following Ernst Lohmeyer) "the Jewish story [from *Leviticus
Rabbah*] of a priest who rejected the offering of a handful of
meal from a poor woman, and was commanded in a dream
during the night: 'Despise her not; it is as if she offered her
life.'"[15] Taylor understands such parallels to challenge "the
genuineness of the story," that is, the probability of its historical occurrence. The genuineness can also be questioned, he
admits, because "we do not know" how Jesus knew so completely the widow's economic circumstances. But neither of
these points, he argues, is "a valid objection to the historical
value of the narrative."[16] On the one hand, "The story is not
so distinctive that similar incidents, with differences, could not
happen in the case of other teachers,"[17] and, on the other hand,
the Markan narrative simply "betrays no interest in the question" of the *how* of Jesus' knowledge.[18]

For Taylor, as for Swete, the point of the story is the
widow's exemplary giving of all that she had. The phrase *holon
ton bion autēs* Taylor translates as "even her whole living," and,

13. Ibid.
14. Ibid.
15. Ibid.
16. Ibid., 498.
17. Ibid., 496.
18. Ibid., 498.

he comments on the phrase, it "is in accordance with Mark's style, and effectively describes the measure of the widow's generosity."[19] The use of the phrase "Amen, I say to you" "indicates the earnestness with which Jesus spoke."[20] Furthermore, Taylor asserts, "the story is in harmony with [Jesus'] teaching elsewhere,"[21] citing Mark 9:41, "Amen, I say to you, whoever gives you a cup of water to drink because you bear the name of Christ, will by no means lose his reward," and Luke 12:15, "Take heed, and beware of all covetousness; for a man's life does not consist in the abundance of his possessions."

Dennis E. Nineham's commentary on Mark was first published in England in 1963, just eleven years after Taylor's, but it reflects a significant development in New Testament scholarship in general: Taylor's orientation is form critical, Nineham's is redaction critical; Taylor asks about the history and tradition before Mark, Nineham asks about what Mark does with that tradition.[22] Nineham is skeptical about the by now traditional comments on the historical background of this passage. He does point out that *lepton* means literally "a tiny thing" and "was used for the smallest coin in circulation."[23] But, following Henry Cadbury, he cautions that it is "unsafe to deduce any conclusions about the Gospel's place of origin" from Mark's explanatory transliteration of the Latin word *quadrans* into Greek.[24] Nineham also mentions the traditional interpretation of "what is meant by *the treasury*" (the thirteen trumpet-shaped receptacles described in the Mishnah), but he notes as well that the Greek word used here, *gazophylakion*,

---

19. Ibid.

20. Ibid., 497.

21. Ibid., 496.

22. D. E. Nineham, *The Gospel of St Mark*, PNTC (Baltimore: Penguin, 1963).

23. Ibid., 335.

24. Ibid.

elsewhere is used for "the rooms or cells in which the temple valuables or deposits were stored."[25] Nineham concludes that "it is probably simplest to suppose that a story related *by* Jesus (on the basis of a current Jewish parable) has been transformed into a story about him"—in which case "St Mark himself may have had no very clear idea what *treasury* was intended."[26]

Nineham considers the "number of quite close parallels [that] are known from both pagan and Jewish sources" (he quotes the one from *Lev. Rab.* 3:5) as evidence in favor of understanding the story as an enacted parable, "a Jewish parable which Jesus took over in his teaching and which was later transformed into an incident in his life."[27] Nineham, as a redaction critic, is particularly interested in the context of this parabolic story in Mark's Gospel. "The present setting of the story," Nineham admits, "may in part be due simply to the catchword *widow* (vv. 40 and 42), but a more apt position for it could hardly be imagined. Not only does it form a fitting contrast to the previous section ('In contrast to the bad scribes, who "eat" widows' property, we now have the tale of the good widow and her sacrifice' [Montefiore]), but with its teaching that the true gift is to give 'everything we have' (v. 44) it sums up what has gone before in the Gospel and makes a superb transition to the story of how Jesus 'gave everything' for men."[28] This brief statement is Nineham's full comment on this idea, an idea that moves away from a focus on the poor widow's gift as exemplary *financial* stewardship to an openness to the poor widow's giving as paradigmatic service or self-sacrifice; it is an idea I will develop further below.

---

25. Ibid.
26. Ibid.
27. Ibid., 334.
28. Ibid., 334–35.

An Intriguing Article

Most of the interpretive work on the story of the poor widow in Mark has been done in commentaries, such as those by Swete, Taylor, and Nineham, rather than in journal articles. An intriguing exception is an article by Addison Wright that appeared in the *Catholic Biblical Quarterly* in 1982.[29] This article will serve as my fourth and final example. Wright's essay is entitled "The Widow's Mites: Praise or Lament?—A Matter of Context," and his thesis cuts against the grain of all those interpretations—the vast majority, including Swete's and Taylor's—that focus on the exemplary financial generosity of the poor widow. To a large extent I agree with Wright's diagnosis of the common interpretive disease, but I differ with him on the appropriate prescription for a cure. Yet I concur completely in finding the issue "A Matter of Context."

Wright opens his study with a tabular survey of the few articles and many commentaries that offer information relevant to or interpretations of the story of the poor widow. Most of the articles deal with some aspect of the coins, and most of the commentaries conclude that the point of the story is the extraordinary and exemplary financial generosity of the poor widow, a model contributor. Wright's chief complaint about these interpretations is as follows. Many commentators recognize, explicitly or implicitly, "that Jesus' observation [about giving] is a commonplace, and that indeed it is not a specifically Christian idea but a universal and human one. Thus they conclude that there must be some further depth to the saying and they supply that further depth by relating Jesus' remark to some element from the larger context of his preaching (blessed are the poor, a cup of cold water in his name, do not be anxious about what you shall eat or wear, you cannot serve

---

29. Addison G. Wright, S.S., "The Widow's Mites: Praise or Lament?—A Matter of Context," *CBQ* 44 (1982): 256–65.

God and Mammon, you shall love the Lord your God, etc.)."
"This procedure of attempting to read in context is laudable,"
Wright judges, but "the proper context has not been rightly
identified in any of the commentaries. . . ."[30] In fact, Wright
suggests, the interpretive context has usually been imported
into the text for external religious reasons. "Critical exegesis is
supposed to inform preaching, piety, and church thinking," he
writes, "but one wonders to what extent preaching, piety, and
church interests have affected critical exegesis in the history of
the interpretation of this text."[31]

According to Wright, "The context is immediately at hand"[32]
in the three immediately preceding verses (12:38–40): "And in
his teaching he said, 'Beware of the scribes, who like to go about
in long robes, and to have salutations in the market places and
the best seats in the synagogues and the places of honor at feasts,
who devour widows' houses and for a pretense make long
prayers. They will receive the greater condemnation." "If,
indeed, Jesus is opposed to the devouring of widows' houses,"
Wright asks, "how could he possibly be pleased with what he
sees here?"[33] Wright argues that Jesus could not, that the story
of the poor widow, "if viewed as an approbation, does not
cohere any better with the immediately preceding widow-
saying, than it does with the Corban-statement,"[34] in which the
truly "religious values are human values."[35] Wright asserts that
we must

> see Jesus' attitude to the widow's gift as a downright
> disapproval and not as an approbation. The story does
> not provide a pious contrast to the conduct of the
> scribes in the preceding section (as is the customary

---

30. Ibid., 259.
31. Ibid., 265.
32. Ibid., 261.
33. Ibid., 262.
34. Ibid.
35. Ibid., 261.

view); rather it provides a further illustration of the ills of official devotion. Jesus' saying is not a penetrating insight on the measuring of gifts; it is a lament, 'Amen, I tell you, she gave more than all the others.' . . . She had been taught and encouraged by religious leaders to donate as she does, and Jesus condemns the value system that motivates her action, and he condemns the people who conditioned her to do it.[36]

"If one seeks further context," Wright adds, "the lines that follow the story should not be neglected"[37]—in fact the next two verses are all one needs. Mark 13:1–2 reads: "And as he came out of the temple, one of his disciples said to him, 'Look, Teacher, what wonderful stones and what wonderful buildings!' And Jesus said to him, 'Do you see these great buildings? There will not be left here one stone upon another, that will not be thrown down.'" Wright comments: "It is hard to see how anyone at that point could feel happy about the widow. Her contribution was totally misguided, thanks to the encouragement of official religion, but the final irony of it all was that it was also a waste."[38] "Instead of reaching ahead one chapter to connect the story with Jesus' self-offering in the passion narrative, as a few commentators [including Nineham] do," Wright proposes, "let us simply be content with the lines that immediately follow both in Mark and in Luke."[39] Thus for Wright the proper interpretation of 12:41–44 is "a matter of

---

36. Ibid., 262.

37. Ibid., 263.

38. Ibid.

39. Ibid. Strangely enough, the moralizing (and unconvincing) interpretation of 12:41–44 offered by Ernest Best (*Following Jesus: Discipleship in the Gospel of Mark*, JSNTSup 4 [Sheffield: JSOT Press, 1981], 155–56), while the very type of thing against which Wright argues, is based not on a link back to 12:40 (widows' houses) but on "a better link forwards" to 13:2 (and chap. 13 as a whole), the very thing for which Wright argues.

context," and the proper context is 12:38–40 and 13:1–2, no less and no more.

But why should we be content to consider only the preceding three verses and the succeeding two verses *the* context of the poor widow's story? Does *the* context or *the proper* context of a passage even exist? Is it a sensible notion? It would seem more appropriate to consider a number of overlapping *contexts* in which the story of the poor widow can be read. I am especially interested in the multiple *narrative* contexts in which this little story functions in the larger narrative of Mark's Gospel.

Six Narrative Contexts

Wright is correct in calling attention to the three immediately preceding verses (about the typical behavior of scribes) as an important narrative context. I would, however, interpret the significance of this (first) context along the lines of what Wright complains of as "the customary view."[40] The poor widow who gives all, her whole means of living, is in striking contrast to the scribes who take all, who "devour widows' houses" (12:40), that is, their means of living. The scribes who seek to call attention to themselves by means of wearing their long robes about and soliciting salutations in the marketplaces as well as claiming the best seats in the synagogues and at feasts are in striking contrast with the poor widow who is so unobtrusive that only Jesus notices her; it is he who calls her action to the attention of the disciples. From beginning to end, Jesus' ministry itself is in striking contrast to the scribes' activities and attitudes. Many citations could be given, of which the first, Mark 1:22, is perhaps emblematic: "And they were astonished at his teaching, for he taught them as one who had authority,

---

40. Wright, "The Widow's Mites," 262.

and not as the scribes."[41] Thus Jesus is unlike the self-centered scribes and like the self-denying widow in being one who gives.

Wright's argument to the contrary seems more ingenious than convincing. Of course the widow's gift of "her whole life" is not reasonable, but that is the same complaint that Peter makes (in 8:31–33) of Jesus' willingness "to give his life as a ransom for [the] many" (10:45). Wright's narrow contextual focus results in an unfortunate, if not unusual, case of "blaming the victim." Perhaps we *are* to assume that the poor widow has been victimized by scribes who devour widows' houses and by the authority of traditional religious teaching;[42] surely the Markan Jesus is victimized by the chief priests, scribes, and elders, those who traditionally hold authority in the temple and in the broader religious tradition. At an important transitional point in the Markan narrative, Jesus calls attention to the poor widow's action; the focus seems to be on giving, but not just of money. The *last* words of the passage are those left echoing in our ears: *holon ton bion autēs*, "her whole life."[43]

41. See also 2:6, 16; 3:22; 7:1, 5; 8:31; 9:11, 14; 10:33; 11:18, 27; (12:28, 32 refer to the exceptional scribe); 12:35, 38; 14:1, 43, 53; 15:1, 31.

42. Swete observes: "It may have been the intention of the two Synoptists to compare her simple piety with the folly of the rich widows who wasted their substance on the Scribes (Victor), or she may once have been of the latter class, and reduced to destitution by Pharisaic rapacity; at least it is worthy of note that Mt., who does not mention this feature in the character of the Scribes, omits also the incident of the mites, whilst Mc. and Lc. have both, and in the same order of juxtaposition" (*Commentary on Mark*, 293).

43. See Joseph A. Grassi, *The Hidden Heroes of the Gospels: Female Counterparts of Jesus* (Collegeville, Minn.: Liturgical Press, 1989), 22 and 35–39. See also Bonnie Bowman Thurston's discussion of the recurrent early Christian imagery of the widow as "altar": "An individual's obedience to God is a form of sacrifice offered to God in imitation of Christ's sacrifice." "It is in this sense that the widow as altar becomes an effective agent; she too is a living sacrifice. The key New Testament texts on widows (Mark 12:41–44; Luke 2:36–38; 4:25–26;

Wright also appropriately calls attention to the succeeding two verses, Jesus' prediction of the destruction of the temple, as an important (second) context for the story of the poor widow. He argues that the foretold destruction of the temple indicates the absurdity of the poor widow's gift. I would argue, rather, that the *overall* temple context of the poor widow's story adds to the impressive *irony* of the Markan passion narrative. Jesus' summoning his disciples to observe the poor widow's action and to consider its significance is his final act in the temple. The Markan Jesus' initial act in the temple was the driving out of those who bought and sold there (11:15–19). This passage, as several of us have argued, is to be understood as a symbolic closing down of the temple, not a cleansing of it.[44] The account of Jesus' conflict with the buyers and sellers

---

7:11–17; 18:1–8; Acts 6:1–7; 16:11–15; 1 Tim. 5:3–16) do not explicitly connect widows with sacrifice. If, however, love of God, love of neighbor more than self, and prayer are Christian sacrifices, then the widows embody Christian sacrifice. Anna worships 'with fasting and prayer night and day' (Luke 2:37). The widow who makes an offering at the treasury exhibits love of God and care for neighbor above self, especially since the offering is her 'whole living' ([Mark] 12:41–44). It is noteworthy that both these widows are placed within the temple environs, near the altars." "In the words of Saint Basil, the altar is for the purpose of the holy remembrance of Christ in which Christ comes near himself as a sacrifice. Christ provides the atonement through his sacrifice; the altar [i.e., metaphorically the widow] reminds Christians of his sacrifice (Heb. 13:10)" (Thurston, *The Widows: A Women's Ministry in the Early Church* [Minneapolis: Fortress, 1989], 111).

44. Elizabeth Struthers Malbon, *Narrative Space and Mythic Meaning in Mark*, New Voices in Biblical Studies (San Francisco: Harper & Row, 1986; reprint, The Biblical Seminar 13; Sheffield: Sheffield Academic Press, 1991), 120–26, 131–36; Werner H. Kelber, *The Kingdom in Mark* (Philadelphia: Fortress, 1974), 97–102. But see also Craig A. Evans, "Jesus' Action in the Temple: Cleansing or Portent of Destruction?" *CBQ* 51 (1989): 237–70, esp. 238–42, where Evans argues against E. P. Sanders that the Gospel writers, especially Mark, manifest an anti-temple theme and thus would *not* be likely to change accounts of Jesus' historical temple action as a portent of destruction

in the temple is intercalated with the account of the cursing and withering of the fig tree (11:12–14, 20–26), which is generally recognized as a parabolic pointing to the destruction of the unfruitful temple whose time or moment (*kairos*, 11:13) has passed. The episode of the poor widow's gift of her all might well be understood as an enacted parable parallel to the fig tree incident (as L. Simon has argued[45]) or parallel to the intercalated fig tree/temple incident as a whole. The fig tree episode introduces a series of controversies between Jesus and Jewish religious authorities in the temple; the account of the poor widow's action closes the series.

As the withering of the fig tree alludes to the destruction of the temple itself, which is made explicit in Jesus' prediction in 13:2, so the widow's gift of "her whole life" alludes to Jesus' gift of his life, which is enacted in chapters 14–15. Furthermore, Jesus' death is related to the temple's downfall, not in the sense in which the false witnesses accuse Jesus of claiming to be the *agent* of the temple's destruction (14:57–59; see also 15:29–30), but in the sense in which the *kairos* of the temple (alias fig tree) is surpassed by the *kairos* of the kingdom and of the Messiah who proclaims that "The *kairos* is fulfilled, and the kingdom of God is at hand . . ." (1:15a). Thus Jesus' first action in the temple, the driving out of the buyers and sellers, points

---

(affirmed by Sanders) to narratives of a temple cleansing; thus the temple cleansing idea must be in the Gospels, including Mark, because of its historical authenticity. Evans's focus is "the historical Jesus," not the Gospel of Mark, and he concludes "that the cleansing idea is too firmly entrenched in the tradition to be so easily set aside. Since the cleansing idea, if properly understood (i.e., not as an attack against the sacrificial system itself), coheres well with what we know of Jesus and the background against which we must interpret him, it is appropriate that we let it stand [as authentic history]" (269). I do not find Evans's arguments concerning "Jesus" or Mark convincing.

45. L. Simon, "Le sou de la veuve: Mark 12/41–44," *ETR* 44 (1969): 115–26.

to the temple's end; and Jesus' final action in the temple, or rather his reaction to the poor widow's action, points to his own end. And, most importantly, the temple's end and Jesus' end are carefully interrelated in the Markan Gospel, not only in the juxtaposition of Jesus' death on the cross (15:37) and the tearing of the temple curtain (15:38), but also in the intercalation (admittedly in the broadest sense) of the accounts of the passion of Jesus (chapters 11–12 and 14–15) and the passion of the community (chapter 13).[46] The crises the community of Jesus' future followers will face—being delivered up to councils, being beaten in synagogues, and standing before governors and kings (13:9), for example—are to be interpreted, and coped with, in the light of the crises Jesus does face in Jerusalem.[47]

---

46. The phrase "the passion of Jesus and the passion of the community" comes from John R. Donahue, S.J. (lectures given at Vanderbilt Divinity School, fall 1977). But see Norman Perrin, *The New Testament: An Introduction* (New York: Harcourt, Brace, Jovanovich, 1974), 148, 159. The positions of Perrin and Donahue represent developments, based on more detailed literary analysis, of the more historically oriented positions of Etienne Trocmé and Rudolf Pesch. My designation of chaps. 11–12/13/14–16 (including the resurrection in 16 along with the passion in 14–15) as an intercalation is in line with the literary analysis of Perrin and Donahue and does not judge the issue of the historical creation of the Gospel of Mark. Frank Kermode also recognizes chap. 13 as "the largest of his [Mark's] intercalations," but in Kermode's view the insertion is not between chaps. 11–12 and 14–16 but between chaps. 1–12, Jesus' ministry, and 14–16, Jesus' passion (*The Genesis of Secrecy* [Cambridge, Mass.: Harvard University Press, 1979], 127–28).

47. See also Robert Tannehill, "The Disciples in Mark: The Function of a Narrative Role," *JR* 57 (1977): 404, and R. H. Lightfoot, *The Gospel Message of St. Mark* (Oxford: Clarendon, 1950), 48–59. Kermode's further expansion of the concept of intercalation is well taken: "Should we think of the whole gospel as an intercalated story? . . . It stands at the moment of transition between the main body of history and the end of history; and what it says has a powerful effect on both" (133–34).

This brings us to a third narrative context of the poor widow's story: beyond its immediate juxtaposition with the scribes who devour widows' houses and its closing out Jesus' activities in the temple, the story of the poor widow's gift of her last two coins serves with the story of the unnamed woman's anointing of Jesus as a frame around chapter 13. Chapter 13, the eschatological discourse, is intrusive within the larger story of Jesus' passion in Jerusalem, which begins in chapters 11–12 and culminates in chapters 14–15. Even though the frame and middle of this large-scale intercalation are to be interpreted together, one can skip from the end of chapter 12 to the beginning of chapter 14 with no noticeable gap in the story line. The central discourse is framed by two stories about exemplary women in contrast with villainous men. Jesus' condemnation of the scribes' typical actions and his commendation of the poor widow's exceptional action immediately precede chapter 13; the accounts of the chief priests' and scribes' plot against Jesus and the woman's anointing of Jesus immediately succeed chapter 13.[48] One woman

---

48. Interestingly enough, if the three criteria John R. Donahue, S.J., established for a Markan insertion (*Are You the Christ?* SBLDS 10 [Missoula, Mont.: Scholars Press, 1973], 241) were to be expanded from the level of the phrase to the narrative level, at least two of the three would be met in the case of chaps. 11–12/13/14–16. First, "close verbal agreement" would become "close narrative agreement" and would be satisfied by the two stories about self-denying women, each following a reference to devious and self-centered men in official religious positions. Second, "synoptic alteration" at the narrative level is clear: both Matthew and Luke parallel Mark 13, but Matthew drops the preceding account of the poor widow, and Luke drops (or moves and significantly alters) the succeeding account of the anointing woman.

Grassi suggests that "the whole tone for Jesus' final testament in chapter 13 is set by a deliberate 'inclusion,' a literary device that links the beginning and end of a section by means of repetition. In dramatic presentation, this device focuses audience attention on their own response to Jesus' example. At the beginning we find the story

gives what little she has, two copper coins; the other gives a great deal, ointment of pure nard worth three hundred denarii, but each gift represents self-denial.

It is, of course, ironic that the poor widow's gift occurs in the doomed temple; and it is ironic that the anointing of Jesus Christ, Jesus Messiah, Jesus the anointed one, takes place not in the temple but in a leper's house (14:3), and not at the hands of the high priest but at the hands of an unnamed woman. A further irony is manifest in the juxtaposition of the unnamed woman, who gives up money for Jesus and enters the house to honor him (14:3–9), and Judas, the man who gives up Jesus for money and leaves the house to betray him (14:10–11).

As a fourth narrative context of the story of the poor widow, the character, her action, and its significance may be read in the context of all the women characters of Mark's Gospel. As I have tried to work this out elsewhere, I will not repeat myself here.[49] I will simply point out that the poor widow, along with three other important women characters (the hemorrhaging woman, the Syrophoenician woman, and the anointing woman), takes decisive action to which Jesus makes a significant *re*action. The hemorrhaging woman touches Jesus' garment and is immediately healed; Jesus reacts in admiration of her faith (5:24–34). The Syrophoenician woman argues with Jesus in his own metaphorical terms about bread for children and for dogs; Jesus reacts to her "word" (Greek *logos*) by healing her daughter at a distance, in spite of his initial refusal to do so (7:24–30). The poor widow gives for others her last two coins, "her whole

---

of the poor widow. . . . At the end of Jesus' last discourse, just before Judas' betrayal of Jesus, we have the story of the . . . woman . . . at Bethany who anointed Jesus' head with oil as he sat at table (14:3–9)" (*Hidden Heroes of the Gospels*, 35). Grassi presents "the significant parallels" of the two stories in parallel columns (36).

49. Elizabeth Struthers Malbon, "Fallible Followers: Women and Men in the Gospel of Mark," *Semeia* 28 (1983): 29–48, esp. 37–40 and 43 [here chapter 2].

life"; Jesus summons his disciples to attend to her action. The anointing woman anoints Jesus' head with expensive ointment; Jesus reacts by proclaiming that the story of her anointing him "beforehand for burying" will be told in memory of her wherever the gospel is preached (14:3–9). Perhaps the historical reality of women's lower status and the historical reality of women's discipleship together support in Mark's Gospel the surprising narrative reality of women characters who exemplify the demands of followership, from bold faith in Jesus' life-giving power to self-giving in parallel to, or in recognition of, his self-denying death. Perhaps women characters are especially appropriate for the role of illuminating followership because in the Markan community women were in a position to bear most poignantly the message that among followers the "first will be last, and the last first" (10:31).[50]

A fifth narrative context of the story of the poor widow is the context of Jesus as teacher. Several verbal clues in Mark 12:41–44 underline Jesus' words about the poor widow as a significant teaching. The pericope opens by noting that Jesus was "sitting." Sitting was the authoritative position of the rabbis while teaching. Jesus is sitting in the boat on the sea (4:1) as he speaks to the crowd in parables in chapter 4, an extended teaching discourse with interesting parallels to chapter 13, where Jesus is sitting on the Mount of Olives (13:3) as he speaks to four of the disciples about the eschaton. Jesus called his disciples (*proskaleō*) to himself in the temple treasury as he had earlier called them from the Sea of Galilee (1:16–20) and

---

50. In reference to *actual* widows (i.e., not characters in stories) in the early church (from the time of Jesus to 325 C.E.), Bowman Thurston notes: "The widow was an effective agent in a spiritual transaction within the Christian community. First, she interceded for the community. Her prayers perhaps sanctified the gifts brought to her. Second, the example of her life of sacrifice provided the community with a living reminder of their Lord's sacrifice" (*The Widows*, 111).

on the mountain where he appointed twelve (3:13–19) and in preparation for sending them out (6:7) and for feeding the five thousand (8:1).

The three references to Jesus' calling his disciples immediately prior to the reference at 12:43 are especially revealing in their juxtaposition of calling, saying to them, on one occasion sitting, and teaching about self-giving service. Mark 8:34 reads: "And calling the crowd with his disciples, he said to them, 'If any one intends to follow after me, let that one renounce himself or herself and take up his or her cross and follow me.'" Mark 9:35 reads: "And sitting, he called the twelve, and he said to them, 'If any one intends to be first, that one will be last of all and servant of all.'" And 10:42–45 reads:

> And Jesus, calling them, said to them, "You know that those supposed to govern the peoples lord it over them, and the great among them domineer them. But it is not so among you; but whoever would wish to become great among you will be your servant, and whoever would wish to be first among you will be slave of all. For the Son of humanity also came not to be served but to serve, and to give his life as a ransom for the many."[51]

Finally, Jesus prefaces his statement about the widow's gift of her all with "Amen" (RSV, "Truly"), as he does also on a dozen other significant occasions, including "Amen, I say to you, whoever gives you a cup of water . . . will by no means lose his reward" (9:41), and "Amen, I say to you, there is no one who has left house or brothers or sisters . . . who will not receive a hundredfold . . ." (10:29–30). The Jesus who sits and calls and says, "Amen, I say to you" is Jesus the teacher, and the moment

---

51. Author's translations in this paragraph. Although a parallel between 10:45 and 12:44 is clear from the larger narrative contexts, the words for "life" differ: at 10:45 it is *psychē*, "life" or "animating principle," and at 12:44 it is *bios*, "life" or "means of living."

so portrayed is a solemn proclamation about the kingdom—its coming now and in the future, its Messiah, and the demands and rewards that fall to the followers of such a Messiah of such a kingdom. Giving one's "whole life" is required of this Messiah, and it may also be required of his followers.

A sixth and final narrative context of the poor widow's story to which I wish to draw attention is the overall pattern of Markan characterization. As I have suggested elsewhere, the author of Mark wishes to show who Jesus is and who Jesus' followers are. To do this he schematizes the characters of his story; he paints extreme cases of enemies and exemplars as the background against which the trials and joys of followers may stand out more boldly.[52] The enemies and exemplars are similar in their "flat," one-sided characterization;[53] they differ in their negative or positive value as models for the reader. The unclean spirits and demons, as well as most of the Jewish leaders, are "flat" and "bad." The minor characters, or "little people,"[54] tend to be "flat" and "good." The twelve disciples, however, are "round," or multisided in their characterization, and also multivalent as models: they present both positive *and* negative models for the reader to follow or to avoid. It would be inappropriate to focus on the "goodness" of the poor widow in opposition to the "badness" of the twelve disciples without also

---

52. Elizabeth Struthers Malbon, "The Jewish Leaders in the Gospel of Mark: A Literary Study of Marcan Characterization," *JBL* 108 (1989): 279, see 275–81 [here chapter 5].

53. The terms "flat" and "round" are associated with E. M. Forster, *Aspects of the Novel* (New York: Harcourt, Brace & Co., 1927; reprint, 1954), 103–18.

54. The phrase is employed by David Rhoads and Donald Michie, *Mark as Story: An Introduction to the Narrative of a Gospel* (Philadelphia: Fortress, 1982), 129–35. However, the phrase is not continued in the second edition of *Mark as Story* (Minneapolis: Fortress, 1999), with Joanna Dewey added as second author; rather, the category is simply labeled "People"; significant revisions are also made to the entire discussion of minor characters.

observing her "flatness" in contrast to their "roundness." All the Markan characters work together for the sake of the Markan story, its teller, and its hearers. Thus the little story of the poor widow who gives "her whole life" is thoroughly integrated into the larger Markan story of who Jesus is and what it means to be his follower.

Multiple Readings

There may well be other narrative contexts that would contribute significantly to our understanding of the story of the poor widow in Mark, but these six are more than enough to illustrate my methodological point. The three commentaries I have surveyed here (Swete, Taylor, Nineham) represent three different foci in New Testament studies: the historical Jesus, the oral tradition of the early church, the redactional (or editorial) activities of the evangelists. Each makes some contribution to our understanding of the poor widow's story. It helps in a basic sort of way to know of the existence of *Shopharoth* and the value of *lepta*, but it does not take us far in the task of interpretation. It is most interesting to know of a quite parallel Jewish story, but looking elsewhere for parallel teachings of Jesus may have led us astray as *interpreters of this text*. It is enlightening to consider the widow's story in its broader context of Mark's telling of Jesus' story. Wright's article represents a literary approach seeking to be free of prior theological presuppositions, and for that I offer praise, not a lament. Yet my own brief analysis moves beyond Wright's in calling attention to six literary or narrative contexts and especially in leaving open the possibility of additional relevant contexts, seeking neither *the* proper context nor *the* final interpretation.

All the readers mentioned here have read the Markan text, 12:41–44, in context—some context, but a contextual reading in itself provides no guarantee of the adequacy of a textual interpretation. *The* context does not exist, and a text's multiple contexts seem to raise as many interpretive questions as they answer. Yet, to understand the text we must have contextual readings, and multiple contextual readings, and, in most cases, multiple contextual *readers.* The critical question is how to interrelate the multiple readings of a single text that result from multiple interpreters focusing on multiple contexts. How do we listen to and talk with each other about our different or differing observations? Does our wealth of scholarly readings overwhelm other readers? Are we rich in diverse readings and poor in our overall understanding of the situation of reading itself?

James Kincaid, writing in *Critical Inquiry,* has observed that "Readers proceed with the assumption that there must be a single dominant structuring principle and that it is absurd to imagine more than one such dominant principle."[55] But texts themselves resist such "coherence," as he calls it: "most texts, at least, are, in fact, demonstrably incoherent, presenting us not only with multiple organizing patterns but with organizing patterns that are competing, logically inconsistent"—with "a structure of mutually competing coherences."[56] The story of the poor widow in its Markan contexts seems not quite so extreme, but Kincaid's general observation applies nevertheless. As he argues against the text's single determinant meaning, Kincaid is not arguing for the text's indeterminacy.[57] These seem to him, and to me as well, false alternatives. We are not free to assume that the text can mean anything just because it can mean many things.

Perhaps the image of advocacy, from the field of law, can shed light on the situation of juggling and judging multiple contextual readings. Perhaps we interpreters are like attorneys

55. James R. Kincaid, "Coherent Readers, Incoherent Texts," *Critical Inquiry* 3 (1977): 781–802; quotation from 783.

56. Ibid., 783.

57. Ibid., 789–90. [With this chapter's conclusion, cf. pp. 124–30 above.]

defending our clients (our contextual readings), always dedicated to our own clients' best interests. One obvious advantage of this metaphor is that it makes room for areas of expertise; if one wanted to argue an interpretive case concerning the relative value of *lepta*, one would surely retain Swete as a consultant. Another useful application of the metaphor is this: just as attorneys have limited free choice of their clients (specialty, location, financial needs or desires dictate accepting some clients; others may be assigned by the court system), so many interpreters select the context or contexts on which they focus neither at random nor with perfect freedom and fully conscious deliberation (I doubt that the feeling of being "drawn" by one's approach—or one's text—is rare). In addition, the image of advocacy suggests the strength of the bond between an interpreter and his or her contextual reading. But the legal analogy breaks down in the end. Scholarly debates, although sometimes heated, are not basically adversarial situations. To suggest that one contextual focus or one contextual reading could be adjudicated "innocent" and another "guilty" assumes not only an acknowledged judge and jury of interpretation but also a standard that all are sworn to uphold: *the* (right, best, whatever) context. In fact, it may make more sense to conceive of the text as the client of all its interpreters, in which case our common advocacy defuses our adversarial relations. Thus the advocacy image is inadequate.

A second image that might provide direction as we struggle to interrelate multiple contexts of multiple readings is neither as concrete nor as striking as the first, but it may prove more useful. It is the image of complication. Jonathan Z. Smith has asserted that the "historian's task is to complicate, not to clarify."[58] Perhaps the same might be said not only of the task of the interpreter but of that of the text as well. Texts, at least

---

58. Jonathan Z. Smith, *Map Is Not Territory: Studies in the History of Religions* (Leiden: Brill, 1978), 129.

"good" texts, "classic" texts, including most biblical texts, "complicate" readings of themselves. Thus interpreters of such texts take up their task from the text itself: to "complicate," not to "clarify," interpretation. The process of "complication" requires dialogue, listening as well as speaking. As Dominick LaCapra has observed: "The point here is to do everything in one's power not to avoid argument but to make argument as informed, vital, and undogmatically open to counterargument as possible," although "the process of gaining perspective on our own interpretations does not exclude the attempt to arrive at an interpretation we are willing to defend."[59]

LaCapra's words (argument, counterargument, defend) return us to the other image, advocacy, which, despite its final limitations, is not without useful application. I am willing to *defend* my reading of the poor widow's story in multiple narrative contexts as more revealing of the text's depth and power than Wright's reading of it in its most immediate narrative context. But I am also willing to appreciate how Wright's reading *complicates* numerous other readings that I am, it is true, less able to appreciate because they seem to import a context in which the poor widow serves as an exemplum for a stewardship campaign. Poor widow, indeed; poor woman to be so trivialized by being placed on the wrong pedestal!

But poor readers, indeed, are we, if we cannot deal with a wealth of readings as "complications" of one another because of our own need to "clarify." Not that all readings are equal. Some are richer, some are poorer. But many are worth more than two *lepta*, and the dynamic *process* of reading and of reading readings may be for some of us worth a "whole life."

---

59. Dominick LaCapra, *Rethinking Intellectual History: Texts, Contexts, Language* (Ithaca, N.Y.: Cornell University Press, 1983), 38, 45.

7

The Major Importance of the Minor Characters in Mark

Not everyone who theorizes about biblical narrative investigates characterization per se.[1] Robert Funk, for example, in his monumental *Poetics of Biblical Narrative*[2] focuses on plot, with detailed attention to segmentation of narrative units and sequences of narrative events. One who looks up "characters"

---

1. I wish to acknowledge the major importance of some minor characters in my life as I began to reduce to writing these thoughts on Markan minor characters: (1) the contributors to *Characterization in Biblical Literature* (*Semeia* 63 [Atlanta: Scholars Press, 1993]), which I have edited with Adele Berlin, containing nine essays and four responses dealing with theory and exegesis of characterization in the Hebrew Bible and the New Testament, and especially Adele Berlin, who graciously extended her editorial service to read this essay; (2) Joel F. Williams, who sent me a copy of his dissertation, "Other Followers of Jesus: The Characterization of the Individuals from the Crowd in Mark's Gospel" (Ph.D. diss., Marquette University, 1992), now published as *Other Followers of Jesus: Minor Characters as Major Figures in Mark's Gospel*, JSNTSup 102 (Sheffield: JSOT Press, 1994). Since my essay was completed before the publication of Williams's book, all citations to Williams here are to the unpublished version of his dissertation.

2. Robert W. Funk, *The Poetics of Biblical Narrative* (Sonoma, Calif.: Polebridge Press, 1988).

in Funk's index is referred to "participants." Characters are not abstracted from the plot and examined in themselves or in relation to one another but are considered only as participants in narrative events.

Not everyone who investigates characterization in biblical narrative attends to the role and significance of "minor" characters. Meir Sternberg, for example, in his equally monumental *Poetics of Biblical Narrative*[3] devotes two chapters (9 and 10) to characterization, and three columns of entries under "character" and "characterization" appear in the index. Yet "minor" characters are not specifically discussed, anonymous characters are considered "faceless,"[4] "typal" characters are said to be resisted in the (Hebrew) Bible,[5] and greatest attention is given the relation between "the truth" (i.e., "explicit statements made about character") and "the whole truth" (i.e., "the secrets and consequences of character"[6]) with regard to such major characters as the patriarchs and Saul, David, and Absalom.

Some who do attend to the role and significance of "minor" characters in biblical narrative misconstrue these on the basis of overgeneralization on the one hand or dismissive labeling on the other. David Rhoads and Donald Michie, for example, overgeneralize that "minor characters in the gospel [of Mark] consistently exemplify the values of the rule of God" and that the "narrator consistently introduces the little people favorably."[7]

---

3. Meir Sternberg, *The Poetics of Biblical Narrative: Ideological Literature and the Drama of Reading* (Bloomington: Indiana University Press, 1985).

4. Ibid., 330.

5. Ibid., e.g., 347–48, 362.

6. Ibid., 321.

7. David Rhoads and Donald Michie, *Mark as Story: An Introduction to the Narrative of a Gospel* (Philadelphia: Fortress, 1982), 129, 130. These statements do not appear in the second edition of *Mark as Story* (Minneapolis: Fortress, 1999), with Joanna Dewey added as second author. The section on "People" (not "The Little People") is considerably revised.

As we shall see below, the Markan depiction of minor characters is more complex than that. Markan redaction critics, at the other extreme, frequently ignore or dismiss the minor characters because they are generally labeled as coming from "the tradition" rather than from "the redaction."[8] Perhaps contemporary readers have a tendency to dismiss minor characters because they are "flat"—one-dimensional, static, stereotypical—rather than "round"—multidimensional, developing, individual.[9] However, not only must attention to characterization be integrated with analysis of plot, settings, rhetoric, and so on, but also all the characters—"minor" as well as "major"—must be observed in relation with one another if we are to be competent and sensitive readers of biblical narratives.

What makes a Markan character minor rather than major? It is some lack. Is it the lack of a name? Minor characters frequently are anonymous: the leper, the poor widow, the centurion. But minor characters may also be named: Bartimaeus, Simon of Cyrene, Joseph of Arimathea. Is it a lack of a "rounded" portrayal? Minor characters are frequently "flat": trusting suppliants and antagonistic demons. But "flat" characters are not always minor: the Markan "Pharisees" are one-dimensional in their opposition to Jesus, but that opposition is critical to the movement of the plot; the "Pharisees" are not minor characters. Is it the lack of a contribution to the major plot line that makes a character minor? This is much more difficult to judge, since it would require, at least, clear delineation of the major plot line. If the major plot line of Mark were considered the outworking of who Jesus is as "Christ, the Son of God" (1:1), would those who, as recipients of his healing power, bring out his authority and those who bring about his death, and thus enable him to give his life as a ransom for the

---

8. See Williams, "Other Followers," 28–31.

9. The terms "flat" and "round" are from E. M. Forster, *Aspects of the Novel* (New York: Harcourt, Brace & Co., 1927; reprint, 1954).

many (10:45), be minor characters? If the major plot line were considered the outworking of who Jesus is *and* what following him entails, even fewer characters could be labeled "minor." It does seem, however, that minor characters tend to present commentary on the plot more than contribute to its movement; yet the role of providing narrative commentary is not unique to minor characters. Neither anonymity nor "flatness" demarcates "minor" characters. And "contribution to the major plot line" is not a clear enough criterion to prove useful.

For my purposes a "minor" character is one who lacks a continuing or recurrent presence in the story as narrated. For the most part, minor characters appear only once: the Gerasene demoniac, the Syrophoenician woman, the anointing woman. Occasionally minor characters appear two or three times.[10] If the appearances of Jesus' family at 3:21 and 3:31–32 are considered two separate scenes, rather than (as is more usual) one scene into which a scene with the scribes has been intercalated (3:22–30), then Jesus' family (3:21)—or mother and brothers (3:31)—appears twice. If "the centurion" whom

---

10. The nonhuman characters, which will not be discussed here (but see n. 22 below), appear—or are alluded to—more than three times each: Satan (1:13; 3:23 twice, 26; 4:15; 8:33), demons (1:34 twice, 39; 3:15, 22 twice; 6:13; 7:26, 29, 30; 9:38), unclean spirits (1:23, 26, 27; 3:11, 30; 5:2, 8, 13; 6:7; 7:25; 9:17, 20, 25 twice), the (Holy) Spirit (1:8, 10, 12; 3:29; 12:36; 13:11), and God (speaking: 1:11; 9:7; alluded to: numerous references). The crowd (*ochlos*), which appears many times, is a special case, and I have commented on it elsewhere ("Disciples/Crowds/Whoever: Markan Characters and Readers," *NovT* 28 [1986]: 104–30 [here chapter 3]). Thus neither the nonhuman characters nor the crowd lack a continuing or recurrent presence in the story as narrated. The Sadducees appear only once (12:18), but because this appearance is part of a series of appearances of religious leaders (11:27–12:27) I have found it more appropriate to discuss them as part of the general category of (Jewish) religious leaders ("The Jewish Leaders in the Gospel of Mark: A Literary Study of Marcan Characterization," *JBL* 108 [1989]: 259–81 [here chapter 5]) than as a minor character group.

Pilate summons to confirm Jesus' death (15:44) is the same centurion who commented at his death, "Truly this man was Son of God" (15:39), and if the death and the confirmation of it are considered two scenes (narrative material does intervene), then this minor character appears twice—in close succession. If the *neaniskos* (young man) who flees naked at Gethsemane (14:51–52) and the *neaniskos* who greets the women at the tomb (16:5) were to be considered the same character—a much more dubious denotative hypothesis, although the two reverberate connotatively—this minor character would appear twice. The women characters who appear at the crucifixion (15:40–41), at the burial (15:47), and at the empty tomb (16:1–8) are a more complicated case. Three are named in the first and third instances, and two in the second; and the second Mary (not Mary Magdalene) is named in three slightly different ways. These three scenes are consecutive, so by their presence in them these women characters do not really achieve a continuing presence in the story as narrated. What is most complicated, of course, is that the narrator comments at 15:41 that women, including the three named characters, did have a continuing presence in the story in Galilee that was *not narrated*. These named women characters would thus meet my criterion for minor characters—characters who lack a continuing or recurrent presence in the story as narrated—although they also challenge that criterion, as they challenge much else in a reading of Mark's Gospel.

My present goal is to suggest—illustratively, not exhaustively—that the minor characters of Mark do have major importance. (1) They, alongside the major characters, extend the continuum of potential responses to Jesus in an open-ended way, providing implicit narrative comparisons and contrasts with the responses of the continuing or recurrent characters and providing a bridge from the (internal) characters to the (borderline) implied audience. (2) They mark where the implied audience is to pause, reflect, connect; that is, they provide overall narrative punctuation—parentheses, exclamation points, and colons especially. As is probably already clear in my way of stating these functions, and as will become increasingly clear in my discussion of them, they are entirely intertwined.

Extending the Response Continuum

A narrative represents a communication event that involves an author (real and implied), a text (read or heard), an audience (implied and real, listening or reading), and various contexts (historical, literary, social, etc.). All the characters internal to the narrative exist not for their own sakes but for the sake of the communication between author and audience external to the narrative, with the implied author and implied audience marking the boundary between. The implied author and the implied audience are abstract constructions made by external interpreters on the basis of internal clues. It is important to acknowledge the dynamic relationship between external interpreters and internal clues; implied readers mask real people (you and me) who construct them on the basis of their readings of the text.[11] I read Mark's Gospel as not only the story of Jesus as the Christ, the Son of God, but also the story of others' responses to him in that role. In this book I have been investigating the characters around the Markan Jesus, especially the religious leaders and the disciples or followers. Here, at its close, I wish to show how the minor characters extend the continuum of responses to Jesus that these major characters present.

---

11. See Marianne Meye Thompson, "'God's Voice You Have Never Heard, God's Form You Have Never Seen': The Characterization of God in the Gospel of John," *Semeia* 63 (1993): 177–204, esp. 184.

Enemies and Fallible Followers

The Jewish leaders—including scribes; Pharisees (and Herodians); chief priests, scribes, and elders; and the high priest—respond to Jesus almost overwhelmingly as enemies. Early and continuing conflicts and arguments (see especially 2:1–3:6 and 11:27–12:27) lead to plots to destroy Jesus (see 3:6 and 14:1–2), which lead in turn to a Jewish trial and condemnation as prelude to a Roman crucifixion. Mark's narrative clearly depicts the Jewish *leaders* as a whole, and not the Jewish *people*, as enemies to Jesus. Nearly all the characters in the Markan narrative are Jewish, and from them come friends and followers as well as foes of Jesus. Thus it makes more sense to refer to the *religious* leaders than to the Jewish leaders. Nor are the religious leaders portrayed unilaterally as enemies; there are significant exceptions. Jairus, "one of the leaders of the synagogue" (5:22), is exceptional in his faith in comparison with the religious leaders as a whole; he is more like many of the minor characters who exemplify faith in Jesus' healing power; in fact, his story is intercalated with the story of one such minor character, the hemorrhaging woman. The story of the exceptional scribe who commends and is commended by Jesus (12:28–34) comes as a surprising contrast after a series of conflicts between Jesus and various religious leaders (11:27–12:27). Joseph of Arimathea, "a respected member of the council [*bouleutēs*]" (15:43), is also an exceptional religious leader, performing the role of a disciple in burying his master (cf. 6:29, John's disciples), rather than the role of the enemy taken on by "the whole council [*synedrion*]" who "held a consultation [*symboulion*]" (15:1). The anticlerical or antiestablishment stereotyping of the Markan narrative is very much a part of its early Christian context, but Mark's Gospel challenges rather than absolutizes that stereotyping by narrating the disciplelike and exemplary actions of Jairus, one of the scribes, and Joseph of Arimathea. It is not a character's social group that is decisive for the Markan narrative, but the character's response to Jesus.

An enduring debate in contemporary Markan scholarship is whether the disciples in Mark are portrayed negatively or positively, or, better, whether the disciples, with their positive and negative aspects, are portrayed polemically or pastorally.[12] I am not at all convinced by the polemical interpretations that the disciples are "transparent" to some historical enemies of the real author of Mark,[13] and I have argued elsewhere for the pastoral interpretation.[14] The disciples are fallible followers— strong in their callings but also misunderstanding of the nature of Jesus' Messiahship and, as they begin to understand, frightened of the implications for their own followership. The implied author encourages in the implied audience both identification with and judgment of the disciples as a way of eliciting self-judgment and offering hope. Because even Jesus' chosen twelve found it difficult to follow Jesus, the latter-day followers (the implied audience) must take care. But if Jesus never gave up on the twelve, then there is hope for the implied audience as well.

Hope and critique, identification and judgment, are not direct opposites. "Identification with" characters is not simply equivalent to "admiration of" them, and "judgment of" a character group does not necessarily mean "dissociation from" it. I am in firm disagreement with interpreters who assume that the audience identifies only with the characters with pos-

---

12. See, e.g., Williams, "Other Followers," 31–44; C. Clifton Black, *The Disciples according to Mark: Markan Redaction in Current Debate*, JSNTSup 27 (Sheffield: Sheffield Academic Press, 1989).

13. Cf. Williams, "Other Followers," 44–48.

14. Elizabeth Struthers Malbon, "Fallible Followers: Women and Men in the Gospel of Mark," *Semeia* 28 (1983): 29–48; Malbon, "Disciples/Crowds/Whoever"; Malbon, "Texts and Contexts: Interpreting the Disciples in Mark," *Semeia* 62 (1993): 81–102 [here chapters 2, 3, and 4].

itive traits or only with one character or character group—or even only with one character or character group at a time. The key issue for the implied audience is *not* identification with positive characters versus dissociation from negative characters (as Williams assumes) but developing sympathy, empathy, and community particularly with the paradoxical characters within a range of characters and character groups.

The implied audience is encouraged both to identify with and to judge the fallible followers of Jesus, and the category of fallible followers is open-ended in Mark. It can include the women at the cross and tomb;[15] it stretches outward from the disciples to the crowd to "whoever"—"whoever does the will of God" (3:35), "whoever gives you a cup of water to drink because you bear the name of Christ" (9:41).[16] It provides a bridge from the characters internal to the narrative to the implied audience at the boundary of the narrative and the external world.

Enemies and fallible followers are two general categories of respondents to the Markan Jesus. Religious leaders are generally, but not always, depicted as enemies. The disciples, but not the disciples alone, are portrayed as fallible followers; and "fallible followers" itself is a paradoxical category. The open-endedness of the categories is crucial to the Markan narrative. An assumed enemy, like council member Joseph of Arimathea, can take on the actions of a disciple, an exemplary follower. And Judas, "one of the twelve" (14:10, 20, 43), can become such a *fallible* follower that he gives essential aid to Jesus' enemies. What is implied in Mark is more a response continuum—from enemies to fallible followers—than rigid, stereotyped categories of characters. The minor characters extend that response continuum.

---

15. Malbon, "Fallible Followers" [here chapter 2].

16. See Malbon, "Disciples/Crowds/Whoever," 124–26 [here chapter 3].

Exemplars

As the religious leaders are *generally* depicted as enemies of Jesus in Mark, and the disciples are *generally* portrayed as fallible followers, so the minor characters are *most often* presented as exemplars. In their brief moments of narrative time they serve as models for attitudes and behaviors appropriate also for the major characters of the narrative and especially for the implied audience. The division of Mark's narrative into two parts, often observed in relation to narrative space (Galilee/Jerusalem[17]) or the unfolding of Jesus' Messiahship (power/suffering), is obvious as well with regard to the minor characters as exemplars.

In the first half of the narrative the minor characters exemplify primarily faith in Jesus' healing power. Healing and exorcism stories tend to be narrated in pairs, and sometimes in triplets, in ways that suggest inclusiveness of males and females, Jews and Gentiles, among those who have faith in the in-breaking power of the kingdom of God manifest in the Markan Jesus. A male with an unclean spirit is healed in the (public) synagogue in Capernaum (1:21–28); a female with a fever is healed in a (private) home in Capernaum (1:29–31). A leper expresses his faith by imploring Jesus, "If you choose, you can make me clean" (1:40), and the friends of a paralytic express their faith by digging through the roof to present their paralyzed friend to Jesus for healing (2:4–5). Although an attitude of faith may also be implied on behalf of the man with a withered hand (3:1–6), the conflict theme completely overwhelms this healing narrative. The Gerasene demoniac is male and Gentile; Jairus's daughter and the hemorrhaging

---

17. See Elizabeth Struthers Malbon, *Narrative Space and Mythic Meaning in Mark*, New Voices in Biblical Studies (San Francisco: Harper & Row, 1986; reprint, The Biblical Seminar 13; Sheffield: Sheffield Academic Press, 1991).

woman, whose stories are intercalated, are female and Jewish. Since these three healings are especially difficult ones (the Gerasene was so desperately ill that he lived among the tombs, the woman had been hemorrhaging for twelve years, and Jairus's daughter died while Jesus was en route), they serve to exemplify Jesus' mighty power and the certainty that the kingdom of God has come near. The two intercalated healings also serve to exemplify the profound faith of Jairus and the woman (see esp. 5:23, 28). Jesus' words to the woman are not lost on the implied audience: "your faith has made you well" (5:34).

The Syrophoenician woman is, obviously, female and Gentile; and her faith—and boldness and cleverness—in pleading for her daughter echoes, and elaborates, that of the male Jew, Jairus, in pleading for his. The healing of the most definitely Gentile woman in the region of Tyre (7:24–30) is followed almost immediately by the healing of a very possibly Gentile man in the region of the Decapolis (7:31–37). The response of the crowd, a usual aspect of healing stories, in the case of the deaf-mute of the Decapolis is unusually elaborated, serving, it turns out, as the conclusion to a certain kind of healing story in Mark: "They were astounded beyond measure, saying, 'He has done everything well; he even makes the deaf to hear and the mute to speak'" (7:37). From the exorcism of the man with the unclean spirit in the Capernaum synagogue to the healing of the deaf-mute in the Decapolis, the Markan Jesus has done all things well. He has exemplified his power and authority as the Christ, the Son of God, the proclaimer and bringer of the kingdom of God. Only minor characters, never major characters such as the disciples or the religious leaders, are healed by Jesus in the Markan narrative, and the minor characters whom he has healed exemplify faith in Jesus' power and authority. Their stories of faith and healing are absolutely essential to Mark's story of Jesus as the Christ. Their responses of exemplary faith extend the Markan response continuum: from enemies to fallible followers to exemplars.

While in the first half of Mark minor characters appear primarily as suppliants, in the second half they appear in that role only three times, and all of these occur in the middle section, 8:22–10:52: the blind man of Bethsaida, the father of the "epileptic" boy, and blind Bartimaeus of Jericho. Commentators generally recognize the symbolic significance of the two stories of giving sight to the blind, made more obvious by their functioning as a frame around the section in which the Markan Jesus is attempting to give his disciples insight into his passion— and theirs. But the symbolic significance of the story of the healing of the epileptic boy, embedded as it is in this same section, generally goes unmentioned. The healing story begins with double manifestations of fallibility: the disciples have failed in their attempt to cast out the unclean spirit (9:17–18), and Jesus expresses his frustration with the faithlessness of the entire generation (9:19). Rather than being a straightforward exemplar of faith, the epileptic's father presents dramatically the image of a fallible follower: "I believe; help my unbelief!" (9:24).

The sequence of scenes in 8:22–10:52 focused on minor characters but bearing symbolic significance not only for the major characters but also for the implied audience is impressive. The two-stage healing of the blind man at Bethsaida (8:22–26) prepares the implied audience for a second stage of seeing and understanding, one that the major character Peter has not yet reached (8:27–33). The healing of the epileptic boy (9:14–29) also takes place in two stages: the disciples' attempt at healing fails, Jesus' attempt succeeds. The boy's father is caught between faith and unfaith; he seeks to follow in faith, but he is fallible. However, his request *is* granted by Jesus; the Markan Jesus does not give up on one struggling between faith and unfaith. Fallibility is forgiven. The final healing story in the second half of Mark is that of blind Bartimaeus of Jericho, who is an exemplar not only of faith and perfect sight but also of followership: he "followed him [Jesus] on the way" (10:52). But before the story of Bartimaeus there occurs one more story of a minor character—not a healing story, but the encounter of Jesus and the rich man. After a conversation about eternal life and the commandments, Jesus asks the rich man to give up his possessions and "come, follow me" (10:21). This is a call—not unlike the call of the four fishermen (1:16–20) or the call of Levi (2:13–17)—but the rich man turns away. Interpreters have observed that the so-called healing story of Bartimaeus manifests many aspects of a call story.[18] Whereas the rich man abandons an explicit call, Bartimaeus follows one that is only implicit. Two minor characters, the blind man of Bethsaida and the epileptic boy's father, not unlike the major character Peter, struggle betwixt and between—between sight and no sight, between faith and no faith. One minor character, the rich man, not unlike Judas, turns away from the struggle. And one minor character, Bartimaeus, perhaps as a special invitation to the implied audience,[19] follows on the way, the way of discipleship, the way to Jerusalem.

The implied audience approaches Jerusalem with Bartimaeus (10:52–11:1). For the remainder of the Markan narrative the minor characters are not suppliants who exemplify faith in Jesus' healing power but exemplars who model service, sacrifice, and recognition of Jesus' identity as Teacher, Christ (Messiah), Son

---

18. See Williams, "Other Followers," 228–44.

19. For Williams, Bartimaeus becomes the pivotal "individual from the crowd" in Mark's Gospel, portrayed as "both an exemplary figure and a transitional figure" (ibid., 228). According to Williams, Bartimaeus's story marks the place where "the reader" begins to associate with a series of exemplary individuals from the crowd and to dissociate from the disciples, although still maintaining sympathy for them (253; see 227–54). My view of the idea of association versus dissociation was stated above. I find that Williams inflates the "unique" position of Bartimaeus, dismissing Levi—who also follows Jesus—as an individual from the crowd (155 n. 36) and underestimating the parallel between the blind man of Bethsaida and Bartimaeus as symbolic characters whose stories of healing become subsidiary to their significance as narrative representations of the nature of followership.

of God. We have mentioned above the exceptional scribe who says to Jesus, "You are right, Teacher" (12:32), and to whom Jesus says, "You are not far from the kingdom of God" (12:34). We will note below the significant framing (or parenthetical) placement of the stories of the poor widow (12:41–44) and the anointing woman (14:3–9). The poor widow symbolizes Jesus' death by giving her whole life (*holon ton bion autēs*, 12:44); the anointing woman prepares for Jesus' death by anointing his body beforehand for burial (14:8). It is also entirely possible that the implied audience sees in her action of anointing Jesus' head a recognition of Jesus as the Christ (Greek), the Messiah (Hebrew), "the anointed one." It is paradoxical, to say the least, for the Messiah to be anointed by an unnamed woman in a leper's house (14:3) rather than by the high priest in the temple, but Mark's Gospel has nothing against paradox!

The centurion's role as a minor character is certainly paradoxical: he assisted with Jesus' crucifixion, and then, when he saw how Jesus "breathed his last, he said, 'Truly this man was Son of God!'" (15:39, author's translation). The scene is a dramatization of a central thrust of Mark's Gospel: Jesus is a suffering messiah; Jesus can only be truly seen as Son of God when this reality is experienced. It is paradoxical that one of the executioners expresses this experience. It is paradoxical that a minor character completes the halfway confession of a major character (Peter, 8:27–33). It may even be paradoxical that the centurion, like the chief priests and the scribes who mocked Jesus on the cross as "the Christ, the King of Israel" (15:32), does not comprehend the significance of his own words within the narrative. But I find it a more natural reading to assume that the centurion is portrayed as knowing what he is saying,[20] just as the anointing woman is depicted as know-

---

20. Cf. R. H. Lightfoot, "The Connexion of Chapter Thirteen with the Passion Narrative," in *The Gospel Message of St. Mark* (Oxford: Clarendon, 1950), 48–59, esp. 56–57.

ing what she is doing. His words and her actions, like the actions of the poor widow, of course, take on for the implied audience a symbolic significance; these minor characters are exemplars of the paradox of suffering service as a manifestation of the power of the kingdom of God.

With the remaining minor characters in the Markan narrative we continue this major paradox and add the paradoxical application of quite specific names to minor characters we would have expected, on the basis of the preceding narrative, to be anonymous: Simon of Cyrene, the father of Alexander and Rufus; Joseph of Arimathea; Mary Magdalene; Mary the mother of James the younger and of Joses; and Salome. Simon of Cyrene, described simply as "a passer-by, who was coming in from the country" (15:21), suffers and serves by carrying Jesus' cross to Golgotha (15:21–22). The implied audience can easily be supposed to hear in this action an echo of Jesus' words: "If any want to become my followers, let them deny themselves and take up their cross and follow me" (8:34). Joseph of Arimathea, described amazingly as "a respected member of the council"—presumably the council that had turned Jesus over to Pilate (15:1)—"who was also himself waiting expectantly for the kingdom of God" (15:43)—with echoes of the exceptional scribe "not far from the kingdom of God" (12:34)—suffers and serves by bearing the expense, the labor, and the risk of burying Jesus' body (15:42–46). Mary Magdalene and the other Mary watch the burial (15:47), as they, and also Salome, had watched the crucifixion (15:40–41). The three women take action in the following scene. Their suffering is grieving; their offered service is to complete the hurried burial by anointing the body. Of course there is no body in the tomb to anoint, the symbolic anointing having been sufficient for the narrative. The specificity of personal names—as well as place names and times—focuses the attention of the implied audience on the passion of Jesus. Minor characters serve not only as witnesses but also as exemplars of the necessity and possibility of suffering service in the kingdom of God Jesus proclaims as having come near.

The narrative situation—and thus the interpretation—of the three named women at the close of the Markan Gospel is more complex than that of the other minor characters. Not only are the women present at the crucifixion *and* the burial *and* the empty tomb, whereas most minor characters appear but once, but the three named women—and nameless others—are reported, retrospectively, to have followed (*ēkolouthoun*, 15:41) Jesus and to have ministered to him (*diēkonoun*, 15:41; cf. 1:31 and 10:45) in Galilee. They were really major characters in the story behind the narration, although minor characters in the narrative itself. And like another group of major characters, the disciples, they seem sometimes to be exemplars, but are, in the end, fallible followers. The women stay with the Markan Jesus longer than the twelve, but even they look on the crucifixion "from a distance" (15:40; cf. Peter following "at a distance" at 14:54). The women come to the tomb as faithful followers, but they depart in stunned silence rather than proclaiming the young man's requested message. They too are fallible followers.[21]

Thus the minor characters around Jesus, generally presented as exemplars, occur in three sequential sets in the Markan narrative. From 1:1 through 8:21, the minor charac-

---

21. In my 1983 article focused on the woman characters of Mark ("Fallible Followers" [here chapter 2]), I discussed all the woman characters under the category of fallible followers. Although I discussed each character separately, the label fallible followers was actually applied to the entire group as a whole. I now find that the characters I described then as "Bold and Faithful Women" (hemorrhaging woman, Syrophoenician woman) and "Self-denying, Serving Women" (poor widow, anointing woman)—each of whom initiates action in a striking way, to which Jesus responds ("Fallible Followers," 35)—are better described as exemplars, while the three named women at the cross and the tomb are indeed best described as fallible followers.

ters are generally suppliants who exemplify faith in Jesus' healing power and authority as proclaimer of the kingdom of God. In 8:22 through 10:52, the middle section of Mark, three suppliants appear—all with rich connotative and symbolic significance for understanding the nature of followership, especially fallible followership—as well as the rich man who is a negative exemplar of followership. From 11:1 through 16:8, the passion story, the minor characters are generally exemplars of suffering and service as paradoxical aspects of the Messiahship of Jesus and the kingdom of God, although Pilate and the soldiers, of course, act as enemies. Like the disciples as fallible followers and the religious leaders as enemies, the minor characters as exemplars manifest a certain rhythm in their appearance, but the rhythm of each group is distinctive. If the disciples may be said, schematically, to move from their best, to worse, to their worst, and the religious leaders from bad to worse to the worst, then the minor characters as exemplars might be said to move from good to mixed to best. The implied author is concerned to illustrate who Jesus is as the Christ and who can be his followers and how. As the disciples increasingly manifest the difficulty of followership by their fallibility, the minor characters are increasingly called on to manifest the possibility of even difficult followership. The unfolding of the plot demands and depends on changes in the characters and groups of characters. Such changes are particularly evident with the minor characters, who are not in themselves a group, but simply a collection of characters.[22]

---

22. Because of their distinctive status, the nonhuman characters (see n. 10) are not entirely comparable to human enemies, fallible followers, and exemplars of Jesus, but if enemies represent the extreme negative value and exemplars the extreme positive value on the response continuum, the nonhuman characters might be arrayed as follows: Satan—demons and unclean spirits—enemies—fallible followers—exemplars—Holy Spirit—God.

Parallel Characters

A few minor characters are not clearly enemies, fallible followers, or exemplars in relation to the Markan Jesus; these
related characters include John the Baptizer, Herod, and
Herodias. Perhaps John could be considered an exemplar of
Jesus' proclamation since John, like Jesus, preaches repentance (1:4–5, 14–15), but John is Jesus' precursor more than
exemplar. John goes out to preach, is rejected and handed
over, and is killed; Jesus goes out to preach, is rejected and
handed over, and is killed.[23] Thus John is more accurately
described as a character parallel to Jesus than as an exemplar
(or fallible follower). John appears three times in the narrative,
but the second and third times are retrospective (1:2–8; 1:14;
6:14–29). In his final retrospective appearance John is intertwined with Herod and Herodias. Perhaps Herod could be
considered an enemy of Jesus since when Herod hears of Jesus'
activity he worries that Jesus is John (whom he beheaded) resurrected (6:14–16), and Jesus warns his disciples to "beware of
the yeast of the Pharisees and the yeast of Herod" (8:15), but
Herod is really John's enemy more than Jesus' enemy. (The
Herodians, however, in concert with the Pharisees, do act as
Jesus' enemies at 3:6 and 12:13.) Thus Herod is more accurately described as a character parallel to Pilate, Jesus' political enemy, than as a direct enemy of Jesus. By a similar
narrative analogy Herodias and her daughter are parallel to
the chief priests, scribes, and elders (the council) and the
crowd because the former (Herodias; the council) stir up the
latter (the daughter; the crowd) to influence another (Herod;
Pilate) to bring about a desired death (John's; Jesus').[24] This
parallel story, presented as a narrative flashback, is intercalated

---

23. Elizabeth Struthers Malbon, "Echoes and Foreshadowings in
Mark 4–8: Reading and Rereading," *JBL* 112 (1993): 211–30, esp.
222–23.

24. Malbon, "Fallible Followers," 46 [here chapter 2].

between the sending out and the return of Jesus' twelve disciples to preach and heal as he had done. The Markan narrative rhetoric discloses a parallel between the preaching, being rejected and handed over, and death of John, Jesus, and the disciples (see 13:9–13). At chapter 6 John is dead, Jesus is rejected (6:1–6), and the disciples are preaching. What will happen to Jesus next? What will happen to the disciples?[25]

There are other parallels between characters who can be designated enemies, fallible followers, or exemplars of Jesus, or between such characters and Jesus. An unnamed woman provides a positive parallel to Jesus by giving "her whole life" (12:44). An unnamed follower of Jesus provides a negative parallel to Jesus by striking the slave of the high priest and cutting off his ear (14:47) while Jesus is being arrested with no personal resistance to be taken to the high priest.[26] Parallels also exist between Judas who betrays Jesus and the rich man who turns away from him, and between Peter and both the half-healed blind man of Bethsaida and the half-faithful father of the epileptic boy. Peter also provides a negative parallel to Jesus in the intercalated scenes of Jesus' trial by the high priest and Peter's "trial" by one of the servant-girls of the high priest (14:53–72).[27] These parallel scenes serve to underscore the movement of Judas from fallible follower to enemy and the movement of Peter from initial exemplar (1:16–18) to most definitely fallible follower.

Thus, overall, the minor characters of the Gospel of Mark extend the response continuum by adding the category of exemplars. The characters around Jesus respond to him as

---

25. Elizabeth Struthers Malbon, "Narrative Criticism: How Does the Story Mean?" in *Mark and Method: New Approaches in Biblical Studies*, ed. Janice Capel Anderson and Stephen D. Moore (Minneapolis: Fortress, 1992), 41 [here chapter 1].

26. Malbon, "Jewish Leaders," 269 n. 34 [here chapter 5].

27. Malbon, "Fallible Followers," 46 [here chapter 2].

enemies, as fallible followers, or as exemplars. Generally the (Jewish) religious leaders respond as enemies, the disciples as fallible followers, and the minor characters as exemplars, with the continuum of responses providing the framework for understanding any particular response. But the exceptions are crucial to the narrative. Not all religious leaders exhibit enmity; a few are exemplary (Jairus, the exceptional scribe, Joseph of Arimathea). And not only religious leaders are enemies; so are political leaders (Herod, Pilate) and even one disciple (Judas). Not only disciples are fallible followers; so are some minor characters. Thus not all minor characters are exemplars; while some are fallible followers (the epileptic's father), others are enemies (Pilate, perhaps the rich man).

For the most part, the exceptional characters within a given category appear late in the Markan narrative. The passion story, an exceptional story indeed, is filled with exceptional characters: the exceptional scribe and Joseph of Arimathea are exceptions to the religious leaders as enemies; the centurion is an exception to the political leaders (Pilate and his soldiers) as enemies; Judas is an exception to the eleven disciples who, however fallible as followers, are certainly not enemies actively contributing to Jesus' death; the three named women at the cross and tomb are exceptions to the more usual exemplars because of their suggestive presentation as fallible followers. There are several obvious reasons for the late appearance of exceptional characters: (1) Unless the general expectations of characters were presented first, the exceptions would not clearly stand out as such. (2) The entire narrative turns on a reversal of expectations—not only power but suffering is a manifestation of Jesus' Messiahship and the kingdom of God. (3) The plot requires certain actions late in the narrative—for example, a centurion commenting on how Jesus died must appear at the close of the crucifixion scene. The requirements of the plot also explain why the exceptional religious leader Jairus does *not* appear late in the narrative: he is one of the leaders of the synagogue (5:22, 35), and, with Jesus' rejection in the synagogue in his *patris* ("hometown"; 6:1–6), the synagogue is left behind as a spatial setting in the Markan narrative.[28] While the more typical characters contribute to the implied audience's perception of the response continuum of enemies—fallible followers—exemplars, the exceptional characters contribute to the implied audience's sense of the dynamism and open-endedness of the response continuum. Enemies can become exemplary followers, but fallible followers can become enemies. Nothing is static. Nothing is absolute.

Narrative Punctuation

In addition to their significance in extending the continuum of responses to the Markan Jesus, minor characters often appear at significant points in the narrative. Especially when Mark's Gospel is heard rather than read, certain stories of minor characters serve to "punctuate" the narrative. Here I wish to apply this evocative metaphor of narrative punctuation to several stories of minor characters that mark where the implied audience is to pause, reflect, connect. Most familiar are paired stories serving as "parentheses" around a larger narrative unit. Other examples include stories functioning as "exclamation points" to indicate surprising end points or conclusions, or as "colons" to direct attention to narrative material that follows as an explanation or spelling out of implications. My examples are not intended to be exhaustive; nor do I intend to construct a systematic "narrative punctuation," analogous to a "narrative grammar." My goal is, rather, to complement the primarily synchronic, or paradigmatic, look (shown above) at the way minor characters extend the

---

28. See Malbon, *Narrative Space.*

response continuum by a more diachronic, or syntagmatic, look at when in the narrative sequence some stories featuring minor characters occur.

8:22–10:52

One of the most consistent observations of Markan redaction critics and literary critics has been that the material in 8:22–10:52 is artfully arranged. Three times the Markan Jesus predicts his passion and resurrection; three times the disciples display their misunderstanding (or denial of the implications of Jesus' passion for themselves, his followers); three times Jesus instructs his disciples concerning the nature of his suffering/ serving Messiahship and the parallel nature of followership. (Of course, as Jesus teaches the disciples, the implied author teaches the implied audience.) These three passion prediction units (passion prediction/misunderstanding/instruction; 8:31–9:1; 9:30–50; 10:32–45) form the well-recognized and substantial framework of 8:22–10:52, the center section of the Gospel.

Less attention has been paid to the overall arrangement of four intervening passages: Peter's confession (8:27–30), Jesus' transfiguration (9:2–13), his healing the "epileptic" boy (9:14–29), and his teaching on household themes and/or metaphors: marriage and divorce, children, riches, a new "family" (10:1–31[29]). But these four passages also appear to be significantly placed. To the question "Who is Jesus?" the story of Peter's confession gives the answer "Christ." To the question "Who is Jesus?" the story of Jesus' transfiguration gives the answer "Son of God." Manifesting Jesus as Christ, Son of God (1:1), is central to chapters 1–3 of Mark. In the midst of

---

29. See Timothy R. Carmody, "'What God Has Joined Together . . .': Mk 10:2–9 as a Metaphor for the Covenant Community" (unpublished paper, 1993).

a section structured around foreshadowings of Jesus' suffering death, the healing of the epileptic boy and the teaching on household themes and/or metaphors provide a flashback to Jesus' powerful life as healer and teacher, which is central to chapters 4–8. Minor characters come to the fore in these two scenes: the epileptic boy and, especially, his father (9:14–29) and the rich man (10:17–22).

Minor characters also come forward in the two scenes that frame this entire section—the two-stage healing of the blind man of Bethsaida (8:22–26) and the healing of blind Bartimaeus of Jericho (10:46–52)—and this framing pair has received much attention from commentators.[30] Clearly these two stories of the gift of sight, the only two such in Mark's Gospel, lead the implied audience to reflect on the gift of insight. The half-sight/half-blindness of the Bethsaida man as he sees persons as trees walking is immediately paralleled by Peter's half-sight/half-blindness as he sees Jesus as only a powerful Christ and not also a suffering servant. The man from Bethsaida receives a second healing touch directly and immediately; Peter's second healing touch is indirectly indicated (chapter 13, especially v. 9; 14:68; 16:7) for the story's future: the Markan Jesus predicts—and he is a faithful predictor of the future—that Peter "will see" him in Galilee and that Peter and others "will stand before governors and kings . . . as a testimony" to him. Bartimaeus not only receives his sight immediately and completely but also follows Jesus "on the way"—in narrative context, both the way to Jerusalem and the way of discipleship—bringing to closure 8:22–10:52 with its predominant theme of discipleship and its dominant setting of "the way." Thus these two stories of minor characters serve as a pair of parentheses or brackets around the central section of the Gospel, marking it off for audience reflection. In oral presentation such a device would be "say-able" and

---

30. See, e.g., Williams, "Other Followers," 9–24, 227–54.

"hear-able" as echoing.[31] In written form it can be presented as a simple diagram:

8:22–26	D*	healing blindness (man of Bethsaida)
8:27–30	A	Peter's confession (Who is Jesus? Christ!)
8:31–9:1	C	first passion prediction unit
9:2–13	A	Jesus' transfiguration (Who is Jesus? Son of God!)
9:14–29	B*	healing "epileptic" boy
9:30–50	C	second passion prediction unit
10:1–31	B*	teaching on household themes/metaphors
10:32–45	C	third passion prediction unit
10:46–52	D*	healing blindness (Bartimaeus of Jerusalem)

A = review of chapters 1–3 (now especially for disciples)

B = review of chapters 4–8 (now especially for disciples)

C = preview of chapters 11–16 (especially for disciples)

D = view of proper viewing

 * = involvement of minor characters

Although most of the material in 8:22–10:52 involves major characters (especially Jesus and the disciples but also the Pharisees), the crowd is never far in the background, and four minor characters come to the foreground at significant points in the narration. Two stories of renewed seeing (D*) frame the overall unit as appropriate narrative parentheses or brackets around material concerned with seeing something new. Within this frame, or echo, two additional stories of minor characters (B*) surround the middle passion prediction unit. Although many minor characters in the Markan narrative are entirely exemplary in their actions—for example, Bartimaeus, who models not only faith but also followership—the epileptic's father and the rich man are not. Nevertheless, it is entirely appropriate that, as part of a larger narrative segment in which

---

31. See Malbon, "Echoes and Foreshadowings."

the disciples struggle with the implications of following Jesus, one minor character struggles with half-belief/half-unbelief (9:24) and another turns away from following Jesus on the way (10:22). As the epileptic's father echoes the man from Bethsaida (both *do* finally receive the healing they request), so the rich man foreshadows the road not taken by Bartimaeus.

2:1–3:6

Also consistently observed by Markan interpreters is the concentric arrangement of the five conflict stories in 2:1–3:6.[32] This is a smaller narrative unit, but, like 8:22–10:52, it is framed, encircled, or echoed by a pair of stories focused on minor characters. The opening narrative of the healing of the paralytic is complemented by the closing narrative of the healing of the man's withered hand. Stories of useless legs and a useless hand set off (and are part of) stories in which Jesus' opponents, the established religious leaders, are depicted as more concerned with "useless" regulations regarding when and with whom to eat and not eat than with the persons to whom the rules are applied. The Markan Jesus, or course, triumphs in these conflicts; the legs and the hand are restored to usefulness. It is not insignificant that minor characters form the parentheses or brackets around this collection of stories that enacts the importance of just such characters in the kingdom of God the Markan Jesus proclaims has come near (1:14–15).

Obviously the echo effect of 3:1–6 (the withered hand) with 2:1–12 (the paralytic) cannot be heard until 3:1–6 has been sounded. "Framing" is a label that reflects a previously completed hearing or reading; terms such as "framing" or "narrative parentheses" are signs of rereading.[33] In the immediate

---

32. See Joanna Dewey, *Markan Public Debate: Literary Technique, Concentric Structure, and Theology in Mark 2:1–3:6*, SBLDS 48 (Chico, Calif.: Scholars Press, 1980).

33. On rereading, see Malbon, "Echoes and Foreshadowings."

process of hearing or reading Mark's Gospel, the audience first catches an echo of 1:40–45, the healing of the leper, in 2:1–12, the healing of the paralytic. In each case a person with a serious physical need comes or is brought to Jesus, and the encounter leads to restored health for the individual, a minor character who exemplifies faith in Jesus' power to heal. In the former instance the leper's open proclamation apparently creates such a clamor for Jesus' aid that he can no longer enter a town openly (1:45), a problem already noted in the narrative (1:33, 37). In the latter instance the silent dialogue with some of the scribes about Jesus' words of forgiveness to the paralytic begins to enact a conflict only implied earlier (1:22, "for he taught them as one having authority, and not as the scribes") and not fully developed until 3:6 (they "conspired . . . against him, how to destroy him").[34]

In addition to the two stories of its frame, 2:1–3:6 includes a third story focused on a minor character, who is frequently not recognized as such: Levi.[35] Levi does bear a name, of course; and the striking parallels between the narrative of his call (2:13–14) and that of Simon and Andrew and James and John (1:16–20) lead the implied audience to anticipate his name in the list of the twelve (3:13–19), but his name does not appear. Levi lacks a continuing or recurrent presence in the story as narrated. The fact that this apparent "disciple" is not among the twelve expands for the implied audience the category of Jesus' disciples or followers.

---

34. A similar first echo and second echo effect occurs at 8:22–26, the healing of the blind man of Bethsaida. The healing of the blind man has striking parallels with the healing of the deaf man in 7:31–37 (see, e.g., Robert M. Fowler, *Loaves and Fishes: The Function of the Feeding Stories in the Gospel of Mark*, SBLDS 54 [Chico, Calif.: Scholars Press, 1981], 105–12); both men suffer communicative disorders; both healings are quite physical. The two stories are not consecutive, as with 1:40–45 and 2:1–12, but in each case the second story becomes the first story in a *new* echoing—and framing—pair.

35. See, e.g., Williams, "Other Followers," 155 n. 36.

12:41–44 and 14:3–9

The eschatological discourse of the Markan Jesus is framed by stories of two exemplary women: the poor widow who gives her last two coins to the temple treasury and the woman who gives an entire jar of ointment in anointing Jesus.[36] The Markan Jesus comments that the poor widow has given "her whole life" (*holon ton bion autēs*, 12:44) and that what the anointing woman has done will be told "wherever the good news is proclaimed in the whole world" (14:9). Between these distinctive stories Jesus presents his eschatological discourse or his farewell discourse. This speech, the longest in the Markan narrative, produces a pause in the immediate narrative unfolding of Jesus' passion as it projects parallel trials and suffering for the followers of Jesus in the narrative's future. The passion of the community is to parallel the passion of Jesus;[37] the community is to see and understand its suffering in the context of Jesus' passion. Again a pair of stories focused on minor characters forms a set of parentheses or brackets around a larger narrative unit.

The frame provided by the two giving women is not as obvious as that provided by the two blind men because another small story, that of the chief priests and scribes plotting against the Markan Jesus (14:1–2), intervenes between the close of the eschatological or farewell discourse and the story of the anointing woman. In fact, the story of the exemplary woman is itself framed by two stories of evil men: the religious leaders' plot and Judas's betrayal. The contrast with Judas is especially marked: an unnamed woman gives up money for Jesus; a named man, even "one of the twelve," gives up Jesus

---

36. See Malbon, "Fallible Followers," 39 [here chapter 2], and Malbon, "The Poor Widow in Mark and Her Poor Rich Readers," *CBQ* 53 (1991): 589–604, esp. 598–99 [here chapter 6].

37. See Malbon, *Narrative Space*, 151–52.

for money.[38] The immediately following story narrates the appropriate Passover preparations of Jesus and the disciples (14:12–16), in striking contrast to the inappropriate Passover preparations of the traditional religious leaders (14:1–2). And, of course, the story of the woman who anoints Jesus "beforehand . . . for burial" (14:8) is echoed in the story of the three women who go to the tomb to anoint Jesus after his burial (16:1–8). The story of the anointing woman is a striking example of how one passage functions in multiple ways: it is a reverse parallel to the Judas story, together with which it is framed by the reverse parallels of the Passover preparations of the chief priests and the scribes and of Jesus and the disciples; it is echoed by the story of the would-be anointing women at the empty tomb (also minor characters); and, along with the story of the poor widow, it sets off a narrative unit (chapter 13) by encircling it by stories focused on minor characters.

The opening parenthesis of this set, the poor widow, also functions in multiple narrative contexts.[39] In terms of the metaphor of narrative punctuation, it functions as an exclamation point to the extended and final teaching session of Jesus in the temple, 11:27–12:44. The Markan Jesus is challenged by all the major groups of Jewish leaders: chief priests, scribes, and elders (11:27–12:12), Pharisees (and Herodians) (12:13–17), and Sadducees (12:18–27); and he beats them all at their own argumentative games. Then Jesus is questioned by one scribe alone, who turns out to be an exceptional scribe, one "not far from the kingdom of God" (12:34a). This friendly encounter with a scribe ends all questions to Jesus (12:34b), but it is succeeded by two unfavorable comments about scribes made by Jesus, underlining the exceptional attitude of the one scribe. Scribes, of course, are recurrent and continuing char-

---

38. See Malbon, "Fallible Followers," 40 [here chapter 2]; Malbon, "Poor Widow," 599 [here chapter 6].

39. See Malbon, "Poor Widow" [here chapter 6].

acters in the Markan narrative. When the one scribe steps out from that group he functions as a minor character, and his story stands in striking contrast to the immediately preceding stories of Jesus' encounters with religious leaders. The most striking contrast, the final exclamation point in this compound sentence, is then provided by the story of the poor widow. Recurrent and continuing characters, functioning as a group, engage in verbal conflict with the Markan Jesus; one individual separates himself from the group by verbal agreement with Jesus; a total outsider to the group is singled out by Jesus as a model of appropriate *action*!

The story of the poor widow also serves as a narrative colon, a colon being a punctuation mark used primarily to direct attention to material (such as a list, explanation, or quotation) that follows. What follows is Jesus' eschatological or farewell discourse, illustrating how Jesus' followers will be called on to give their whole lives, as he will, as the poor widow has done. Willingness to give oneself is called for *and possible* (12:41–44): here are the immediate circumstances in which the disciples within the narrative and the implied audience at its edge will find this to be the case (chapter 13). Thus the poor widow is both the opposite of the religious leaders of chapter 12 ("!") and the model for the disciples (and the implied audience; see esp. 13:14, 37) of chapter 13 (":").

12:41–44 and 3:31–35

Mark 3:31–35 is a scene in which Jesus' mother and brothers appear as minor characters; the passage (just as 12:41–44) serves both as an exclamation point, in relation to the material it follows, and as a colon, in relation to the material following it. The parallels between 12:41–44 and 3:31–35 extend not only to their double functions as narrative punctuation but also to the nature of the surrounding narrative material. First, both 2:1–3:6 and 11:27–12:27 narrate controversy stories, the former in Galilee, the latter in the Jerusalem temple.[40] Secondly, both 3:7–19 (3:7–19a in the English text) and 12:28–34 present a break in the pattern of controversy. In the former situation a great crowd follows Jesus; unclean spirits, who certainly are opposed to Jesus, surprisingly fall down before him, saying, "You are the Son of God"; and Jesus chooses twelve of his followers to be disciples (or apostles) in sharing his work of preaching and healing. In the latter situation an exceptional scribe is in surprising agreement with Jesus, who commends him, saying, "You are not far from the kingdom of God." Thirdly, in 3:20–35 (3:19b–35 in the English text) and 12:35–44 a character or characters juxtaposed with scribes culminates the series of encounters in an exemplary way. Finally, in chapters 4 and 13 a longer discourse of the Markan Jesus follows the example scene, bringing out its implications not only for the characters within the narrative but also for the implied audience at its border. The overarching pattern is controversy—cooperation—example (negative and positive)—implications:

2:1–3:6	controversy	11:27–12:27
3:7–19	cooperation	12:28–34
3:20–35	example	12:35–44
	(negative and positive)	
4:1–34	implications	13:1–37

No doubt it is 3:20–35 that most calls for explanation within this pattern. Commentators often note the intercalation of the coming of Jesus' family at 3:21 and 3:31–32 and the Beelzebul controversy with the scribes at 3:22–30.[41] The family of Jesus may appear twice as a minor character, yet it all but disappears from the narrative scene under the pressure, first, of the strong negative example provided by the scribes, a continuing charac-

---

40. See Dewey, *Markan Public Debate*.

41. See Malbon, "Fallible Followers," 35 [here chapter 2].

ter group, and, second, of the strong positive example provided by the metaphorical heirs of Jesus' family, "whoever does the will of God," a group that includes both characters within the narrative and especially the implied audience at the narrative's edge.[42] Although some interpreters have argued that the family of Jesus is portrayed negatively in Mark,[43] this assertion strikes me as an overreading of the three verses in which they are mentioned (3:21, 31–32). The family's motive for coming to Jesus is left ambiguous; some were saying Jesus is "outside himself" (*exestē*, 3:21), but not necessarily the family. Was the family trying to protect its honor or to protect Jesus? The narrative seems very little interested in the characters constituting the literal family of Jesus; all interest lies in those becoming part of the metaphorical family of Jesus (cf. 10:28–31), the latter of course not being limited to the former, and the former not necessarily being excluded from the latter.

Who will be followers of Jesus? Not the established religious leaders (2:1–3:6 and 11:27–12:27), and especially not the scribes (3:22–30 and 12:35–40)—with a notable exception (12:28–34, the one scribe). Not—or not just—the biological family of Jesus (3:31–35). The disciples are indeed especially chosen followers (3:13–19). But "whoever does the will of God" is kin to Jesus, part of his new metaphorical family! This surprising conclusion—that membership in the family of the Son of God, participation in the community witnessing the in-breaking of the kingdom of God, depends not on the usual high status criteria (roles as established religious leaders or as designated disciples or relatives of the new leader) but on doing the will of God—this surprising conclusion comes as a narrative exclamation point at

---

42. See Malbon, "Disciples/Crowds/Whoever," 124–26 [here chapter 3].

43. E.g., John Dominic Crossan, "Mark and the Relatives of Jesus," *NovT* 15 (1973): 81–113; Werner H. Kelber, *The Oral and the Written Gospel: The Hermeneutics of Speaking and Writing in the Synoptic Tradition, Mark, Paul, and Q* (Philadelphia: Fortress, 1983), 102–4.

the end of a series of controversy stories and a discipleship story. As the exceptional scribe "not far from the kingdom of God" (12:28–34) echoes the called and chosen disciples (3:13–19), so the negatively valued scribes and the positively valued new family encountered and spoken of by Jesus (3:20–35) are echoed by the negatively valued scribes and the positively valued poor widow (12:35–44) observed and commented on by Jesus.

The passage about family (3:31–35) also functions, like the passage about the poor widow (12:41–44), as a narrative colon: a mark that directs attention to a list, explanation, or quotation that follows. What follows the poor widow's story of suffering and sacrificial giving is the Markan Jesus' eschatological discourse concerning future suffering for his disciples (chapter 13), a discourse that serves as a narrative interlude in the midst of Jesus' own passion story. What follows the passage about Jesus' family as those who do God's will, while his biological family is waiting "outside" (3:31–32), is Jesus' parables discourse concerning those inside who have been given the mystery of the kingdom of God and "those outside" for whom "everything comes in parables" (4:10–11). The parables discourse serves as a narrative interlude in the midst of Jesus' messianic activity as powerful teacher and healer, decisive proclaimer and bringer of the kingdom of God. Both of Jesus' major discourses have obvious implications for the implied audience. According to R. H. Lightfoot, both are concerned to give assurance: the parables of chapter 4 "give an assurance . . . of the final, ultimate certain success of His [Jesus'] mission in spite of present, temporary difficulty and hindrance"; and the sayings of chapter 13 provide "a great divine prophecy of the ultimate salvation of the elect after and indeed through unprecedented and unspeakable suffering, trouble, and disaster."[44] Both of Jesus' major discourses are preceded by a story focused on an appropriate minor character or characters.

44. Lightfoot, "The Connexion of Chapter Thirteen with the Passion Narrative," 48.

The above examples should serve to illustrate the point: one aspect of the major importance of the minor characters in Mark is that they provide overall narrative punctuation—especially parentheses, exclamation points, and colons—marking where the implied audience is to pause, reflect, connect. Of course, stories focused on minor characters do not provide the only narrative punctuation for Mark's Gospel. Mark 4:35–8:21, for example, is strongly punctuated by three stories involving Jesus and his disciples on the Sea of Galilee, two of which frame the narrative unit. However, stories centered on minor characters do occur at significant points in the narrative: setting off material as parentheses; bringing surprising closure to a series of narrative events as exclamation points; and, as colons, introducing discourses that develop the broader implications of the preceding stories.

Narrative punctuation is an aspect of the syntagmatic or sequential dimension of a narrative. The opening parenthesis occurs prior to the closing parenthesis. The exclamation point follows a series; the colon introduces one. By extending the continuum of responses to Jesus, the minor characters of Mark also make a major contribution to the paradigmatic or schematic dimension of the narrative. When viewed simultaneously, all the characters—major and minor—throughout the narrative form a system based on comparisons and contrasts with one another, and this system enlightens understanding of each character.

Conclusion: Characters and the Implied Audience

Characters around the Markan Jesus are not to be judged by the implied audience according to their social location in the narrative world (disciples, religious leaders, diseased persons, etc.), nor by the extent of their time on the narrative scene (major or minor), nor by the development of their narrative portrayal (round or flat), but only by their response to the Markan Jesus. This is not to say that the distinctions major or minor and round or flat are without significance for interpreting the Markan narrative.[45] The minor characters, like the religious leaders, are flat in comparison with the more rounded disciples. But the religious leaders are like the disciples in being major characters. The minor characters who are exemplars are positive in value from the point of view of the implied author and implied audience, whereas the religious leaders who are enemies are negative in value and thus the opposite of the exemplars. The disciples and others who are fallible followers manifest both positive and negative values. It is not surprising that the paradoxical fallible followers are generally the rounded disciples, since showing more than one trait is what moves a character from flatness to roundness. Nor is it surprising that there are positive, flat, minor characters (exemplars); negative, flat, major characters (religious

---

45. In actuality, I think of major and minor and flat and round as extremes of continua. Along with a number of biblical interpreters, I have found the terms flat and round useful heuristic devices for investigating patterns of characterization (see Malbon, "Jewish Leaders," 277, 280 [here chapter 5]; Malbon, "Poor Widow," 601 [here chapter 6]; Malbon, "Texts and Contexts," 93 [here chapter 4]). See especially Adele Berlin's reformulation of Forster's "flat" and "round" characters into three types (thought of as points on a continuum), also cited here in chapter 5, n. 52: "1) the agent, about whom nothing is known except what is necessary for the plot; the agent is a function of the plot or part of the setting; 2) the type, who has a limited and stereotyped range of traits, and who represents the class of people with these traits; 3) the character, who has a broader range of traits (not all belonging to the same class of people), and about whom we know more than is necessary for the plot" (*Poetics and Interpretation of Biblical Narrative* [Sheffield: Almond Press, 1983], 32). For discussions of the limits of the flat/round distinction, see a number of the essays and responses in *Characterization in Biblical Literature*, ed. Malbon and Berlin. The main significance of the flat/round distinction is not that it allows us to label some characters flat (and possibly dismiss them) and others round (and possibly emphasize them) but that it forces us to consider each character in relation to all other characters. Flat and round are relative—and thus relational—terms.

leaders as enemies); positive and negative, round, major characters (disciples as fallible followers); but no round, minor characters of whatever value. (The closest would be those minor
characters who display in brief encounters the role of fallible followers: the epileptic's father and the three women at the cross
and tomb.) Flat and minor, and round and major, are not
required linkages; but flat and major seems to be a more feasible
category than round and minor.

A close look at these overlapping but not equivalent distinctions helps solve a puzzle encountered by Markan interpreters: Why do some of the minor characters seem to be
better models of followership than the disciples? Some interpreters have even thought that these minor characters make
the disciples look so bad in comparison that the disciples are
to be interpreted as enemies! That designation, of course,
washes out the disciples' even greater contrast with the religious leaders as enemies, as well as ignoring all the positive
characterization of the disciples. It is not narratively fair (or
reasonable) to judge round major characters and flat minor
characters over against one another in abstraction, rather than
judging both in terms of the entire response continuum and
the narrative as a whole. In art as in life (let the reader understand) many could probably be considered exemplary if only
one well-chosen story were recounted! If Levi is exemplary in
his response to his call (2:13–14), and he is, why do we not consider Simon (Peter) exemplary in his parallel response to his
call (1:16–18)? Because we know more about Peter, maybe too
much about Peter for Peter's sake, but just what the implied
author wants us to know for our own sakes as the potential
implied audience. The minor characters and the disciples contribute differently to this communication.

In the Markan narrative the exemplars (positive, flat, and
minor—and female and male, Gentile and Jew) communicate to
the implied audience that anyone can be a follower of Jesus. The
disciples (positive and negative, round, and major) communicate

that no one finds it easy. Both messages are essential to the Markan Gospel.[46] We see now why the three named women at the cross and the tomb are so distinctive and important in the Markan narrative. As minor characters and exemplars they open up the possibilities of discipleship: anyone can be a follower. As almost-major and almost-round characters they manifest fallibility: no one finds it easy. As the characters who have the final word, or rather the final silence, the women communicate both the inclusivity and the challenge of following Jesus.

The women characters at the cross and the tomb are on the border between flat and round, between minor and major, between exemplars and fallible followers. Perhaps it is for this reason that they form a natural bridge to the implied audience, also on the border—the border between the internal world of the text and the external world of its hearers and readers. Is the women's final silence an exclamation point—marking the surprising turn of events (resurrection) following the surprising turn of events (crucifixion) in the story of Jesus?! Is the women's final silence a colon—directing attention to what will follow: . . . ?

Only by knowing where a minor character is in the unfolding narrative of the Markan Gospel (for example, does her or his story provide narrative punctuation?) and where a minor character is in relation to other characters (how does his or her response to Jesus compare with others' on the response continuum?) do we know who that character is for the implied audience and how that character aids communication from the implied author to the implied audience. Although real (external) interpreters construct the implied audience, we do so on the basis of an understanding of internal evidence. The otherness of the text is a constraint on the interpreter. While it is true, as Paul Armstrong notes, that "a text is not an independ-

---

46. See Malbon, "Fallible Followers," 46 [here chapter 2].

ent object which remains the same regardless of how it is construed,"[47] it is also true that an interpretation *of a work* is not independent or autonomous. In fact, the literary work that we interpret is "heteronomous," that is, "paradoxically both dependent and independent, capable of taking on different shapes according to opposing hypotheses about how to configure it, but always transcending any particular interpreter's beliefs about it."[48] It is my understanding that, by presenting a response continuum (with some surprises to general expectations about characters) rather than absolutely stereotyped characters, the Markan narrative constrains and shapes not only the implied audience's response to Jesus but also its response to other respondents to Jesus. Perhaps the implied audience is to generalize experiences of nonexclusivity of followership among narrative characters to experiences of inclusivity among other members of the implied audience. Indeed, all the characters internal to the narrative exist not for their own sakes but for the sake of the communication between author and audience external to the narrative, with the implied author and implied audience marking the boundary between. For the implied author of Mark, the minor characters are of major importance, but the implied audience is the most important character of all!

---

47. Paul B. Armstrong, *Conflicting Readings: Variety and Validity in Interpretation* (Chapel Hill: University of North Carolina Press, 1990), 11.

48. Ibid., x.

Appendix to Chapter 1

Further Reading on Narrative Criticism

General

Chatman, Seymour. *Story and Discourse: Narrative Structure in Fiction and Film*. Ithaca, N.Y.: Cornell University Press, 1978.

A classic presentation of the elements of "story" and "discourse" that has been widely influential in biblical narrative criticism; includes thorough discussions of plot, setting, characters, implied author, types of narrators (covert versus overt), and point of view, with examples drawn from secular literature and film.

Genette, Gérard. *Narrative Discourse: An Essay in Method*. Translated by Jane E. Lewin. Ithaca, N.Y.: Cornell University Press, 1980.

An attempt at a comprehensive, systematic theory of narrative and simultaneously a study of Proust's *A la recherche du temps perdu*, which focuses on careful delineations of the order, duration, and frequency of narrated events and the mood and voice of narratives.

Rimmon-Kenan, Shlomith. *Narrative Fiction: Contemporary Poetics*. London: Methuen, 1983.

A clear, concise, and very helpful overview of narrative aspects: events, characters, time, characterization, focalization, levels and voices, speech representation, the text and its reading, with examples drawn from various periods and various national literatures.

Biblical

Berlin, Adele. *Poetics and Interpretation of Biblical Narrative*. Sheffield: Almond Press, 1983.

A thoughtful and accessible discussion of aspects of (theoretical) poetics and (practical) interpretation of Hebrew Bible narratives, focusing on character and characterization in the stories of David's wives and on point of view; includes also an extended analysis of the book of Ruth and a reflection on the interrelations of literary and historical methods.

Culpepper, R. Alan. *Anatomy of the Fourth Gospel: A Study in Literary Design*. Philadelphia: Fortress, 1983.

A thorough and rich reading of the narrative of John's Gospel, exploring, in turn, the narrator and point of view, narrative time, plot, characters, implicit commentary, and the implied reader.

Funk, Robert W. *The Poetics of Biblical Narrative*. Sonoma, Calif.: Polebridge Press, 1988.

An extensive presentation of narrative grammar, how narratives work; especially strong in analyzing smaller segments within narratives.

Kelber, Werner H. *Mark's Story of Jesus*. Philadelphia: Fortress, 1979.

A brief, dramatic retelling of the Markan narrative focused on the negative portrayal of the disciples.

Kingsbury, Jack Dean. *Matthew as Story*. 2d ed. Philadelphia: Fortress, 1988.

A literary critical reading of Matthew with emphasis on the plot or story line of Jesus and the story line of the disciples.

Malbon, Elizabeth Struthers. *Narrative Space and Mythic Meaning in Mark*. New Voices in Biblical Studies. San Francisco: Harper & Row, 1986. Reprint, The Biblical Seminar 13. Sheffield: Sheffield Academic Press, 1991.

A detailed analysis of the spatial settings of Mark based on a (literary) structuralist methodology; suggestions of their significance to the Gospel as a whole.

Moore, Stephen D. *Literary Criticism and the Gospels: The Theoretical Challenge*. New Haven, Conn.: Yale University Press, 1989.

A lively, scholarly critique of narrative criticism and reader-response criticism from the point of view of deconstruction and postmodernism; includes an extensive bibliography.

Petersen, Norman R. *Literary Criticism for New Testament Critics.* GBS. Philadelphia: Fortress, 1978.

A rich, yet accessible, introduction to literary criticism of the New Testament; includes helpful discussions of the differing approaches of historical and literary criticism, contributions of structuralism, story time and plotted time in Mark, and narrative world and real world in Luke-Acts.

Poland, Lynn M. *Literary Criticism and Biblical Hermeneutics: A Critique of Formalist Approaches.* AAR Academy Series 48. Chico, Calif.: Scholars Press, 1985.

A critique of the New Critical influence on biblical studies, focusing on examinations of the work of John Dominic Crossan, Dan Otto Via, Jr., and Hans W. Frei.

Powell, Mark Allan. *What Is Narrative Criticism?* GBS. Minneapolis: Fortress, 1990.

A clear and inclusive introduction to narrative criticism of the Gospels, moving from a sketch of the relationship of narrative criticism to other critical approaches (biblical and secular) to an overview of narrative elements (story and discourse, events, characters, settings).

Rhoads, David, Joanna Dewey, and Donald Michie. *Mark as Story: An Introduction to the Narrative of a Gospel.* 2d ed. Minneapolis: Fortress, 1999.

An indispensable and inviting introduction to narrative criticism of Mark, focusing on the rhetoric, settings, plot, and characters; includes a fresh translation of Mark.

Tannehill, Robert C. *The Narrative Unity of Luke-Acts: A Literary Interpretation.* Vol. 1, *The Gospel according to Luke.* Philadelphia: Fortress, 1986.

An exploration of the narrative and theological unity of Luke, with emphasis on the shifting and developing relationships between Jesus and other individual characters and groups of characters.

Appendix to Chapter 3

Specific Markan References to the Disciples and the Crowd

	The Disciples (of Jesus)	**The Crowd**
1:16, 19	Simon, Andrew, James, John	
1:27		*pas*
1:29	Simon, Andrew, James, John	
1:32		*pas*
1:34		*polloi*
1:36	Simon	
1:37		*pas*
2:2		*polloi*
2:4		*ochlos*
2:12a		*pas*
2:12b		*pas*
2:13		*ochlos*
2:15	*mathētai*	*polloi*
2:16	*mathētai*	
2:18d	*mathētai*	
2:23	*mathētai*	
3:7	*mathētai*	*plēthos*
3:8		*plēthos*
3:9	*mathētai*	*ochlos*
3:10		*polloi*
3:14	*dōdeka*	
	[*apostoloi*]	
3:16	[*dōdeka*]	

	The Disciples (of Jesus)	**The Crowd**
3:16–19	the twelve by name	
3:20		*ochlos*
3:32		*ochlos*
4:1a		*ochlos*
4:1b		*ochlos*
4:10	*dōdeka*	
4:34	*mathētai*	
4:36		*ochlos*
5:20		*pas*
5:21		*ochlos*
5:24		*ochlos*
5:27		*ochlos*
5:30		*ochlos*
5:31	*mathētai*	*ochlos*
5:37	Peter, James, John	
6:1	*mathētai*	
6:2		*polloi*
6:7	*dōdeka*	
6:30	*apostoloi*	
6:31		*polloi*
6:33		*polloi*
6:34		*ochlos*
6:35	*mathētai*	
6:39		*pas*
6:41	*mathētai*	*pas*
6:42		*pas*
6:45	*mathētai*	*ochlos*
7:2	*mathētai*	
7:5	*mathētai*	
7:14		*ochlos*
		pas
7:17		*ochlos*
	mathētai	
7:33		*ochlos*
8:1		*ochlos*
	mathētai	
8:2		*ochlos*
8:4	*mathētai*	
8:6a		*ochlos*
	mathētai	

	The Disciples (of Jesus)	**The Crowd**
8:6b		*ochlos*
8:10	*mathētai*	
8:27a	*mathētai*	
8:27b	*mathētai*	
8:29	Peter	
8:32	Peter	
8:33	*mathētai*	
	Peter	
8:34		*ochlos*
	mathētai	
9:2	Peter, James, John	
9:5	Peter	
9:14	*mathētai*	*ochlos*
9:15		*ochlos*
9:17		*heis ek tou ochlou*
9:18	*mathētai*	
9:25		*ochlos*
9:26		*polloi*
9:28	*mathētai*	
9:31	*mathētai*	
9:35	*dōdeka*	
9:38	John	
10:1		*ochlos*
10:10	*mathētai*	
10:13	*mathētai*	
10:23	*mathētai*	
10:24	*mathētai*	
10:28	Peter	
10:32	*dōdeka*	
10:35	James, John	
10:41	*deka*	
	James, John	
10:46	*mathētai*	*ochlos*
10:48		*polloi*
11:1	*duo tōn mathētōn*	
11:8		*polloi*
11:11	*dōdeka*	
11:14	*mathētai*	
11:18		*ochlos*

	The Disciples (of Jesus)	The Crowd
11:21	Peter	
11:32		*ochlos*
12:12		*ochlos*
12:37		*ochlos*
12:41		*ochlos*
12:43	*mathētai*	*pas*
12:44		*pas*
13:1	*heis tōn mathētōn*	
13:3	Peter, James, John, Andrew	
13:6a		*polloi*
13:6b		*polloi*
14:2		*laos*
14:10	Judas Iscariot, *heis tōn dōdeka*	
14:12	*mathētai*	
14:13	*duo tōn mathētōn*	
14:14	*mathētai*	
14:16	*mathētai*	
14:17	*dōdeka*	
14:20	*heis tōn dōdeka*	
14:29	Peter	
14:32	*mathētai*	
14:33	Peter, James, John	
14:37	Peter (Simon)	
14:43	Judas, *heis tōn dōdeka*	*ochlos*
14:54	Peter	
14:56		*polloi*
14:66	Peter	
14:67	Peter	
14:70	Peter	
14:72	Peter	
15:8		*ochlos*
15:11		*ochlos*
15:15		*ochlos*
15:41		*pollai*
16:7	*mathētai* Peter	

Index of Authors

Index of Biblical References